2/03

If Nights
Could Talk

If Nights Could Talk

a family memoir

Marsha

Recknagel

THOMAS DUNNE BOOKS
ST. MARTIN'S PRESS
NEW YORK

THOMAS DUNNE BOOKS.
An imprint of St. Martin's Press.

www.stmartins.com

Design by Kathryn Parise

Photograph on page 259 courtesy of Bobby Aldridge (1939–
2001)

ISBN 0-312-26809-2

10   9   8   7   6   5   4   3   2

For Dante

and

for Moragh

contents

1.	The Arrival	1
2.	The First Day	9
3.	Louisiana: The Dream State	16
4.	Magical Realism	32
5.	Our House Is Haunted	44
6.	Family Circle	65
7.	A Decade of Disasters	98
8.	If Nights Could Talk, Stars Would Sing	115
9.	Disorders of the Sleep State	134
10.	The State We're In	142
11.	Emancipation Day	148
12.	For Those Who Wait	167

Contents

13. Food Not Bombs   199

14. The Fog   207

15. Weddings and Funerals   213

16. The Fog Lifts   224

17. Nearing the End   241

acknowledgments

There have been many who supported me through the lived as well as the writing part of this story. My thanks to Carolyn Anderson, my dear friend, who talked me through many a bad time. Marcia Carter's advice as a mother and a reader were invaluable. Karen Shepard kept me honest and kept me writing. The following friends loaned me their belief in the book when mine sometimes flagged—David Alexander, Pearlie Burns, Amelia Giles, Linda Leavell, Thad Logan, the Montoya guys, Kelly Thomas, and Red Vanderkuy. Susan Wood was always on the other end of the line. Patti Fullerton saw a vision of the story for the big screen and thrilled me with the prospect. I also want to thank Geoffrey Reed Pike, who consoled or celebrated, whichever was necessary. My sister, Jan Glasgow, and her daughter, Jenifer Revere, taught me that family can also be friends. I want to thank my cohorts from the Bennington Writing Seminars, who helped me find my story even though they each had their own to tell. Sally Kim, my editor, threw herself into the project with great energy and insight. And finally, I want to thank Leslie Daniels, my agent, who knows all sides of the story.

If Dante had not trusted me with his story, this book would not exist. It is *our* book. For Dante's generosity in allowing me to make his private life public, I am deeply and forever grateful.

And I walk out now,
In dead shoes, in the new light,
on the steppingstones
of someone else's wandering,
a twinge
in this foot or that saying
turn or *stay* or *take*
forty-three giant steps
backwards, frightened
I may already have lost
the way: *the first step*, the Crone
who scried the crystal said, *shall be*
to lose the way.

   —GALWAY KINNELL,
    "The Shoes of Wandering"

1

the arrival

Jamie was on my porch. Standing in the door in his black leather jacket, black jeans, and combat boots, he blocked out the porch and streetlights, even the light from the moon. His eyes were hard to see behind the long swath of greasy hair pulled down to cover half of his face. At first, I only saw the wild hair falling around his shoulders. I remembered the way my father often had brushed my bangs out of my eyes and I would swat his hand away. I knew not to touch Jamie. The writing on his black T-shirt looked as if it were scrawled in blood; slowly it came into focus: The Dead Kennedys. I had been in the sixth grade when Kennedy was shot.

"Hey, Jamie," I said. I heard myself say it as if from far away. The name, which had meant so much for so long in our family, didn't seem to fit him. "Hey, Jamie," I said again as if to assure myself he was really

Jamie. He seemed to grow larger the longer we stood facing each other, and I imagined if I let him in the house he would fill it with darkness.

We stood in the triangular wedge of the opened door, which seemed perpetually ajar, half-open, half-shut, held as if by its own geometry, but really suspended by the drama of the one who stood asking, though without words, to come in. I remembered my high school boyfriend, Pike, warning, "He'll follow you. He'll end up on your front porch some-day." Pike had meant my brother, Jimmy, and at the time I'd been angry at the prophecy and at his fear of the prospect. How incredible, I thought, that it was my brother's son who was finally on the porch, and he looked so much like my brother I couldn't move my body in space, couldn't make my mouth say "Come in."

My house glowed lamplit yellow behind me, and I felt its particulars pressing forward—the portrait my friend from New York had painted of me in pinks, reds, and purples; the two dogs, one yellow, one brown and black, both jolly at the prospect of a visitor, tapping their paws on the honey-colored oak floors as they came to see who was at the door. We were all lively commotion in contrast to Jamie, who was part of the night, a question waiting for an answer. I wanted to tell the hulking boy that I'd carved and shaped and clawed this bright life into existence. I wanted to shout, "You can't come in. You will bring it all in with you."

Jamie ducked his head as he stepped into the foyer, pulling his jacket around him as if trying to hide how large he was, as if trying to make himself smaller to accommodate me. The last time I'd seen him he'd still been a boy, but now he was a teenager who had shot up to over six feet with shoulders like a linebacker's. He reminded me of a Matisse sculpture in which the human figure is barely emerging from the black stone, still at war with the inert mass that holds it back.

My next memory of that night is of Jamie sitting on the edge of my bed, playing a video game he'd brought with him, sitting like a hypno-tized six-year-old, mouth gaping, blasting small scurrying figures into splintered flashes. There was a dull look of deep satisfaction each time he pressed the button on the Sega CD control. I sat behind him on the bed and felt he wished I'd vanish too, along with the rest of the world. Slack-jawed, mesmerized, Jamie looked stoned. Here, I thought, finally, the boy I dreamed about for ten years, who in my mind was perpetually sweet and vulnerable and at the mercy of his parents. And he was now grown monstrous, a furrowed, overhanging-browed Frankenstein grunting his yeses and no's.

I watched him watching the screen and saw the familiar fat cheeks that many of the Recknagels have, saw the creamy skin marked with huge red splotches, places where he'd scratched pimples into sores. His eyes were those of my brother. Hound dog eyes.

I left him zapping enemies while I made up the bed in the guest room as if I too were hypnotized. Over the bed is a mahogany-framed set of photographs: black-and-white portraits of my brother and me taken when we were five and six. Thinking Jamie wouldn't want his father— even as a small boy—peering down on him, I took it down, but before hiding it away, I stared into the faces, studying the girl with her Buster Brown haircut dressed in a starched pinafore, and the boy with a buzz cut wearing a white shirt almost the same color as his pale face. In the portrait I'm smiling a coy, shy smile. I'd recently had surgery to correct my crossed eyes, but when I was nervous they still crossed, and I remember the photographer becoming frantic, making me look up, then to the side in an effort to trick my eyes into coming together. In his photograph my brother isn't smiling. He is holding his arms over his head as if in an appeal to be lifted up. The pallor of his face blends into the parchment white of the background as if about to disappear.

A friend once questioned why I kept the portraits on the wall, thinking it was some sort of self-torture. The portraits were a shrine for me, a place to honor the dead relationship between me and my brother. In 1958 when my brother and I walked down the stairs to sit for the portraits, we'd held hands. The photographer had looked up from under the brim of his hat as he bent over his suitcase of bulbs and lenses, and asked my mother, "Twins?" It was a common mistake, and my mother laughed as if pleased.

I could hear the beeps of Jamie's video game in the next room as I sat with the portraits in my lap, looking out the upstairs window and rubbing the dust from the glass with my shirttail until, as if I'd rubbed Aladdin's lamp, I saw the other house, the one where my brother and I grew up—where we grew up together. The house in Shreveport—the family speaks of it now as "the old house"—was a two-story stucco surrounded by trees with a wide front porch and yellow French doors. In spring green mold crept up the stucco. Sometimes whole years would go by in which my brother and I wouldn't see any neighbors. Across the street lived Old Mr. Jones, one of Shreveport's first oilmen. At the end of his winding driveway was a miniature oil derrick kept painted bright white; the street number sat on top in black letters as if oil were spilling over—a gusher that had made possible this stately southern mansion. Next to his house was a Christian Science church, a behemoth of Greek architecture. On our block there was only one other house that was visible from across a wild hedge of azaleas and camellias, dogwood and pecan trees. It belonged to the Hamiltons. In the eighteen years I lived there, I never met the Hamiltons. I knew Alfred, their black gardener, who tended the roses that hardly anyone ever saw. The Hamiltons were old money, Mother had told us, and spent most of the year in Florida, living off their oil production. I would sneak into their still garden and bend down to look into the goldfish pond to catch sight of the huge imported orange-and-white fish. A statue of a young boy, whose penis spouted water in a graceful arc, was in the middle of the pond. My brother, timid and scared to follow me, would be peeking from behind the bushes, his expression, as usual, midwhine, ready, as always, to break into tears. He always seemed to know I'd leave him behind. Now, I thought, we are estranged, a perfect word for what it describes—being a stranger to someone who was once beloved. The night Jamie appeared at my door, I hadn't seen or spoken to my brother in ten years.

I heard Jamie's snoring in my bedroom and went in to see him slumped over sideways, his mouth open, his mustache like a shadow. The two dogs looked from the sleeping giant to me as if questioning what we were to do with him. Jack, the corgi mix that had followed me home the year before, curled on the edge of my bed, his fox face alert and questioning. Rose, the Airedale, sniffed Jamie's boots, wagging her tail at the power of the odor. Bending down, I looked him over, inspecting the big hands spread open in his lap, his forearms, the scraggly beard that was shocking in its blackness. As he lay in a heap in my room, I examined the Celtic cross he wore around his neck and scanned his neck and arms, looked at his fingers. His feet were splayed out, the laces of his boots untied. He didn't have on socks. His feet, I knew, must be raw and blistered from the long walk—eighteen miles, he'd said—from his parents' house to the bus station, and as I stared at his feet, I noticed a small round yin-yang tattoo on his ankle bone. I could tell it was home-made, a pen-and-ink-and-knife do-it-yourself, dug in and painted by hand. What else, I wondered, was beneath his bulky clothes?

I squatted down and looked at the face in repose, a face I'd know anywhere. The resemblance of Jamie at sixteen to the way my brother had once looked was like having the past doubled and redealt. While staring at the TV screen, Jamie had worn the same vacant and dreamy expression I'd seen on my brother's face when he'd escaped into the world of *The Three Stooges, Tarzan, The Late Movie;* it's the look deaf people sometimes have. My brother had made himself deaf when he was sixteen by placing his head between large stereo speakers, one for each ear. He'd wanted to block out the world. He had been sent away from home, first to a school for the learning disabled, then to a military school from where he wrote our father, "I hate you so much I hate myself." After military school, where the cadets teased him mercilessly and ran him around campus, lap after lap, for being plump and afraid and home-sick, he came home six feet tall, on Ritalin, and chain-smoking one cigarette after the other. During his teens he was silent most of the time, bathed a pale blue from the television screen that he watched in the dark sunroom. Those had been the terrible years—for my brother, for me, for the family.

That night, looking at Jamie, I told myself, as if chanting a mantra:

This is Jamie, not Jimmy. This is Jamie, not Jimmy. As I stared at him, I wondered if this were some cruel cosmic joke—that I had to relive what I had tried so hard to put behind me.

I shook Jamie awake, and with his movement the smell of the Greyhound bus he'd traveled on to Houston was released into the room. The whiff of diesel and old grease and smoke and bad times reminded me of the oil fields and the filling stations where I'd hung out as a kid. I stepped back and onto Rosie's paw. She yelped and Jamie awoke.

"Jamie," I said, "you have to get up."

He grunted and looked around him like a drunk old man and stumbled into the guest room, falling onto the covers face first.

I'd just fallen asleep when I heard the first roar. Rosie raised her head to look at me with surprise. I stayed very still, listening, thinking perhaps it had been a car outside revving its engine. Again the sound—impossible to identify: beastly, hollow, ragged. I got up slowly, moving the covers away, then placing one foot on the floor, then the next, and walked on tiptoes toward Jamie's room, barely breathing in anticipation of what I might see. There was only Jamie, making a sound like a drowning man's last gasps amplified over a loudspeaker. I held on to the doorjamb and saw his back arch until only his head and feet were touching the bed, and then he'd let out a rasping wet moan before he crashed back to the bed. I held my T-shirt in a fist, perspiration rolling from under my arms down my waist. I began to pant rhythmically, the way an asthmatic will do when she hears the breath of others coming hard. The dogs shuffled behind me as I whispered over and over, "Shit. Shit." Jamie seemed possessed or dying or both. He'd shudder after each spasm, then collapse back into deadweight. Then I'd count: one, two, three, and on until ten seconds would pass by, then fifteen. Suddenly he'd be gulping, gasping, grabbing for air, seeming to rise up from the bed to find the place of peace. He was more movie than real to me that night.

I can't say how long I stood and watched him rock the bed. My mind must have let loose chemicals that numbed me, made the sight seem unreal or faraway or both. In the dark Jamie seemed unreal. Or I did. I thought of the many nights I'd slept in the single bed he was riding as if it were a bucking bronco. I'd often moved from my double bed into the smaller room and the twin bed when I felt the house too big and empty. On some of those nights I'd longed for a child, knowing that the time for having one was passing me by. Looking at Jamie, I knew why I'd never had a child. I'd been scared I'd have a Jamie, a child like my brother had been, a child that would bring a family down. I tiptoed away as if Jamie were a bad dream I didn't want to awake. Like a child I clambered into bed, and instead of stuffed animals, I pulled the nervous dogs to me, held Jack and Rose as tightly as I wanted to hold my life close.

I was scared of Jamie.

Maybe, I thought, he'd kill my dogs in the night with one of the daggers I'd heard he collected. I imagined finding blood smeared down the hallway walls, a trail that I'd follow to the terrible finale: Rose, sacrificed to Satan. As the fantasy played out in my mind, tears squeezed from my eyes, but I didn't know it until Rose licked my face, nudging me with her nose. "Oh, God," I whispered to her, the matriarch of my dog family. "Rose, Rose, what are we gonna do?"

I'd heard he worshipped the devil.

The next morning I opened my eyes and tried to hear if he was up. I felt furtive and sneaky, venturing into the foyer, listening for sounds. Suspicious sounds. I slowly walked into his room where every cover and both pillows were on the floor as if blown there by a bomb in the bed. The mattress was soaked in urine. Now I remembered my brother had wet his bed until he was in his teens. I stood still, feeling the lineage short-circuiting, loose and live.

Then I heard water splashing in the bathroom. The simple sound of Jamie bathing made me feel better. In the bath he sounded like a four-year-old at play, or a seal, or a Labrador puppy. Water, I could tell, was everywhere, but I didn't care. He was washing off some of my brother. It was a beginning.

I placed my hands on the banister of the stairwell and looked at them.

My right ring finger is crooked—the memento of a motorcycle accident at fourteen—and I often think of it as the part of me that can't think straight. I gripped my hands around the wood of the banister and took heart in the strength of my hold. *I can do this,* I thought. I went downstairs to see what there was in the kitchen to feed such a strapping boy.

2

the first day

I don't cook and never have. I suppose I went on strike as a teenager when I refused to cook or do dishes if my brother didn't have to do the same chores. Later my first forays into feminism gave me a doctrine to back up my dogma. On that first morning in the kitchen, waiting for Jamie to descend, I felt foolish as I looked in the refrigerator and saw the barrenness as if through his eyes. I sat down in the wicker chair that looks out from my unused kitchen into my garden, a windowful of crepe myrtle and ivy, and watched the birds searching for seeds in between the bricks of the patio. I always kept plenty of birdseed.

My refusal to learn to cook, I knew, was an adolescent rebellion that had lasted way past its usefulness, but my resistance to pots and pans and smoke and the smell of food cooking ran deep. In the midst of my reverie about those who cook, those who don't, I heard a horrible racket that sounded as if Jamie had fallen down the flight of stairs. I was just getting to my feet when Jamie appeared in the doorframe of the kitchen.

"Jesus Christ," I said, "what in the hell happened?"

Jamie looked at me as if he didn't understand English.

"That noise!" I said.

Jamie had no sense of the chaos he created in a room. When he sat down in the wicker chair across from me, he collapsed into it, dropping all of his weight and six-foot-plus frame into the chair, which gave off a sound as if someone had just broken a fistful of sticks. The kitchen rag rug clumped around his feet; the dog bowl was suddenly in flight from an accidental kick across the room. I got up and told him to take my chair—I didn't say because it was sturdier but that's what was going through my mind. Do you like smoothies? I asked, not telling him that it was his only choice. I despised the fakeness of my voice as I made small talk while adding the ingredients to the blender, the roar of which was a relief, filling in the silence between us as the bananas and milk and juice swirled together into a creamy mixture. Handing him the frothy smoothie, I visualized the healthy liquid working like Drano to cut through the nicotine and fast food. He took a big gulp and came up with a milk mustache but no smile. "Is it sweet enough?" I asked in my new bubbly voice.

No, it wasn't sweet enough, he said.

I handed him the sugar bowl and then watched in horror as he put one spoonful after another into the glass.

To me sugar and mental illness go hand in hand. I always remembered the patients at the mental health center where I'd worked in my twenties. I'd watch them in the snack bar pouring endlessly from the sugar dispenser. Always I'd recoiled at the sight, which brought to mind my brother, who used to eat sugar with a spoon straight from the bowl.

To keep from commenting, I began to rub Rose's stomach and sweet talk to her.

"She smells like an old bathmat," Jamie said.

He might as well have kicked Rose across the room. His cold assessment made me grit my teeth and hold my tongue as I kept rubbing Rose's stomach, trying to think before I spoke my hurt. I held her muzzle in my two hands, and stared into her eyes that were hazy with cataracts. Jamie's presence loomed outside that bond. And he must have felt exiled when I'd baby-talked to her, banishing him from my thoughts and from the room. His resentment was swift. It was not a coincidence that Rose was ten years old, bought the year Jamie had been returned by the courts to his parents, taken away, I'd thought then, forever.

Smoothies, Rose grown sour with old age, the cramped kitchen and the buzz-saw sound of the blender are what I remember of that first morning. Instead of mounting a defense of Rose, I'd left the kitchen to go to the living room, where I drew the curtains back and looked up and down the street. Jack, the young yellow dog, was already keeping a vigil on top of an old trunk that made a perfect perch for him to watch the front yard from the window. I checked the lock on the front door. The house was so open, I thought. Where I'd always felt safe, I felt exposed.

The phone rang and I stared at it, going through a list of who could be calling—my brother, demanding his son; the police, looking for a runaway; any of my friends, who would be, I knew, astonished to learn that Jamie was at my house. The return of the repressed, I'd say to my friends. "You aren't gonna believe this!" I'd begin the story.

I picked up the phone.

"Dayna is really in a state," Mother said. She said Jimmy and Dayna suspected Jamie was either in Shreveport with my sister, Gail, and her husband, Bobby, or in Houston with me. They were in the car, she said. "They were headed out," she said. "Lookin' for Jamie," she said. "I just don't know," she kept saying in between bursts of information. She was all warning and worry. "I just don't know."

How was I to know? By now, I thought, by this time in my life, I should know what to do in a family crisis. There'd been enough of them.

But I hadn't a clue. Run away with the runaway? Hold my ground? I pictured Jamie in a physical tug-of-war—Dayna and Jimmy with one arm, me with another, pulling him to pieces.

I hung up the phone and paced around my house, went upstairs and pulled the blinds back to look out on the street, looking up and down for the patrol car that might be coming to get me. Mother had mentioned kidnapping charges. I wasn't sure who I'd hate to show up the most: Dayna and my brother or the police.

I'd seen Dayna's "states" before. "Really on the warpath," Mother had said. Would she have a gun? I wondered. I'd looked out my window to see if Dayna was perhaps stalking my house, peeking in the window. Years before Dayna had decided I was her mortal enemy, the sister-in-law she swore was a witch or worse.

"Let's pack," I said to Jamie, who sleepily put his palms on the jeans he'd arrived in and said, "This is it." Actually he'd come with the clothes on his back, an electric guitar, a big hardback book with medieval gold script on the cover, and the Sega CD.

I decided we should go to New Orleans and find a lawyer. I needed something to do, a plan to organize my thoughts around. Gail had sent Jamie money to his parents' house for a bus ticket to Shreveport, which she'd hidden in the pages of a *Rolling Stone*. But once he got to Shreveport, she'd realized his parents would certainly look first for him at her house. She'd sent him on to me in Houston. I thought I'd soon be returning him to Gail and Bobby with whom, it was assumed by the rest of the family, he belonged. He had been raised from infancy until he was six and a half by the Aldridges. But Gail had grown terribly fragile since she lost Jamie in the custody suit ten years before. She'd seemed to have slipped further and further away from the family, who talked to her across a barrier of cigarette smoke and her three cantankerous, unpredictable Pomeranians. She'd hunkered down. Though she feigned cheerfulness, there was a deep dark sadness that shimmered behind her eyes. Jamie, who wasn't there, was always there.

I packed, rampaging through my closet to find a conservative outfit appropriate for visiting lawyers. Everything I had was loose and casual, the wardrobe of a literature professor, not clothes for warfare. I stuffed some slinky things into the suitcase thinking, You never know. Maybe, I thought, the lawyer I'd hire would be cute and would want to go out for oysters and to hear some music. You never know, I thought, and laughed out loud at the irony of what all I'd never known and also at my infinite capacity for surprise, even though I'd grown up in a family full of surprises.

I planned to hire a Louisiana lawyer, a good, tough, young one because this time, unlike when Jamie was six years old, I intended to win Jamie his freedom. I didn't know what would happen after that. I just knew that this time he would not be sent back to his parents. Never, I thought. Once and for all, I said to myself with focused fury that could have matched Dayna's. "Once and for all," I said aloud to myself as I stuffed some panty hose and heels into the bag. What years before had seemed complicated now seemed simpler. Now there was evidence. Now Jamie could speak for himself, or so I thought.

I didn't think much beyond winning, which in my mind really meant beating my brother and his wife—especially his wife—in this battle of wills that had raged for more than ten years. This is what Daddy would do, I thought, as I checked my wallet for credit cards and cash. He would win. If he were still alive.

I looked over at the prize. He was hunched over, rolls of fat rippling over the waist of his jeans, staring glassy-eyed at the television screen where small figures were splintering, then disappearing. He was folded deep into himself. He was a big mess, but he didn't look like a Satanist to me.

Jimmy and Dayna had become TV fundamentalists who were devotees of Jimmy Swaggart, the charismatic Louisiana preacher who pranced around stage like a rock and roll star. Jamie's parents had enrolled him the year before in Swaggart's school from which he was quickly expelled. That expulsion became for them proof that Jamie was under the sway of the devil.

"What do you mean, devil worshipping?" I'd asked Mother when she'd told me that Jamie had been kicked out of school. I was suspicious of the faddish diagnosis. She'd said he was collecting daggers. "And?" I'd prodded, attempting to tamp down her tendency to believe in the worst-case scenarios. The rest of the family seemed to sigh collectively as if they'd known it would happen sooner or later: devil worshipping. Of course. On the phone I'd asked Mother sarcastically: "Any dead animals? Sacrifices?" She'd become defensive: "He plays some video game all the time," she offered. "What game?" I'd asked. "Something called Daggers and Dragons," she'd said. I was silent on the other end of the line, considering the helplessness of the boy at the mercy of so many people for so long. When I'd tried to argue with her—my students, I said, at Rice University play Dungeons and Dragons—she'd stubbornly ended the conversation with her final evidence: "He claimed he's one."

I was sure—then—that he had just wanted out of that awful school. His pronouncement—that he worshipped the devil—got him out of the Swaggart school, but landed him first in a mental hospital in Baton Rouge, then in one in New Orleans, committed by his parents, who'd claimed they feared for their lives. He'd been put away for months, and home for a week when he ran away.

Jamie seemed to be sleepwalking instead of running away. By my first afternoon with him, I caught myself speaking to him as if he were a disobedient dog, something I was used to. Sharp, direct commands seemed to work best to shake him into semiconsciousness: "Let's go," I shouted at him, a suitcase at my feet, waiting for him to turn off the Sega CD, waiting for him to come to. He put down the control, lumbered to his feet, exhaled a long dramatic sigh, and followed me. I was on a mission, and he was in a daze as we set off on our first trip together.

First, I took him to lunch at the Hobbit Hole, a health food restaurant that had '60s murals of Bilbo Baggins, the protagonist of the *Lord of the Rings* trilogy, books I'd read and reread in my teens. Bilbo, on the wall behind Jamie, had his back to us as he walked on furry feet down a winding path. Bilbo had taken off for parts unknown, ventured far from home, going against his nature to seek adventure, or was it something else he was seeking? I couldn't remember. Had Bilbo gone in search of the dragon or had the dragon happened along the way?

"Have you read the trilogy?" I asked Jamie as I puzzled over Bilbo's motives for heading out from the comfort of his home, leaving those honey cakes and tea. Jamie looked at me, considering, it seemed, if I was worth any effort at all.

"Yeah," he said.

I could see it was no use asking him if he remembered why Bilbo had left home.

When the food came, Jamie scraped from his hamburger the bean sprouts and tomatoes. "I hate avocados, too," he said in a monotone to his plate. I would learn over the next year just how much and how intensely he hated. There was a list, a litany ready for recitation: he hated children, he hated yuppies, he hated bugs, and big hair on women. He hated what he called porch sitters, beer-bellied rednecks. He hated bow heads, the girls with their hair neatly pulled back in clasps, the girls who had played with Barbies. He hated mushrooms, would gag at the thought of eggs. He hated anything both mushy and sweet, which meant almost any dessert. He hated anything thick and rich, like chocolate. He hated to take showers, would only take baths. But particularly he hated his mother.

3

Louisiana:

the dream state

Jamie and I had our next meal in New Orleans, where we arrived late in the afternoon. The first hotel I checked us into was expensive, a charming sequestered place on the edge of the French Quarter. I had some notion that while getting Jamie a lawyer, I could vacation on the side: sip a glass of wine in the afternoon at the Old Absinthe House, listen to music at my favorite bar at St. Ann's and Bourbon, the 544 Club. Going to New Orleans had always been like a pilgrimage for me, a respite, a reminder of roots, a return of sorts. I'd gone twice a year for the last fifteen years.

On this trip I thought I could show my rowdy, irresponsible family how to take charge but stay sane and enjoy oneself. I was still in my teaching mode—my literature classes had ended the week before. To me Jamie was like a student with a problem I didn't doubt I could solve. Rolodex mind, my students called it, the way I searched for solutions, wracked my brain, was a model of mind over matter. A flaky rationalist. A ditzy pragmatist. They came to me for advice, standing in the hall outside my office, waiting to enter, to be advised. I liked being able to steer them, help them find their way, trying, I knew, to give them what I'd never had—someone to give me direction.

That night Jamie and I ate in the candlelit restaurant that opened onto the courtyard. White-jacketed waiters pirouetted like dancers around the filigreed tables, potted trees, and overhanging ferns. Jamie seemed like a big grizzly bear trying to balance on the ice cream parlor chair. His eyes roamed around the tabletop for food before he took a pat of butter onto his fork and placed it on a large dinner roll. He took the roll with its icy wedge of butter into his mouth with one bite. My brother's face rose before my eyes, his chipmunk cheeks stuffed with food. The way my brother had stuffed food into his mouth had disgusted my father. Eventually he, not yet even a teenager, began taking his meals in front of the television on a tray in the dark sunroom. My brother was banished from the table for being a pig, and learned over time to banish himself from my father's sight. Jamie, just like his father, concentrated on the food, never looking up at me during the whole meal, never uttering a word, until he shoved away from the table, rocking the water from the glasses, and said he had to smoke.

He walked into the darkest corner of the courtyard where I could make out the end of his cigarette flaring orange. It was like a signal, on and off, a light from the dark sea to shore. I also moved into the courtyard, situating myself in an opposite corner with another bottle of wine. The spring semester behind me, I was ready to shed the responsibility of students and turn my attention elsewhere: to writing, to fixing up my house, to romance. Jamie walked past my table with a nod that I understood to be good-night. I closed my eyes and leaned my head back to look at the sky that was a small square hemmed in by the courtyard.

At eighteen I lost my virginity on a roll-away bed in the Holiday Inn in the Quarter. I was celebrating Mardi Gras. At twenty-six, I got in a fight with my boyfriend in the St. Ann's and moved down the block to the Prince Conti. At twenty-nine, I read a scholarly paper I'd written on Lillian Hellman at the Sheraton. Afterward I walked for hot hours looking in the Garden District for 1718 Prytania Street where Lillian had lived in a boardinghouse run by her aunts. At thirty-five, I stayed at the Royal Sonesta on Royal Street with a famous novelist who was married. It is not a city you get lost in. It is a city where I'm always finding something or finding something out or being found out.

Jamie was already asleep when I returned to our room. All four of the large white bath towels were soaking wet on the floor of the bathroom and lifting them up to wring out was like moving dead sea creatures. From the bedroom I heard Jamie gasping for breath. He would seem to stop breathing for two to three minutes and then gulp and snore, his body seizing up, his back arching as if trying to physically reach for his breath somewhere over his head. I was drunk and in my favorite city, but my roommate was breathing as if each breath would certainly be his last. He wore the same clothes he'd had on since his arrival in Houston and water from his bath was seeping onto the carpet growing into a stain resembling a Rorschach. Slob. Heathen. Filthy. Lazy. All the names my father had thrown at my brother pressed themselves into my mind as I stared at the dark, creeping stain. For years my brother has slept in all his clothes as if he wanted to be ready to flee or he were too exhausted from simply existing to undress. My father's words, the criticisms and judgments, became mine, and when I looked at myself in the bathroom mirror I started crying, first in a whimper and then in a full-scale sob that went back for its breath to my childhood, our childhood, my brother's and mine, and the air was thin.

↔

Jamie roared and snored through our night in New Orleans while I lay sleepless, shifting in my twin bed and sifting through the past that had now brought me back to Louisiana, the son of my brother in tow. In the morning, we took a cab to see the lawyer, Mark McTernan, whose office was in a renovated Victorian bungalow overlooking Audubon Park.

I was sitting in a newly upholstered wing chair—Jamie sat across the room in the matching chair—when Mark came in, looking at me, then at Jamie. Always I'd felt a sinking in my stomach as I watched someone size up my brother. Now the feeling returned, and I experienced the same conflicted response—the desire to protect and the desire to disassociate myself. Did this hulking, mute monster cancel out all that I was? Could I stay centered and unabashed as I watched the lawyer connect us, link us together as our genes did, chaining me to this miserable evidence of the damage a family could do to its own? Had done. *We are all jinxed,* I thought. *And the lawyer can see that I am too, despite appearances, despite degrees earned.* Ball-and-chained to this damage, I felt the frenzied need to gnaw my leg free from Jamie and run out of the room, run away from all that he had become, all that he represented.

Mark and I shook hands, but then he turned to Jamie, who only stared at the offered hand until Mark let it wilt back to his side. As if to dissipate the gloom that had settled around us, Mark, like an overeager schoolboy, began to ask questions without waiting for answers. He reminded me of the way a day earlier I'd tried to buoy up both Jamie and myself with bubbling banter in my kitchen. Jamie's presence—the way he glared and kept his mouth in a perpetual angry pucker as if he'd been asked a question he refused to answer—made one try to talk for two. He was having that effect on Mark. I wanted to touch Mark's arm, and say, "Settle down." I suppose what I really wanted was for him to touch my arm and say gently that everything was going to be all right. What I wanted more than anything was for him to suggest a halfway house where I could drop off Jamie.

Instead he grilled me for factual information while calling out for the secretary to bring us coffee. "Coffee?" he asked, turning toward Jamie, who didn't answer. I straightened my back and inched to the edge of the chair as if ready to perform. I recited Jamie's history as if I were a social worker giving a case history, speaking of Jamie as if he were really no relation to me. Clearly, I wanted to say, you can see he cannot speak in his own defense; he is incapable of articulating his plight. Clearly, I wanted to shout, he is quite out of it. I was not yet out of it but bordering there, edging toward controlled hysteria. There was so much talk going on in my head that it was difficult to stay tuned in to the room. How old was Mark? I wondered. Was Jamie the worst-looking kid he'd ever tried to save? I couldn't imagine a kid looking less appealing. I half expected that any minute he might bare his teeth and growl at us.

Alan, Mark's partner, who was tall and had wild curly hair, came into the office and interrupted my halting nonlinear story of my brother and Jamie and the past lawsuits. He smiled, held his arm up on the doorjamb and asked me where I was from and where I'd gone to school. We were engaging in small talk. Yes, I thought, school, much school. LSU, I said. Rice University. Barricades between me and them, between me and Jamie's parents. I was glad he could see I'd been schooled. He spoke with a thick New Orleans accent, but said he was from Long Island. I told him I was going to Long Island in July for a writer's residency. To Montauk, I said. "Beautiful," he said, looking homesick. I blathered on and on about Edward Albee's nineteenth-century barn that had been turned into a writers' retreat, then cringed inwardly for trying too hard to let them know I was a writer and a literature teacher, not really part of the mess I was recounting. But Jamie hunkered down in the chair was alarming evidence to the contrary. I wrenched myself away from Alan and the world of pleasant exchanges and back to the room and the problems—Jamie, the family. I tried to begin again.

"My father left a large inheritance," I said, as if that explained the feral boy who was napping and sighing in their office.

When I saw this didn't seem to register as a huge problem, I tried again. "Well, it all started," I began, and then stopped. It had started and never stopped, I thought. It all started, I heard myself say again, trying hard to swallow the sob that was lodged in my throat.

⁓

My father's story was a success story, Horatio Alger. His friends told the stories over and over after his death: how he preferred the oil field trash to the country club crowd; how he discovered the huge gas field that he said would keep us in cash for years, and it did; how he threw down his ruler and pen and drilled for oil where the two intersected, and struck it rich, again. Honest, they'd say, he was honest, as if that were particularly unusual in the oil business. "That Leo," they'd say nostalgically, looking as if the loss of him were truly their loss. I wanted to see the Leo they had known, the one behind their smiling eyes, see what made them proud to have known him, worked with or for him. In memory, I see my father laughing with his friends, his laughter hovering above all the others, which would make me strangely melancholy, a drifting deep sadness that pervades my memory of my childhood that, I think, stemmed from knowing without understanding that my father was not happy. As a child, I'd thought he was not happy with us—the kids. Even as a child, I knew that Jimmy, his only son, was a disappointment. Jimmy was uncoordinated, incapable of running fast without tripping over his own feet. He couldn't catch a ball, hit a ball, throw a ball. I'd watched, holding my breath, the early fall morning Daddy tried to teach him to ride a bicycle. As the bike and Jimmy swayed and tilted and quickly tumbled over, I saw something in my father's eyes that made it hard to like him. Eventually, I'd split my father into two men—the one I loved and who loved me, and the one who looked at my brother as if my brother were a bug, a loathsome creature who he wanted out of his sight.

Now I believe the damage was in the marriage and the spokes of sadness radiated out from that point of origin. I think my brother and my mother became one in my father's mind. They were weak. He was strong. Mother explained his behavior with Jimmy to us and to Jimmy by saying our father had no patience, never had. If you didn't stay afloat in the water the first time you were thrown in, if you didn't straddle that bike and keep it going without wobbling, if you didn't get up the first time on the water skiis, you were dismissed with a disgusted wave of his hand, a shake of his head, the walk which would be away.

In response, I rode a two-wheel bicycle before I could reach the seat by using the picnic table to mount the bike. I swam competitively for seven summers from the time I was six—swimming as fast as I could from one end to the other because I knew my father was watching. I won swimming medals at the country club, and every year I won field day medals at elementary school. Third grade broad jump champion. Fourth grade. Fifth grade. I brought home straight A's. At twelve I won the state poetry contest. I learned to avoid my mother's eyes in the face of my accomplishments. Sometimes I hated myself.

In the first couple of years after he'd died, I'd see his old friends in Shreveport when I was home for a visit. Actually, I'd seek them out. It was a way to be near my father, to bring him back to life through their memories, if only for an evening. I'd go with Mother to the Petroleum Club for buffet and bingo but leave her with her friends, telling her to pick me up at the small, dark bar across the street. An oilman owned the bar. The building had been bought as an investment by him and my dad for the parking garage and gas pump; my dad had officed there right before he'd died.

Walking in the bar, I might see John Tom White, who'd made and lost a fortune. He was short and round but magnetized the space around him, perhaps the mesmerization of money made, money squandered. His wife had been a beauty—a Natalie Wood type—black hair, white skin—who fitted tightly into spandex, wore leopard prints, big gold Gucci buckles and chains hanging on her hips. She'd run off the road coming home from a party—she and John Tom already divorced, sharing two kids—and was paralyzed now from the waist down. Good fortune, bad fortune. Being with a man like John Tom was a risk I like rubbing up against. Flirting with disaster.

I'd be home for a holiday, waltz into the room full of men and hug them, breathe in the smells of smoke and spicy cologne and bourbon. They'd sat with their elbows on the bar, and jostled and teased me: "You ought to buy some breasts," one landman, who used to work for my dad, told me, taking a huge suck off a cigar and smiling a lopsided grin. "You've got the money," he said, and winked at me.

I hung on every word, matched them drink for drink, put on more lipstick in the rest room before taking my place on the barstool. I needed their attention. I needed to hear again about the time my dad threw the nine iron in a tree in a temper, and later, embarrassed, paid a caddie to retrieve it under cover of darkness. Along with the series of photographs in which he stands in his "lucky" brown plaid Bermuda shorts—the same ones from 1959 to 1978, I have framed the golf score cards that show his three holes in one. In the photos he stands among his famous foursome, the men he played with each year for the Oilmens' Golf Tournament. His smile is wide, his knees knobby.

I knew about handicapping before I knew long division.

But I didn't understand odds. During his life I didn't comprehend the luck, against all odds, of the three holes in one. I do now.

His first heart attack struck just as he looked at his gin rummy hand at the Petroleum Club, the sight of which threw him back in his chair. "Some hand," his friends would laugh in the telling. "And you," they'd tease, "what have you done lately, Miss Intellectual Nose in a Book!" Then they'd all roar and order another drink, not waiting for an answer.

⋰⋱

It was 1981. My father was only a few months dead when his banker called a meeting to read the will. My family had filed into the lobby and into the elevator and then into the conference room with hardly a word between us, still stunned from our father's sudden death, from the shock of life without the weight of his gaze, real or imagined, that had kept us steady even in the most chaotic times. We sat at the huge table and each of us folded our hands in expectation of the news. The room was a strangely antiseptic setting for such a dramatic turning point in our lives. "Seven to ten million dollars," the banker said, looking at a sheaf of papers. The news took time to sink in. Bob, my father's close friend, his golfing buddy, had held the papers in shaking hands. He'd been nervous because he had good news and bad news. Keeping his eyes down, avoiding our eyes, he'd said, "Your father put all his assets into a trust." There were, he'd explained, considerable assets. Your father, he'd said, had a large net worth. We were, I thought, slippery fishes caught in the net worth of our father. As we'd sat in the windowless room in the bank that in the '50s had loaned my father the money to start his drilling company, we'd heard words that were difficult to decipher. They were technical words meant to diffuse or confuse their meaning, to buffer the punch and pain they would inflict if spoken in human terms: Trust instrument. Generational-skipping trust. Infinitely reinvested. Interest to go to the children of the children.

I had no children. I couldn't stop staring at Bob's fingernails, which were trimmed and buffed pink with perfect slivers of white at the tips. As he continued to speak of mineral rights, the fluctuation of oil prices, I'd held my hands up in the air. Like a child making shadow play, I looked at my hands, the blunt tips of my fingers, the nails unpainted. My inheritance, I thought, are my father's hands.

When I shook hands with Bob, I couldn't feel his hand or mine, so cold were both with nerves and southern air-conditioning. We were ushered out and into the elevator before we'd fully fathomed the words and implications of Bob the banker and the legalese of the "trust instrument," before we'd quite understood that the bank had control of all of his money, that 10 million might just as well be ten cents for all we would ever see of it.

I'd just taken my nineteenth-century preliminary exam for my Ph.D. Walking toward the elevator, I was struck by how Dickensian the whole scene was. *Bleak House,* I'd thought, as my family stood stunned and quiet, waiting for the relief of the ping of the elevator that would herald our return to the warmth of the summer day. *Dombey and Son,* I'd thought as we all looked up at the lit numbers marking the elevator's approach. *"Little Dorritt,"* I said aloud as we filed into the elevator like third graders on a field trip. When the elevator dropped from the third to the first floor, I'd felt my womb sway lightly beneath my navel like an empty pocketbook.

✌⃛

I saw that Mark and Alan were staring at me, waiting for me to go on with the history I'd started. How long had I sat lost in the past, thirteen years of time travel in a few seconds? My father had been a handsome man whose presence dominated any room. I'd tumbled back into time, perhaps trying to pull his spirit forward into this room, to help me with this trouble. My father, I said, picking up where I thought I'd left off, had been very successful, had been an oilman, a wildcatter. And, I added quickly, he had died under very mysterious circumstances. As their eyes widened, I saw Jamie close his.

I don't talk of my father' death often because when I do I go on a tear of telling, still, I suppose, amazed that I have such a story to tell. I start with "Someone found him crawling down the side of the road one hundred miles from where he should have been." Or, "All the arteries in his gut collapsed, signs of poisoning. Medical records disappeared." I take a deep breath, and say, "There was a lot of money involved." This usually gets attention, and it worked with these frisky family lawyers.

Mark's secretary came in and served rich, chicory-laced coffee, and looked at me with sympathy, glancing from beneath a plume of mall-bangs at Jamie as if afraid to offer him anything.

"Your brother and sister-in-law?" Mark asked. I hated to run through the incoherent mess that was my brother's life. Two years after my father's death, Mother had tried to undo what was done. She told my father's lawyers, now her lawyers, that she wanted to split her interest. She had been receiving the interest from half the 10 million, the other half being kept in trust. She insisted that her half be divided into fourths and dispersed monthly to Gail, Jan, me, and Jimmy. This was a way around my father's will, an end run that wouldn't qualify as breaking the terms of the will. And suddenly we were receiving money, lots of money, more money than I'd ever imagined. In 1983 I received ten thousand dollars a month. I was in my third year of graduate school, reading all of the southern classics, immersing myself in Faulkner's world of legacy, metaphoric and not, while living such a life. As my graduate student friends struggled to make their rent, I had a recurrent dream: I would open a closet door and be buried in cash.

I began a habit that became compulsive. I'd add up the salaries I'd earned over the years before entering graduate school. I'd been a waitress, a freelance journalist, a bookstore clerk, a social worker, an assistant editor. Over those years I'd surprised and impressed my father. But the money I'd made was a pittance compared to what I was now receiving from his life's work. My efforts at being independent seemed puny and pitiful in comparison to the wealth my father had amassed.

Later I was surprised at his wisdom. My father had known the damage the money would do.

"My brother is a gambler," I explained to the lawyers that day in New Orleans as the example of the damage that money can do sat across from me. "Publisher's Clearing House. The horses. Off-Track Betting," I said, explaining my brother's life. Sweat formed on my forehead and between my legs.

In a sense, my father's career was based on gambling, which is the nature of the oil business. My brother had inherited the lust for rolling the dice, playing cards, picking horses.

"His wife," I said, shaking my head, his wife.

"My brother," I explained, "had met her in the private mental hospital when they were teenagers. They married soon after they'd met. Dayna was twenty-two when she had Jamie. They'd divorced when he was three months old, reconciled temporarily when he was six months old, then remarried when Jamie was five." The numbers didn't convey what havoc Jimmy and Dayna had wreaked over the years, what ruins they'd left in their wake. Married, divorced, married, then traveling like gypsies, bankrupt, then not, Jamie pulled along with them in their ten-year journey through three states and a great deal of money.

"They can't even take care of themselves," I said, searching my memory for the anecdote that would make Alan and Mark see what I knew. "Can't take care of themselves," I repeated, "much less a boy." Recently the city had taken away their dog. And that wasn't the first dog that had been taken from them, I explained, trying to bolster my case. Or that had been lost, or died, or something. The city had taken the latest dog—a brown chow—the day after Jamie had run away. "Even their dog," I repeated. I always thought it ironic that the laws protected the dogs more than the child.

I told Mark and Alan a story my mother had recently told me, hoping to convince them to take pity on Jamie and take him away and put him in a safe place. As the city had done for the dog.

My brother's dog had run out of the house before dawn. Dayna, as usual, had been up—vacuuming, watching movies, restlessly pacing, watering plants. Dayna knew Jimmy would be furious that the dog was out so she chased it down the street, still in her nightgown—first on foot and then by car. The sun was just coming up. She carried in her hand a hunk of raw meat to lure the dog, which she held out the window of the car while she steered with one hand. "Blood," I told the lawyers, "was *literally* dripping down her arm as she drove through her Baton Rouge neighborhood."

Mark and Alan had their mouths open as if that were the required response. As she held the meat out the window, I continued, the car wove dangerously from lane to lane, at one point jumping the curb. A neighbor had yelled out to her, "Are you on your medicine?" Even her neighbors knew, I'd thought when Mother told me the story.

Finally Dayna got the chow in the car, but decided instead of going home she would drive to her doctor's office. Why not? She was already out and angry that her latest doctor hadn't refilled her Prozac prescription. She marched into her doctor's office in her nightgown, blood dried on her hands, with her arm in a sling.

I had to stop myself from making it a comedy routine for the lawyers—I'd told it to friends, who knew the sadness that bubbled under the surface of my family stories, who laughed with me when I trotted out the latest. But this story was Jamie's life. Nothing, I knew, really, to laugh about.

"Yeah," Jamie suddenly interrupted, emerging from his coma. "She always keeps a sling to put on. For pity," he said with a world-weary, nonchalant manner, his eyes half-closed.

The receptionist in the doctor's office assumed Dayna was a battered wife. She walked up to her, speaking as if to calm a wild animal, saying they would help her, they would call 911, help would be on its way. Dayna bolted from the clinic, got in her car and pressed the pedal to the floor, which hurled the car up and over a concrete parking barrier. The police arrived to see her careening wildly from the parking lot. There was a chase and when Dayna was caught, she was flailing and furious. They impounded the car, took the chow to the pound and Dayna to the emergency room, where she was given a shot of phenobarbital to calm her down before they took her to jail.

My brother woke up to an empty house. His wife, car, and dog were gone. He was out about a thousand dollars, though he didn't know it yet. His life was spinning out of control even while he slept. Their lives were in perpetual motion, and I was now hurdling headlong into the chaos, caught in the momentum of my brother and sister-in-law's snow-balling messes.

"A life-management problem," I called it. The lawyers, who were big-eyed, were leaning toward me. I felt like I'd run laps, and Jamie seemed asleep again.

It was southern gothic, and I hoped it worked. For so many years, the only way to escape them was to narrate them—the family—to package and recycle the stories.

Mark and Alan looked at each other, grinned, then let out some appreciative whoops and, as if psyched for battle, they began talking to each other a mile a minute.

They threw one hypothesis back and forth until it lost its power, and then pounced on another with excitement. "Emancipate?" Alan asked. "Sue his parents?" Mark countered, smiling diabolically. Such a case was in the news at the time. For a while I was consoled by the game, lulled into the back-and-forth of it. I really thought Alan and Mark were going to take Jamie off my hands. They were full of possibilities. Perhaps a halfway house, an orphanage, an efficiency apartment. I didn't know what people did in such cases, but I was sure the lawyers would know and get it done.

And maybe someday Jamie would show up again on my porch— transformed—to thank me. I could see it all clearly, the before and after: Jamie clean-shaven, fit, and finally fine. I just couldn't picture the in-between.

As I listened to Mark and Alan toss around strategies, it began to dawn on me that this was a mental exercise for them, and that the clock was ticking. I'd almost forgotten they were being paid by the hour. Since my father's death, lawyers had become a part of my family's life, acting out publicly our private dramas. In the beginning, I'd been shocked that these "family members," these friends of my father, who consoled and counseled and gossiped with us over the kitchen table, across one conference table after another, across the white linen tablecloth at the Petroleum Club, across the red-checkered plastic table covering at the seafood place, would actually charge us for their time. How long, I wondered, had we already been in this room? Five hundred dollars' worth? A thousand?

⌐:∿

Two years after my father died, I got a phone call from a former lover who was a lawyer in Shreveport. "Darlin'," he said, "you won't believe who's in my office." Randall and I had hurt many people during our three-month affair: he had been my longtime boyfriend Pike's best friend in law school. His voice instantly reminded me of my worst self, my past self: reckless, selfish, drunken.

The phone became deadweight, full of the sounds of guilt and lust and Louisiana, as he continued to tell me that my brother and Dayna were down the hall and were trying to hire him to gain custody of Jamie. A new picture went into the mental slide show Randall was presenting. Jamie—chestnut brown hair, huge brown eyes, luscious lashes.

Happiness. Jamie, who was growing up—with Gail and Bobby Aldridge, my sister and brother-in-law, was, I realized, in terrible danger. And I was the first in the family to know what was about to happen to him. In that moment, I saw the whole thing play out, envisioned in a second the scale of the sadness that was only a tiny seed at the time of the call. I felt my knees go out from under me as I sank to the couch and waited for Randall to continue.

"Did you know they remarried?" he asked.

"Remarried?" I'd repeated in a way that made Randall know that no one was going to be prepared for what was to come.

"The shit's really about to hit the fan," he said, and I looked up at my ceiling fan, which was circulating lazily. Always, my father had kept my brother in check, had held the purse strings, had convinced him six years before to go on with his life, divorce Dayna, hand over his three-month-old. But Randall's call was the clarion, the opening of a ten-year drama, alerting me that Jimmy was back and ready to reclaim his child, to become the daddy, now that his own father was safely dead and buried.

و∴:ي

Sitting in the lawyers' office, I was thinking about Randall, and about what love we'd made in his trailer long before the phone call, when he was just out of law school and had moved to Shreveport, about how strange the texture of the connections had been throughout this upheaval in my family's history, when I noticed Alan and Mark had stopped jousting and jostling with each other.

"Well, are you?" Mark asked.

"Am I what?" I asked from the fog of memory that was clearing quickly with the obvious change in the pressure in the room.

"Are you willing to adopt?" he asked.

"Willing to adopt?" I repeated.

I think I blacked out for a minute. The question seemed biblical. I mumbled that I'd think about it. I looked across at Jamie and wondered if right in front of him I could deny him. How could they ask me such an earth-shattering—life-shattering—my life shattered!—question in his presence? I remember that mainly I needed to get out of the room where everyone seemed to be waiting for me to answer. This wasn't a soap opera, I wanted to scream. This wasn't a made-for-TV movie. I got up, excused myself, and found the rest room. When I discovered I'd begun my period—a week early—I put my arm out toward the wall to brace myself. I stared at the blood on my underwear and thought that the question had torn something inside of me. This, I thought, is just too much. Returning to the office, I saw that I'd bled through my skirt onto the seat of the wing chair. I quickly took my seat hoping no one had noticed, and felt my face burning with embarrassment. Every which way I'd turned there had been shame. It had filled up the room and leaked onto the lawyer's chair. No one would take me to dinner. No one would want me, I thought.

Then I looked at Jamie. Who on earth would want him? I wondered. I certainly didn't.

"Yes," I said, "I'll adopt him."

4

magical realism

Jamie and I didn't talk as we walked back to the Quarter. Maybe, I thought, I hadn't really spoken the words out loud, taken the vow, made the commitment to adopt him. Jamie didn't seem to have heard the question—Would you be willing to adopt?—much less the answer—I will. Maybe it hadn't happened. There was nothing in writing.

Yet, I thought, what a challenge. I would turn him around. Would save the day! Would succeed where everyone else had failed! It was all playing out in my head—the kudos, the applause—when I glanced over at the incredible hulk of a boy and my fantasy of *My Fair Lady* withered. Who was going to be able to turn him around? I wondered. Turn him around? He didn't even seem present. He was missing, had gone so far inside himself that I doubted there was any chance of anyone hauling him back up into the light.

I looked into the secret courtyard gardens as I always had, imagining the lives being lived down each bricked path. Down one such courtyard I had had my palm read eight years before. The palm reader's face was worth reading itself; the deeply etched lines around his lips made him look like a puppet. "This is the life line," he said with his puckered puppet lips, "and this the marriage line, this the children line," tracing them with a finger. He moved closer to my palm as if he might sniff it. "There is something blurry here," he said. Then he looked up at my face, and said, "Not clear. A child. Perhaps not biological." And then he pushed my palm away as if angry at trying to decipher someone's illegible handwriting.

Only after I was blocks away did I realize I had forgotten to ask what I had gone there to find out. "What about love? Will there be any more love in my life?" I hurried back only to find him holding the hand of another patron, her back to me. He looked up and smiled as if he'd expected me. "Love?" I asked. I only remember his smile. I've tried to remember the words but they float in and out of my fantasies so often I know I can't trust my memory. With time I decided that the child he saw inside my hand would come with the man, an indirect, package deal in which I would be a mother, but tangentially. Perhaps a beloved step-mother. I'd be waiting in a long line at the hardware or Target or Café Express or for someone to arrive on a delayed flight, and I'd look into my palm as if I thought a picture would emerge the way it does from Polaroids. Bird in the hand. Out of my reach. Grasping. Who? Who? Was in my hand?

When Jamie and I got back to the hotel, I decided we should pack and move across the street. Since the lawyer's office, my brain had gone on autopilot and was only receiving cryptic reports from the world around me. Money, I thought, was essential. A key element. Ten years before, Gail and Bobby had gone bankrupt from the lawsuits—the custody, the fight for visitation rights, the appeals.

It was becoming clear this was no longer a vacation.

We moved from our elegant hotel to the Hotel Pension, a ramshackle place that had a hand-painted sign advertising rooms for rent. A fine mist was falling on us as I rang the rusted old doorbell and waited several minutes before the door was finally opened by an elderly black man who was wearing a garbage sack as rainwear.

"Cash only," he said.

"Fine," I said, lugging my suitcase into the hallway.

We followed him upstairs to a lovely room with a twenty-foot ceiling and faded cabbage-rose wallpaper. He said there was a pay phone in the courtyard, that if we wanted he would deny—if asked—that we were registered, and it was up to us if we wanted the cats in our room. I was thinking about what he'd said first, wondering if it were so obvious that we were on the lam, as I felt fur against flesh. Two Abbysinian cats do-is-doed between his legs. Our strange porter crossed the hallway and opened the door to a balcony to show us the miniature wrought-iron staircase custom made for the cats that led from the second floor to a courtyard where banana trees sprouted thick purple blossoms and fruit fitted together like green fists.

The place tended to be anything I imagined—bucolic one minute, eerie the next. We'd not just moved across the street but into a different dimension, I thought. I went back in our room, threw myself down on the bed, and covered my eyes with my hands. When I opened them, I could see Jamie standing at the balcony with his back to me. I could smell him, had smelled him since the first night when the smell had crossed the threshold of my house before he did. He smelled of smoke and urine and nerves. He smelled the way my brother did when he had his first nervous breakdown.

I went down to the pay phone and sat on the lawn chair to make calls. There was a plastic ashtray filled to overflowing and half a dozen books of matches with phone numbers scrawled on them on a little wooden table. Much sweating and agony had taken place in this spot. Lives had been rearranged, desperate transactions had been made. I was making such transactions.

As I made a half dozen calls on the sticky phone—to family, to lawyers, to bankers—I looked up at the balcony and saw Jamie watching me. "You know," he called down to me, "you have a purple aura." His dark hair fell forward, leaving only his nose between curtains of hair. He lifted a cat from the stair, its body going limp and arching into a receptive arc.

He had the cat in his lap when I returned to the room. "It was gray at first," he said. "Your aura," he explained. I hadn't slept a full night since our lives had intersected. I felt gray as a ghost.

He continued to stroke the cat as I considered whether he had just given me a compliment or not.

"Do you know about dervishes?" he asked.

I stared at him. My entire being was gearing up for battle. I was plotting and planning my strategy for launching a huge legal battle that would most probably destroy the fragile regrouping my family had finally settled into after the last trial. For ten years our infrastructure had been like a cracked cup. We stayed together as if by centrifugal force, and I was about to make a critical move that would shatter the illusion of peace and harmony.

"Dervishes?" I asked. I'd actually seen them whirl in the Rothko Chapel a block from my house, their bodies like stamens, the turbans the flowers in a field of foreignness.

"They neutralize the earth's hold by whirling," he explained.

I lay looking at the ceiling, wondering what else he knew, how much he knew, this mystery of a man-child I'd hooked up with, whirling, whirling through time.

"Like glue," he said, delivering this explanation in a didactic tone as if he *knew* I knew nothing.

I started laughing. "Like glue!" I said, suddenly thinking this was the funniest thing I'd ever heard as tears ran down my cheeks and into my ears.

My brother was one of the only people who used to be able to throw me into a fit of giggles. Maybe it was reflexive, the tone of Jamie's voice, a New Orleans hotel room, the sleep deprivation, or just the word "glue"—so unexpected, so perfect—that made me laugh so hard. I remembered other times, times I'd been in New Orleans with my brother and it was as if there had been no time at all.

When I was eight, nine, ten, each year until I was seventeen, my mother, father, and brother and I would drive south to New Orleans for the Thanksgiving weekend opening of the racetrack. We always stayed at the Monteleone, a huge hotel stacked on one city block at the entrance of the Quarter. Always in the past—before I was fourteen—the hotel had been enough adventure with its coffee shop and gilded lobby with burgundy carpet and shimmering chandeliers and room service and doormen dressed in red uniforms with gold epaulets. But at fourteen, the Quarter called. I tapped my toes with impatience as Mother finished her coffee and my father pored over the racing form on the table. "Pick a name," Mother said. She'd place a bet for us—"Flying Fearless?" "Fontenot Favorite?" she asked, opening her big black "track" purse that held her pencils and dollar bills and lipstick. Finally they left in a cab, leaving my brother and me standing in front of the hotel, where the black bellboys in red uniforms ran back and forth to cover with umbrellas women in fur coats for the trip from the hotel to the taxis.

"Take care of your brother," my mother had said as they left. Always I was to take care of my brother. As soon as we thought they were out of sight, we went out the revolving doors of the hotel, the doors seeming to push us with a puff into the streets of the Quarter that were slick from an afternoon rain.

I was in search of the perfect hippie beads. When we got to Jackson Square, I went from one jewelry stall to another, fingering the leather, admiring the feathers and beads, thinking what an impression I'd make in such regalia in Shreveport where there wasn't a head shop yet. Jimmy wandered off, and later I found him sitting on the curb with a guy that looked to my Shreveport eyes to be an authentic hippie. He had a handlebar mustache and wore a serape and a Mexican straw hat with a feather in the band. He asked us if we wanted to go smoke a joint— "Sure, cool," I'd said, trying to be cool as I walked toward what I considered a Salinger adventure. Then he took us to a warehouse on the edge of the Quarter where he opened a door to a long room that smelled of wet concrete and sweet incense. The room was lit by shelf after shelf of torsos, mannequin half-body lamps dressed in girdles. It was a warehouse for department store lingerie mannequins.

The three of us sat in beanbag chairs as the hippie took out a small tin box and began to concentrate on cleaning the marijuana. I knew it was marijuana, not because I'd seen any but because he had Zigzag rolling papers, which I knew had to do with joints because my friends and I had recently used them to roll the banana peels we'd cooked in the oven, having heard that could make you high.

I smoked my first joint and contemplated the various forms of girdles, some of them revolving, some of them short legged, some longer legged, some with a thick V across the midriff. My mother had wanted me to wear a girdle at twelve. By the time I was seventeen she was begging me to wear any underwear at all.

I wouldn't let my brother smoke. "I'm taking care of you, remember?" I said as I began to melt into the beanbag chair and stare at the girdled lamps. Jimmy and I had started giggling and the guy smiled and nodded toward Jimmy, "Contact high," he said, and rubbed his mustache the way I saw Dennis Hopper do a few years later in *Easy Rider*. When my father wasn't around, my brother and I always laughed.

On the way back to the hotel, I was practically levitating down the streets of New Orleans, where everyone seemed smiling at me, probably because I had a euphoric grin on my face. Walking by my side, my brother said, "I hate Daddy." My high evaporated as if it had never been. He said it as if he'd said that the rain had stopped or that the sun was shining. He said it as if it were an irrefutable fact of life, of his life, which it was, though it was also a fact of our life.

I turned over on my stomach and looked at Jamie now, sitting cross-legged on the floor, who was older than either Jimmy or I had been back then. The room we were in was much like the room Jimmy and I had shared as children—the old ceiling fan creaked high above; the ceiling was so high it lent buoyancy to the air around us. Suddenly I thought I could hear all of the doors of all of the rooms I'd ever been in softly shutting, one after another, until there was only this room containing all the others.

I realized that my brother had managed what I hadn't—he'd married and had a child.

Yet Jamie was no longer a child. He had seen so much already, having been in a boarding school, a juvenile home, and two psychiatric hospital units. He wore his cynicism lightly as if it had been with him a long time.

Perhaps I wore mine the same way.

He took off a small pouch around his neck filled with crystals and began to lay them out in a circle on the floor of the room. Like an alchemist preparing his work place, he quietly told me as he arranged and rearranged the stones about positive and negative energy, about how crystals grew, splitting and cracking into wedges of glacier mountains.

"They seem dead, but they're not," he said, holding up a pale pink crystal, and squinting as it reflected the light.

"This one will absorb bad vibes," he said with no hint of irony.

It was the most he had ever said to me at one time.

"Well, we need a lot more of those," I said, and grinned at him, hoping to coax a smile. But he was studying the stones with deadly seriousness. I saw that when serious and alert he was handsome. Like the shadow of something beneath the surface of choppy water, his face suddenly revealed a flash of the six-year-old Jamie, the child whose face had once been open, all huge brown eyes and thick black lashes, heart-shaped lips. "Just a cuddler," Gail would say, pressing her cheek against his—when he was one, two, three, four, five, and six years old. I could not imagine touching this boy who was touching the rocks with tenderness.

My father had often picked up rocks and told me where they'd been, pointed to the place worn by water, or showed me the layers that indicated pressure, revealed how old, how deep, what age. Foretelling the past, not the future. Yet, I supposed, his knowledge of rocks actually did determine our future. He made a fortune reading the lay of the land. I looked down at Jamie's circle of rocks and thought about the ones I collected as a child and kept in cloth bags my grandmother had sewed for me.

"When we were kids your dad and I collected rocks," I told Jamie.

⌇⁓

When pipe is drilled into the ground and brought up, it is filled with rock. It is called a core. On a June night when I was nine, my father had a backyard party to show some impressive core samples to potential investors. The cores were nested in wooden boxes and spread around the perimeter of the backyard, looking like a primitive homemade train looping from the swing set to the patio, which was paved with different-sized stones. Men dressed in short-sleeved cotton shirts and women in starched cotton sundresses wandered around the yard, drinks in hand, pointing at the pieces of gray rock; sometimes the men squatted down to run a finger across the gray surface of a core. A few of the men, those in new blue jeans and plaid shirts, stood among themselves holding on to their beer cans, fingertips white with their grip. They didn't look at the cores. Much later I learned of the hierarchy of the oil patch, which explained the stiffness of these men who had stood around the backyard, hair too recently cut, exposing a white band of skin like slipped halos, fingernails rimmed in black. These were the tool pushers, drillers, and mud men who worked around the clock at the wells, who lived in trailers or motel rooms by the side of highways while they baby-sat the drilling process from setting up the rig to sending down the pipe, changing drill bits, checking samples of earth for sand, salt, and oil. The other guests were bankers and people who had money to play with, sons from the old families or young geologists ready—eager—to strike it rich. My father, it was always said, had moved easily between the two groups, playing gin rummy, drinking scotch, making deals, making money.

It was a roughneck named Johnny who knelt down like a cowpoke from TV to show me the imprint of the sea animal on a core, the fossilized shading of a scorpion-looking creature, tufted tail, like the cray-fish and shrimp my father was boiling for the party in large washbuckets. Johnny, who had lines like small fans on the sides of each eye that bunched when he put his face near mine, looked out beyond the brick fence to the horizon, and said, "Once all of this was underwater." He squinted as if seeing into the past, then dug his bootheel into the grass, and said, "The ocean was right here." And instantly the world was wet, my brother and sisters and I afloat, bobbing in the current. Johnny looked down at the small hole he'd made, then at the bourbon-and-Coke-drinking crowd, then at me, then back at the ground. Is it the ocean, I wondered, that makes him seem sad, perhaps the thought of crabs, stingrays, purple-gray oysters lounging in their shells, the shells that now line the roads to the wells, brought in by dump trucks to fill in the potholes after the spring rains?

He leaped up as my father approached, kicked his tight pants legs down before extending his hand. People always wanted to impress my father. Now I know that Johnny was sad because he was a roughneck, and because he was not my father, not as smart, not as lucky. That was my father—smart and lucky.

⌇⌇

Jamie glanced up at me as I spoke of rocks, core, pipelines, mud and oil, and his brown eyes turned black, and then looked back down without a word. How dare I, he seemed to say, speak rhapsodically about the past?

That night we kept the door propped open with the twenty-pound *Golden Book of Dawn*, a book of medieval magic spells Jamie carried everywhere. Jamie wanted the cats to be able to come and go.

We returned to Houston the next morning.

The lawyers decided that until the papers were signed Jamie should go into Covenant House in Houston, a place where no questions are asked of the runaways who show up to spend the night. This would protect me from kidnapping charges. I knew about Covenant House. It was ten blocks from my house and its spillover kids had caused a lot of trouble in the neighborhood. If turned away—for being high or drunk—the teenagers wandered the streets for the rest of the night or slept wherever they could find a shelter, behind convenience stores, in garages; I'd seen them climbing out of Dumpsters. Two Covenant House residents had shot a neighbor in his garage while trying to steal his car.

I took Jamie to a sporting goods store for supplies. I bought him heavy hiking socks, a kit for bathroom articles, which I stocked with toothpaste and toothbrush, deodorant, acne medicine, vitamins. I would have bought these for a kid going to camp, I thought, under other circumstances.

I drove him to the side entrance of Covenant House, not wanting anyone at the front door to see him arrive by car. At the last minute, I wrote down my phone number and address on a slip of paper as if he were five years old and told him to put it in his pocket. Jamie got out of the car at the building with a sign that read Intake and walked toward the door. I watched him make his way up the wheelchair ramp. He didn't look back. I looked at the adjoining lot where there was a basketball court and a volleyball net, but no one was playing. Sitting on a wall along the entrance were clusters of kids—tattered and pierced Oliver Twists. Many of them had bandannas wrapped around their heads and necks; silver glinted in the sun from wrists and noses and necks and ears; black and blue and red tattoos moved up and down biceps like water lapping. A couple of boys hunched over beers wrapped in brown paper sacks. The heat of the Houston summer was so intense that the kids seemed to move in slow motion as they put cigarettes to lips, flipped butts into arcs in the air, looked over as Jamie trudged up the path. Jamie was hunched over as he made his slow way across the blistering concrete into the building.

I drove home and curled on the couch, holding a pillow and sobbing dramatic hacking sobs.

I cried because I'd left him with the forsaken, the homeless, the un-wanted, the detritus.

I cried because I'd wanted so badly to get rid of him.

⌁

The knock on the door was like an explosion.

Unfurling my sweaty self from my mound of pillows, I pushed my hair back from my face, looked down at my clothes to see if I could possibly go to the door. Finally, I peeked around to see who could have delivered such a loud blow to the door and why.

There stood Jamie, holding his bag, looking sheepish. Next to him was my mailman, Luis. For a few seconds, I just stared. The combination of the two of them left my mind in a total muddle. They didn't fit together. But nothing had been fitting together for the last few days.

I've never understood why Jamie was turned away from Covenant House; his explanation, that the woman behind the desk said he was too old, didn't make sense. I knew from the neighborhood meetings that twenty-one was the limit. It didn't dawn on me for years that probably Jamie had never walked inside Covenant House. That day I didn't argue with Jamie, only looked at him, wondering where I could hide something so large.

The mailman kept saying, "I'm sorry, I'm so sorry." I didn't know what he was sorry about or why he and Jamie were together, both look-ing aggrieved, the one over six feet, the other a short compact Hispanic, a Vietnam vet who'd delivered my mail for nine years. Luis was grim-acing and smacking his head with his hand, saying he didn't know what had happened to him. Sweat dripped off his chin.

Finally I pieced the story together: After leaving Covenant House, Jamie had seen Luis and asked the way to Marshall Street.

"There is no Marshall Street in this neighborhood," Luis had told him. Even when Jamie took out my address and showed him, Luis still insisted that there was no such street as Marshall Street. He was positive.

Adamant. He'd had this route for eighteen years, he told Jamie, and he knew there was no such street.

On the porch, Luis moaned over and over again, "Oh, I'm so sorry," while shaking his head. Luis thought he'd lost his mind, and Jamie thought he'd lost his aunt. And they both stood before me as if expecting me to fix everything.

I don't know what happened to Luis that day. Perhaps Jamie's menacing look had scared him, and he'd been trying to protect me. Or maybe a synapse suddenly sparked, taking away for a moment a familiar place. All I know for sure is that he claimed he'd lost his internal map and it had scared him to death. As I stood on the porch with them, I, like Luis, had the terrible feeling that what used to be would never be again. I too felt that the street I'd lived on for nine years had been picked up and moved to a new location, and I was going to need directions to find my way back.

5

our house
is haunted

I was seven when my sister Jan, who was thirteen, was given a Ouija board for her birthday. The first question Jan, Jimmy, and I asked of the exotic board as we sat cross-legged around it as if it were a campfire was, "Does a ghost live in our house?" The plastic diviner covered by our fingertips sped across the board to "Yes." Pop-eyed, the three of us looked up at each other and didn't say a word, didn't need to, because the board had confirmed what we had known all along. We had a ghost. We'd heard it at night, creaking up the staircase, pausing on the landing before it retreated to the hall closet, where sometimes (especially when Jimmy and I were left with the baby-sitter, fat Mrs. Crawford) it would turn the brass doorknob ever so slowly. Our next question was, "Where does it live?" Slowly the diviner selected the letters: "The hall closet."

From then on, all of the ill will we sensed in the house we attributed to the ghost that lived in the hall closet.

When I was five, Gail, my oldest sister, who was then fifteen, stole my father's Buick while he and my mother were in Hot Springs at the races. I stood in their bedroom, jumping from one foot to the other, screaming as Gail and Jan wrestled for the keys on the floor. Jan, a freckled, tomboy of eleven, who had a keen sense of right and wrong, had tried to grab the keys away from Gail. Jan always wanted all of us to be more normal, to be a calm and placid family, not, as she bemoaned over the years, people who made scenes and provided grist for the city's rumor mill. Daddy's keys had nestled in the china dachshund where he put the stuff from his pockets at night. After Gail wrenched the keys from Jan's fist and ran down the stairs and out the back door, Jan and I watched from the upstairs window. We watched as Gail started the car and began to back it down the winding, steep drive that was shaped like an S. We watched without a word as she backed into the brick wall, which toppled into the flower bed, then watched as the brake lights glowed red as she tried again, swirling down the drive like water down a drain, never stopping on her way out of town. We heard she drove to Oklahoma. She'd heard from a friend about a wild party that was going on there. That was what the two policeman, who came to the house the next day with small spiral notebooks in hand, told our parents. Their voices were deep and calm, not like the voices I'd heard throughout the night as my mother and father turned on each other over what was Gail's latest transgression. Eavesdropping, I heard one of the policeman tell my parents that they hadn't found Gail yet but that there was an APB out on her. APB was the first acronym I ever knew. The next was DWI. My sister was dangerous. I began to think we were all in danger.

I built a house of bricks around the base of a crepe myrtle, using the bricks from the broken wall, stacking them the way the bricklayers did who repaired the wall.

I stayed outside more and more. There was something wrong inside. First inside the house, then inside me. Mother said it all started with Gail. I thought about this as I made mud pies with wisteria pods, sat in the still and quiet of the big yard, often refusing to come in as the sun set, making my mother call and call. I didn't believe her. I never believed it started with Gail.

⚮

Accidents always happen at dusk, Mother told me. That was a lesson I learned, remembered, but also never truly believed. Now I can see some wisdom there, realize that by nightfall we were bone-tired, giddy with play. She'd see the limbs of a child lightly dusted with golden hair one minute and then the next suddenly broken by the misstep, the jaunty recklessness of a child trying to climb the mimosa, or swing on the rope past the brick wall and roll down the slope on the other side, where the daylilies grew.

"Dusk," she'd say when I came in with the bloody knee as the cicadas began their chorus, and the sky went from the buttery yellow of last light to the deep purple of a bruise.

To get to sleep as a child I would count the backyard's flowering trees and bushes instead of sheep, beginning with those on the left of the yard and moving in memory to the right: Four-o'clocks. Bridal wreath. Wisteria. Camellia. Rose of Sharon. I loved the night, the time when I knew my family was peaceful.

⚮

Mother always pinpointed the fault line, the place where the family wasn't ever the same again. I'd look at the ceiling of the living room, cracked into jagged lines, creating continents. Daddy said that the house shifted because it was on clay. "See," he said, putting one hand outstretched on another, "it's like plates stacked, and you carrying them. They slip and slide." Yes, I thought, like us, the family, shifted with time. The first thing he did when Gail was born, Mother told me time and time again, was go down to the bank and open an account for her college education. Mother would shake her head, peer at her lips in her little compact mirror, put it back in her purse and snap it shut while talking to me, to herself: "He was just never the same."

46

He was never the same after Gail got pregnant at sixteen and had to quit high school.

We were, I always sensed, a huge disappointment to him when we weren't a major aggravation. I don't think I believed that there was ever a time when he didn't shake his head if we had a temperature, an asthma attack, a crying jag, a fight with each other, an accident, a broken bone, the giggles. He would throw his hands up in the air with news of us, look at Mother with pursed lips, and say, "It's always something." He'd take his scotch and water and walk outside where he would rattle open the aluminum boat chair with one hand, and then sit and stare at the setting sun. I'd stand by the screen door, wanting to comfort him, crawl into his lap, but staying stock-still in the space that yawned between us, knowing that to go to him would be to betray them.

Before the baby, Gail had hung out with greasers, guys in a gang called the Eight Balls who sprayed graffiti, big black loopy letters, on the youth-center wall. One night they put cherry bombs around our house. I was in bed when the explosions went off, sending me into hysterics. "You just crawled me like a monkey," Mother always said. "You were so high-strung." I was "overly sensitive." I grew to believe that the problem was mine, that my reaction was outsized, that most people would sleep through detonating cherry bombs.

Yet I suppose we were a high-strung, sickly bunch, but Gail, Gail, as Mother said, she "took the cake." She had migraines, would sleep curled next to the toilet, where for days she'd sleep and puke, sleep and puke. Wretched girl. In my mind and memory, pregnancy seemed like another dread disease.

As a teenager, her lips were always so red they looked gooey, her glasses had pointed flares, her blue jeans carefully rolled at the cuff to show her thick white bobby socks. In her room, she had red and pink and blue petticoats that stood up by themselves in the corner. I would go in her room when she was out, put my hand over the netting, turning my palm upward and imagine my skin seen through the diamond cut-outs, try to tell my future, read my fortune in my palm full of underwear.

Just a slip of a girl, I was, but I wanted to be Gail, who had somehow filled the sunroom with boys—boys with slicked-back or buzzed-cut hair, wearing white T-shirts and leather jackets. To my wonder, the boys, like jugglers, would twirl footballs on the tips of their fingers or take lit cigarettes and hide them in their mouths, blowing smoke out of their noses like dragons.

"Come here," one would say. "Come on over here," coaxing me from the dark of the living room by the floor furnace where I'd be watching them in the sunroom. I'd step around the wires of the big television, duck under the rabbit ears wrapped in tin foil, to enter the screened porch with the cane furniture. One of them would snatch me up and put me on his knee where I'd make them all laugh by touching the top of a new haircut as if it were a porcupine. I'd dodge cigarettes and breathe in the smell of the leather jackets until Mother called from the landing for me to come upstairs. I realize now that Mother was afraid of them. I wasn't.

When Gail got pregnant, she and her husband, Hoy, who mother said lived on the wrong side of the tracks—tracks! I wondered, what tracks?— moved to a duplex. Like tracks, duplex was a word I rolled around in my head, fascinated by the sound. They had chickens in the backyard. Gail said the neighbor raised them. And if it rains, Gail told me as I wandered in the dusty yard looking at the chickens, they'll look up at the sky and drown. Gail, in her pedal pushers and flip-flops, bent down and brought an egg from beneath a scraggly bush. She placed it in my hand. It was warm and brown and speckled. I held it in my palm and thought of Scotty, Gail's baby, who my mother had explained to me had come from an egg. What a wonder! I thought. Scotty! From an egg! From under a bush!

One day Daddy didn't go to work, but he and Mother and Gail dressed up as if going to church though it wasn't Sunday, and they went out together, the air electric around them, their eyes averted from each other, Daddy gripping Mother's elbow, Mother watching her step as she made her way across the patio made of odd-shaped stones. As I stared at their receding backs, I felt Lula's presence behind me—Lula the black woman who took care of me and Jimmy. "To court," she said. "Goin' to court."

Not long after the court day, Gail, who had moved back in with us, discovered she was pregnant again. She was eighteen. Just a child herself, my mother said, says still.

Lula wanted to quit. "Way too many children," she told Mother.

I remember my mother clipping camellias and floating them in a crystal bowl. I remember her patent leather high heels, shiny, sharp, and her purse to match. I can close my eyes and smell Pond's and sweet powder bought at the five-and-dime. I see red perfect fingernails. I thought mine would grow that way automatically because I'd never seen her naked nails—still have not. My mother had a veneer that was, strangely enough, soft. She was made of hair spray and lipstick and fingernail polish. She wore nylons and a girdle always. Yet her brown eyes were so kind that they frightened me because they didn't match her hair and hands and mouth—all of which were held in place. She couldn't control the look in her eyes.

I saw my father less and less. He came home later and later. "Making deals," Mother explained, but I saw her watching for his car as evening closed in, saw her begin to pound with a vengeance the steaks she planned to fry, saw her glance at the plastic clock shaped like a skillet that hung in the kitchen. Once she lamented to me that she was a golf widow. I loved the new word but worried that she had put together the wonderful white dimpled balls my father brought home to me with a word that I knew was associated with death. And with spiders.

Gail moved back in to the house after the divorce and took the downstairs guest bedroom, the one next to the haunted hall closet. After her departure to the duplex there'd been a restructuring of the hierarchy: Jan had moved into Gail's old room. I'd moved into Jan's room. Now Gail was to be set apart from us. Gail had always been my big sister yet I'd always sensed her mother love for me, and I'd returned the love by taking it for granted, which seems to me the definition of that kind of love. But then she became a mother twice over, which made me Aunt Marsha. I always thought I was too young to be an aunt, just as Gail was, as mother said, too young to be a mother.

When the new baby came, she looked to me just like the Gerber baby on the box of dry cereal given to Scotty. She was all round and fat and soft where I was skinny and angular and scabby kneed. She was blue-eyed while all the rest of us were brown-eyed. "The beauty of her! The wonder of her!" the family cried. Her name was Stacy. I felt small and dark and secretive. Rooms seemed newly crowded, full of odd contrap-tions—changing tables, strollers, mechanical swings, bassinets, playpens—and a cacophony of sounds—whimpers and gurgles and screeches. There were toys that whistled and whirred and popped. I see myself slowly backing up, taking one step out of the circle of noise, then another, creeping away, watching from farther and farther away.

Mother hired a nurse. I heard Mother and the nurse whisper the word "complications." The nurse wore a white uniform and white hose and white shoes and guarded the downstairs bedroom door where I roamed around trying to sneak a look at the new baby. I worried about Gail, who I heard whimpering and moaning from behind the closed door. The nurse was serious and mean, and as she swished in and out of the door she seemed to always catch my eye and give me a fierce frown. I hid in the hall closet that was next to Gail's room and curled up with my knees to my chest, and sucked my thumb, trying, I suppose, to suck myself up and away, far away from complications. Feeling invisible, I joined forces with the ghost and became more and more wraithlike, slipping around, listening in on conversations, committing everything to memory—snatches of dialogue, pieces of scenes, a bright image here and there. These fragments would take me years to piece together, a task I felt had been given to me. By whom? Perhaps I took too seriously my mother's refrain, which began when I was in elementary school: "You could write book about this family, Marsha."

The same winter that Stacy was born, my father hired a painter to paint the outside of the house. No one noticed his ladder moving from one bedroom window to another except me. No one saw him sit in a clump of bushes swigging from a bottle. The empty bottles were piling up in the azaleas.

"You want to play marbles?" the painter asked me one morning when he came into the kitchen where Jimmy and I were having breakfast and held the screen door with his foot so it wouldn't slam shut. My nylon nightgown was stuck to me in swaths of static electricity from standing with my back to the gas heater. I felt naked, worse, transparent, as the painter paused and took in the kitchen, then me. His cheeks were steep planes, his eyes set back in the sockets giving him the appearance of skeleton, except grizzled, his face unshaven. He bent down near the gas heater and shot a marble across the room, then another and another until marbles were ricocheting off the walls, pinging off the stove and heater, whizzing by fast enough, I thought, to put out an eye. "We're shooting marbles!" he laughed, and his mouth was a broken scene of brown teeth and scarlet tongue. He slowly raised from the squatting marble-shooting position, steadying himself on the old yellow heater with his hand that was streaked with white paint. He chuckled deep and gurgly, and then he grabbed me around the waist and turned me around and around, chanting like a Rumplestiltskin, "We're playing marbles! We're playing marbles!" Then he was out the door, cackling, his skinny scarecrow legs the last I saw of him as I sat spinning on the floor.

In the afternoon I saw him looking into Gail's bedroom, where the nurse was bathing Stacy, or where Gail was nursing Stacy, saw him holding the ladder with one hand and the middle of his pants with the another. To me, he looked as if he were trying to unzip his pants to pee. I saw him swerve and fall backward into the bushes as if they were a safety net under his high-wire act.

Then he didn't come back for two weeks. My father was furious that the house was left half-painted.

"He's back, he's back!" I screamed when I saw the painter's pickup, which was as half-painted as our house, bounce noisily to the curb one morning. My father ran out of the house in his robe, his skinny bare legs as much a shock to me as the fact that he'd picked up Jimmy's plastic bat from the yard on his way down the terrace. "He's swinging the bat, Daddy's swinging the bat at the crazy painter!" I screamed to Lula, who had her hands submerged in sudsy water flecked with brown coffee grinds. "Girl, get away from that window," she said, grasping me by the waist and trying to pull me away. Lula, who'd been there since memory, Lula, who didn't want me to see what I had to see, had to see, had to see.

My father told the swaying, drunken painter not to come back, then he shoved the painter, who fell to his knees and almost tumbled over. My father's legs worked like scissors slicing to walk up the terrace, up the back steps, his robe flapping between them like a flag, his house shoes making soft flaps like fish brought aboard a boat.

The phone calls began the next night.

"I'm gonna cut your family into little pieces and throw them in the bayou," he whispered into the phone to my father at three in the morning, morning after morning until my father called the police, who came to live with us for a week. They tapped the lines, caught the crazy painter and sent him to jail.

I thought of us as little pieces to be fed to fishes. I would go to the neighbor's pond and watch the fishes' quick dive for the pancake remnants I brought them. Their eyes were glass marbles. I thought of us— Mother, Daddy, Gail, Jan, Jimmy, Scotty, Stacy—sliced and diced, bait, chum as my father called it, food for fishes.

⌣⁚⌢

Jimmy and I had always slept in a huge room upstairs that took up a half of the house and had floor-to-ceiling windows that were screened so that you could turn the rusted handles, open the windows, and be in the midst of a huge oak, two pecan trees, birds and squirrels, the outside spreading inside. Now in the big room there was the baby-sitter, the constant chatter of the TV turned to soap operas, and Scotty, who as a toddler was full of feistiness and mischief, who was hardy, unlike Jimmy, who at six was fragile and prone to tears at any nudge.

Scott was a boy—a boy's boy. Jimmy was a Momma's boy. That became the story and set the terms of the competition.

There was a wall of shelves on which toys and games were stacked haphazardly, spilling onto the floor if you tried to remove one; some of the toys dated back ten years from Gail's and Jan's childhoods. Drawers and shelves and closets, once filled, were never emptied. I could look deep into the shelves and find shells that had crumbled into dust, spiders dead and dehydrated into mummies, dolls without heads, spare pieces of old games. I loved the odds and ends, mementos of long, lazy afternoons with my brother. Now Scotty, who at two resembled a little bulldog, rampaged through what had been the languorous peace of what we called the green room, because of the old musty green carpet that had, over the years, grown sticky with spilled Benadryl and baby formula.

I discovered I could trick Jimmy from tears to laughter by pretending to bash my head against the floor. Thus began my comedy routine that developed over the years into full-blown skits, one-woman shows that I used to get them all laughing in the kitchen before dinner—Mother, Daddy, Jimmy, Jan, and later, Scott and Stacy. Constantly scanning faces for tension and impending quarrels, I'd make up stories, place myself as the miserable butt of all my jokes, turn their attention away from each other. Yet the tension was to become a presence that grew familiar, that seemed to be the flesh that held the body of our family together, a skin that pulsed with each of our desires.

Gail wanted her son to reign supreme, to be admired and appreciated. I think she saw Scotty as her finest accomplishment. She pushed him forward—toward our father, perhaps as a gift, a peace offering for the trouble she'd caused. In reaction, Mother coddled Jimmy even more hoping, I know, to protect him yet only managing to turn us against him. "Sissy," Jan and Gail would say under their breaths as he cuddled with Mother, or ran to her to tell on Scotty. "Mama's boy," we derided.

Scotty wasn't more than one year old when he swallowed a Tinkertoy. Emma, an enormous, beautiful black woman with great grace, was supposed to be watching him but instead was watching her program, *The Edge of Night*. When Scott began to choke and turn pink and then purple, Emma grabbed him and turned him upside down while taking the stairs three at a time. I ran before them, down the stairs, out the front door, into the empty neighborhood, screaming, "My baby! My baby is dying!" I returned, pulling Alfred, the Hamilton's gardener, along with me. Emma had slammed Scotty's forehead on the French door as she had run through the space too tight for them both, and the toy had popped out. We all stared at the cherry red toy in a pink gob of spittle. I was stunned at what little evidence there was of such a huge disaster.

Emma was fired. I listened from the top of the stairs, my hands clasping the banister as if I were on a rocking ship, when my mother told Emma she had to leave. Emma cried and later I heard Mother crying in her bathroom. I woke with nightmares. "Emma, Emma come back," I screamed one night, waking myself from the dream of impending doom. I have little memory of my brother during this time. In my recollection he is small and weepy on the margins of the household. Sometimes I felt as if I were watching from a corner of the green room, watching the household teeter off track. My affection for Scotty intensified after I'd felt the near loss of him. Accidents snowballed into more accidents, which became fodder for my comedy routines by day, for my bad dreams and anxieties at night.

Anything could happen, I thought, and at any time.

❧

My mother told the story often. My brother had an asthma attack a few weeks after he was born and for a month was enclosed in an oxygen tent. The tent, my mother said, was made of thick plastic, and she could hardly see through it. She wasn't allowed to touch her tiny, blue boy. So would begin her narrative, the one that had lodged with such permanency that the three girls—Gail, Jan, and I—could, and when particularly exasperated with Jimmy for some new calamity, would recite in unison her story of "what happened to Jimmy." Here we go, I'd think as Mother got a certain wistful expression, a mixture of guilt and regret, as she began: Jimmy, she says, is mildly brain damaged from the pure oxygen given him in the tent when he was a baby and that's why we should look out for him, take special care—"If we *cared*." Then she'd snap a few cards down for her ongoing game of solitaire, and say, "He is so intelligent. I just know he could have gone to college. He should have had his education." If only, if only, if only all the "experts" hadn't failed her in their expert advice. As the story took on recitable form, the real Jimmy seemed to get lost. I never recognized this storybook version of Jimmy. I knew a boy who grew into a master manipulator, playing on the guilt of a mother and the neglect of a father. If only, I'd think in the middle of the night. If only I were a better person who *cared* more for my brother then everything would be all right.

Jimmy was ten when Mother took him to a psychologist with a German name and a wart on the tip of her tongue. He was mesmerized by the fleshy lump, watched it instead of the flashcards she held up for him to add or multiply. She told Mother that if Jimmy was ever to "get on with it"—it being, I supposed, getting good grades, getting friends, getting the baseball as it whizzed past his glove—then he must relive the crawling stage. Mother went to Sears and bought a plastic mat, and I watched Jimmy do his crawling exercises, sliding on his belly like an infant, lifting first one elbow then a knee. "He walks, he talks, he crawls on his belly," I sang as I danced around the edges of the mat, until Mother took both my wrists, her fingernails red and sharp digging into my skin, and looked me right in the eye as if she hated me. That day, to be good, I found a paper-towel cardboard tube from the trash and made the device that Jimmy had to look through to exercise his lazy eye. For a while he wore a patch over his left eye. I did too. For penance. For not spending my afternoons in the humiliating posture of a baby scooting along a gym mat.

When at sixteen Jimmy had a nervous breakdown and was committed to the psychiatric ward of the local hospital, Mother sent me to visit him first. My mother's emissary: I was seventeen.

"I just can't face it," Mother said.

I remember feeling proud that she thought I could.

Jimmy and I had sat opposite each other in an empty visiting room that was all cheap plastic and shiny aluminum. The chair beneath me was hard and orange. Everything about Jimmy was in slow motion as if he were floating in water, a fish in an aquarium separated from me by thick glass. As we sat across from each other almost knee to knee, he told me he had plans. At first I thought he meant plans for escaping the hospital, and I felt elated, though he was all right, was considering rebelling, was not really as sick as he looked.

As he unfolded his plan, spread it before me with steady conviction, I held each side of the molded plastic chair until the tips of my fingers were numb. Each sentence was like a rope tying my insides up tighter and tighter. He told me he was going to dig a tunnel from the downstairs hall closet of the old house out to the washhouse under which he would build a little tentlike house out of twigs from the oak trees. The twig refuge would be part Indian teepee and part beaver dam, he said. "A place where hitchhikers can live," he said.

"Hitchhikers," I repeated, and nodded my head. I couldn't stop my head from bobbing and my feet from kicking nervously under my seat like I was a kid. I could imagine the tunnel, remembering the science fair's exhibits of rabbit burrows, anthills, beaver dams. I tried to hang on to the word "hitchhiker" for consolation just as Jimmy was trying to hang on to the old house that my parents planned to sell. I tried to keep a look on my face that said, This makes perfect sense—hitchhikers under the washhouse.

The way I pictured the tunnel and twig tent that day in the psychiatric ward has not dulled in twenty-eight years. That might be because as I sat across from my broken brother the thought of going back in time or going underground seemed better than facing my brother and the fact that he really was, as my mother had said, "not right." The washhouse, which was cool even in the middle of Louisiana summers and smelled of rain and earth, had been one of our favorite places to play as children. Jimmy and I had spent hours in that washhouse across the yard from the house, talking to Beatrice, the maid, who, while she ironed, chewed gum which every few seconds she would pop, making a sound like the caps exploding in our toy pistols. Usually T. J., the yardman, sat in an aluminum chair while visiting with Beatrice during the hottest part of the day. T. J. loved the pocket watch he'd been given when he retired from the railroad, and to our delight he checked it continually, opening, then holding it far away from his eyes, squinting to see the roman numerals, before snapping it shut with satisfaction, raising up on one hip to slip it back in the pocket of his overalls. It was a ritual. Time was slow and gold and in his pocket.

The hall closet was the exact opposite of the wash house. As children, Jimmy and I had been both terrified and fascinated by the musty closet filled with old winter coats and Jan's sequined net dance costumes. The closet smelled of Pan Cake makeup, sweet as syrup, and Mother's cigarettes. It was where at twelve I'd gotten my first kiss from Scooter Swann as a group of kids held the door tight. On the floor of the closet was a hinged door that I'd never seen anyone open. This was to be the entrance of Jimmy's tunnel.

Sitting across from my brother in the hospital, I wanted out from under the blue-tinted glare of the cold room, wanted to be outside in the fall air, outside this family that had created ghost stories to explain why, as my mother said helplessly, "It was just always one thing after another, just one thing after another. You'd hardly caught your breath before something else horrible happened."

Jimmy had gone crazy just as I was about to go to college.

After his first commitment, he began to check himself in to the new private mental hospital as if it were a motel. He would be on the way home from the park where teenagers gathered when he'd change his mind and change directions, going to the hospital instead of home. Usually, he told me, it was because his hands didn't seem to belong to him.

~:~

One hot bright Sunday in August of 1970, a few weeks before I left for college, the family was in a caravan driving to the lake when Jimmy's car pulled off the road. I stopped and went to his car window and saw him staring at his hands as if they were newly attached, and he was surprised to find them at the end of his wrists. We left the car on the side of the road, and he got in with me, leaning his head back and closing his eyes. Our father, who had no patience with Jimmy's attacks of feeling and no-feeling, said he was just trying to get attention. When we got to the lake, Daddy backed the boat into the water himself, unwinding ropes, wrenching the Styrofoam ice chest from the car, heaving the skis onto the deck. Jimmy, the only son, the long-hoped-for, long-awaited son, stood in the gravel under the hot sun and watched his hands turn as if they were fish flopping. My father would look at him, then continue launching the boat, something he probably had once dreamed he would do with his son.

~:~

When I was five I had a book that showed a brown child and her father on an island with a beautiful beach. The girl had dolls made of shells. Her father wore a bone necklace and a piece of flowered material for swimming trunks. Each day the girl begged the father to climb the palm tree and bring down a coconut for her. On one page the father scaled the tree, reaching across the sky to grab a coconut. On the next there was a picture of the exchange, the girl smiling and holding the gift. This globe of a gift, toy and food, was coveted by the two girls, the one in the book, the one who began to dream of the wonders within the coconut. I turned six and became determined that I had to see a palm tree. "Please," I begged my father every day at breakfast, every single morning for a year, or so I was told. "Take me to see a palm tree." I only remember the stories that became familiar in the telling. When he did take us to a place where coconuts grew on trees, he planned to drive all night so the children—Jimmy and I—would sleep, but I kept scooting from the right back window to the left exclaiming, "The stars! The moon!" And in the retelling everyone would laugh—I suppose thinking it funny that I was unaware of my father's impatience, that I hadn't learned the rules. Exasperated, he gave up and stopped at a motel.

"Took *you* to Florida," Jan corrected me thirty years later as we looked through the old photographs and I'd reminisced about the time Daddy took all of "us" to Florida. "Took you," she said, staring at the photo. "It was for you. Just for you," she said, holding the wrinkled black-and-white snapshot of us at the beach. In the picture, I am on a float on the edge of the water. Like sentinels, a grim-faced sister stands on each side of me. Gail wears sunglasses that flare at the tip and her mouth looks black with lipstick in the photo. Jan wears a sailor cap. I wonder if this is the cusp. Is this right before our family is ruined forever? My father—so young and so skinny—stands right behind me, a hand on each of my shoulders, which I have hunched up near my ears as if I'm cold or expect a wave to break over us. I have a huge grin on my face.

I was in Italy with my boyfriend, Pike, when I was twenty-one. At the sight of street vendors selling coconut on the street, slices piled into pyramids of white trimmed in brown, I shouted as if I were a child, "Coconut!" Only after Pike bought me a slice, and I took a bite did I remember the summer of coconuts. Remember that my father didn't climb a tree but bought one from a store. It was brown and hairy. He had to crack it open with a carjack. The milk was thin and sour. Perhaps this was our last summer together as a family.

⌒⌒

Throughout my childhood, my father would take me along with him in his green Buick to the quiet of the piney woods to check out a well site. Positioning the air-conditioner vent to blow on my face, I'd watch the heat mirages floating right over the car hood as we flew down black-topped roads until veering off the main road into the forest, the car bucking and jumping down a red road carved out of clay by canary yellow tractors. Pine needles shimmered, breaking the sun into streaks, the resin making the trees seem full of prisms. The clearing was always a surprise, the derrick blooming metallically against the blue-green of the pines. "Every time that pump goes up it's fifty cents in your pocket," my father told me once as he pulled me toward him across the plastic pebbled seat. He was smiling the wide smile that showed his front teeth, one slightly overlapping the other, the glint of a gold bridge somewhere within the mystery of his mouth. My father always drove with his left hand, his right arm slung back over the seat, his arms so long he could reach behind the seat with his right hand, fling the top off the ice chest and grab a beer from the rustle of ice cubes. That day he grabbed a beer and popped the top as if in celebration of our riches to come.

⌣⁚◡

One afternoon on a trip to the well site, I awoke to discover we'd already arrived and before I could smooth my hair, wipe the drool from my hot cheek, put my cast back in its sling, I found myself hoisted by my father up toward a man standing on the platform of the rig. Midair, middream, I was suddenly in the arms of my beloved roughneck, Johnny, the one who had spoken to me as if I were an adult at the backyard core party, who had given me a glimpse of his own sadness, and whose voice delivered the messages about the wells over the telephone. As he steadied me in front of his khakis, he smiled for my father's camera, but in the picture I appear dazed, squinting against the noise and sun and the surprise of Johnny. The oil pump was a vibrating roar under my feet, the man who had only been a voice now a set of freckled sun-burnished hands touching my shoulders, tenderly, perhaps wondering if it would be worse to hold on tight to the boss's daughter or to risk her tottering off the edge of the platform. A tattoo of a black dragon with a necklace of roses grew up his forearm, the roses the color of dried blood, the tail of the dragon faded like spilled ink from a fountain pen. In the Polaroid picture, my right arm is in a cast, white and thick and awkward. Johnny has on a hard hat. The well looms behind us.

60

On the way back to the house on Centenary, I held the Polaroid picture my father had taken with his new camera and flapped it in the air, fanning to the surface the image of the girl and the roughneck, both of whom appeared as if from the bottom of a deep well. I often study this black-and-white picture with the saw-toothed edges. I love the way my memory can fill in the missing colors: the purple of my new Capri pants, which were a sign of my new self-consciousness about my appearance. The inscriptions from classmates scrawled in Magic Markers on my white cast. The orangy blond hairs on Johnny's arms. I love the idea of who is outside the frame, the father who had proudly handed his daughter up into the fierce machinery of oil drilling and manhood.

⌣∶⌣

Screen memories. That is what psychoanalysts call those memories that are a scrim that buffer one from the full force of the sharp edges of real memory: I sift them like minnows from the net of association, following the line that sweeps across my childhood, deciding for me which stays, which goes. Where, I wonder now, is my brother when I go with my father to the oil fields? Where is he as I ride my bike that I've named for a race horse down the steep hill ten blocks from home? Most memories I have of him, I realized lately, were formed by the photographs we have, not by my actual recollection. He was sad, I know. His eyes were huge and sad and made me turn my head away. This memory seems real. It is a keeper: I am standing, hands held up, fingers splayed against the screen door, metal and wood worn soft as the house slippers Lula shuffles by in, her heels light as the coffee milk she gives me as she bends down, tilting the cup to my lips. She straightens herself, knees crackling, and I smell the starch of her uniform and the metal of the iron with which it's been pressed. She is not my mother. She is dust and sun and fills the wedge of light where I stand staring out. I want outside. To coax the squirrels down from the oak, to pull the stamens from the azalea blossom and smear the deep orange pollen on my hands. I hear my brother somewhere behind me. I want out. And I am six.

I will not blossom in this house: I would grow spindly and wild. Failure to thrive, a doctor called my asthma attacks that often weakened and transformed me into a sickly girl with purple circles under her eyes.

During the weeks of recuperation from asthma and the bouts of pneumonia, I would long for the backyard where I found solace climbing the trees and flying through the air on thick vines that wove one tree to the next. There was a sharp contrast between my fragile self who gasped for breath over the steam of the vaporizer and the tomboy with scabby knees and boyish biceps who wanted to stay out playing past dark. Over time I ventured farther and father afield—out of the sickroom and onto a bike, then a scooter, then on the backs of motorcycles, gripping the waists of boys who will make me catch my breath, lose my fears.

I fell in love at fifteen. I first saw Pike on a Christmas holiday night around a fire at a field party. I'd swayed between the fire and him; he held up both hands to steady me, then let me go and laughed. "Who is she?" he asked the people he came with. "Who is he?" I wondered, holding the cold can of beer to my cheek to cool the heat from the popping orange fire. She wins beer-chugging contests, he was probably told. She has a rich daddy. She has a real nut case for a brother. She's smart. She's drunk. Just like her sister. She doesn't put out. She's a prick tease. She puts out.

I was told that he was trouble and troubled. "And," a friend said, "he has a real son of a bitch for a father."

We were two troublemakers who helped each other grow up—in spite of our families. He's now a lawyer. And I teach literature at a prestigious private university that I could never have gotten into when I was eighteen. I had a record at eighteen. As a teen, I'd been a drunken, straight-A truant.

⁂

I wanted to be a writer.

In my senior year in high school, I took a creative writing class. On the morning after we'd turned in the first assignment, the teacher, Mrs. Bridger, who looked like a lady golf pro, walked heavily up to the podium, the sound of her thighs rubbing against her hose making a sandy sound. Lifting her glasses to the end of her nose, she began to read my story. In the back row of the classroom, I tried to figure out how I should react, opting for modesty—a subdued surprise that my story was being previewed. The girl in my story wore the same thing I wore that day—an army jacket that was longer than my short skirt. But the story girl had run away from home, jumped onto a freight car of a train and made her way to New Orleans. I believe that M&M's appeared in the story, as well as a hobo she encounters once she disembarks in New Orleans. This old man fumbles with the zipper of his pants with one hand while he holds on to the wine bottle wrapped in a paper sack with the other, until he manages to expose himself to the story girl. Mrs. Bridger shuffled the pages back into order, allowing an uncomfortable silence to settle before she took off her bifocals that hung on a string around her neck and said to me: "Marsha, I don't know when you will get over the notion that you're Holden Caulfield."

I realized Mrs. Bridger hated me. I always had the most trouble with my English teachers. In the fifth grade, Mrs. Miller took me out in the hall and asked me, "Do you call boys on the telephone?" It had never occurred to me that this was against the rules. "She plays with the boys at recess," she told Mother as the reason that despite my good grades, I wouldn't be allowed in Rapid Learners, could not join the elite group who left on a bus once a week to go to another school to learn more than was taught by my teachers. In the seventh grade, Mrs. Tampke accused me in front of the whole class of plagiarizing a ballad—my rhymed version of *The Old Man and the Sea*. In the eighth grade, Mr. Johnson discovered me reading *The Lord of the Rings*, which I'd placed inside the bigger anthology we were reading in class, and threw it against the chalkboard. Later I understood what they really hated. They hated my miniskirts. They hated my reputation. And particularly they hated that I was a bad girl who made good grades.

In college, at LSU, I majored in English, making my slow way through the classics, one survey course after another taught by harried graduate students or English professors whose droning voices drowned out the beautiful rhythms they were attempting to teach. Magazines and newspapers—reading material I'd never had much exposure to while growing up—had begun to enthrall me. Each week I went to the newsstand in downtown Baton Rouge and bought *The New Yorker*, *Harper's*, *Atlantic Monthly*, *Ms. Esquire*, *Mother Jones*, *Life*. I read voraciously about the war in Vietnam. Bernstein and Woodward seemed real heroes, more tangible than Milton or Donne or Chaucer. I was obsessed with current events, especially with civil rights and the burgeoning women's movement. After graduating in 1974, I stayed in Baton Rouge for a year of postgraduate work in journalism.

I wanted to record events. I wanted to travel.

I never wanted to be tied down—like my sister had been, like my mother had been.

6

family circle

In 1976 I moved to Houston, which was all pavement and promise. There were Jewish delicatessens that served new words on a plate— knishes, blintzes. I ate Chilean empanadas and Thai dumplings and Vietnamese noodles. There were yoga centers, East-West centers, drug centers, a Jung institute, and an art institute. All within walking distance of my apartment. I moved into a second floor apartment surrounded by live oaks except for one pear tree, almost strangled by ivy, which filled the living room window. The shade and the hardwood floors made the room a dark frame for the bright white pear blossoms.

Willy, the maintenance man, lived catty-cornered to me in one of the building's twelve apartments and during the day he swept the leaves that fell from the pecan tree that was in the center of the courtyard. He'd stay outside all day, sweeping, raking, standing and looking around him, rake in hand. I'd started a night class in photography, and I took portraits of Willy and still life studies of his rake propped against the tree. We became friends, chatting as I clicked pictures of the shadows cast by the rake, close-ups of his hands gripping the handle. He became my confidant. "Will I find love?" I asked him. Pike was in law school in Baton Rouge, and we seemed like an old married couple ready for divorce. "What do you think, Willy?" And then I'd tell him about the medical student, the musician, the psychology intern. Willy was short and dark and wore dress shirts with the sleeves ripped off to make them sleeveless. He chewed a stub of a cigar and under his eyes were huge stained circles that looked like small leather pouches. On the weekends, he played opera on a record player and Italian arias rattled the windows of his apartment.

One morning I was sitting on the concrete stoop drying my hair while Willy raked. "I don't want to get personal," he said, "but if you want a boyfriend you should curl your hair."

His hair was the strangest invention I'd ever seen. Around the bald crown he had the thin fringe combed up instead of the down. He told me he had once worked in a beauty parlor in Queens.

"This," I said to Willy, tossing my head forward until my long brown hair hung to the concrete and then flipping it all back in one movement, "is a radical feminist head of hair."

"Well, you might comb it at least," he said, frowning down at the clean concrete that he continued to rake.

One spring I dreamed of hair, of wrapping it like Porphyria around the neck of my lover, the head of his penis, around and around my love. Tom was his name and he'd left for medical school in Israel. He wrote me romantic letters in which he told me he saw my face in the faces of others, exotic Jewesses just out of reach, glancing from bus windows. Tom was the cousin of John, whom I'd met first, across the hallway. Tom was the cousin I chose. It was like a fairy tale, choosing which cousin. I made the wrong choice.

At night Willy stood in his apartment, arms akimbo, backlit, and watched the tenants' comings and goings. He worried about us—Lettie, a child welfare worker who came home with tales that sent chills down our spines; Ginny, who was training to be a therapist for children; and me, who he thought stayed out too late. The first year I lived there I did freelance writing jobs during the day and worked as a waitress at a downtown bar at night. I lived on Hawthorne Street for five years, five springs of the pear tree blossoming.

I'd been in Houston two years before I got what I considered my first *real* job. Even before my waitressing job, I'd heard about TRIMS, a research and training institute for mental health. My father had said, "Get your foot in the door." For many weeks I went to the medical center and checked the bulletin board where job openings were posted. When a clerical position came up at TRIMS, I applied and was hired. My job was to keep a census of the mental patients in the fifty-bed locked ward across the street from TRIMS proper. Basically, I did a head count twice daily, which meant that twice a day I went on the ward and scooted stealthily in and out of the door because patients hung around trying to escape. Clerical work, the supervisor had prevaricated when she hired me.

After six months of counting mental patients, the public relations job became available. The title that appeared on my paycheck thrilled me: Journalist I. I helped publish a monthly newsletter with a large circulation outside the institute. I wrote feature stories and six employee profiles a month. Also I became, because of confidentiality laws, the photographed Everypatient. I appeared variously in the newsletter as the woman sipping methadone from a small white pill cup, as a battered wife, as a child abuser, even as a patient undergoing hypnosis in order to recover her many hidden personalities. I'd been determined to leave my family and all of its mental health problems behind when I moved, but it seems I was drawn to the familiar.

During my time as roving reporter for TRIMS, I interviewed psychologists, psychiatrists, social workers, computer scientists, and biochemists. Most had advanced degrees—some had two: an M.D. *and* a Ph.D. TRIMS exuded a kind of kinetic energy. People there were doing cutting-edge research on addictions, domestic violence, psychotropic drugs, geriatric medicine, and family therapy. My task was to boil down the complexity of the research and results into catchy lead sentences for the newsletter. I strained to sound upbeat and hopeful in stories about heroin addicts and schizophrenics. For the newsletter, I translated the highly specialized language of the mental health field into something understandable to the layperson. TRIMS, in the middle of the Texas Medical Center, was across the street from Baylor College of Medicine, where my editor's husband worked in the mechanical engineering lab where the first artificial heart was created. Next to Baylor was TIRR, the rehabilitation center that treated people from all over the world who had spinal cord injuries. Across the next block was M. D. Anderson, the renowned cancer center. I felt in the thick of things. I walked around the halls of TRIMS with my notepad and pen, a camera slung over my shoulder. I felt powerful and full of purpose.

I wasn't surprised and I wasn't happy when my brother and his new wife arrived in Houston a couple of years after I did. He and Dayna moved to the south part of town, the site of oil refineries and billowing yellow clouds of smog; country and western bars and pickup trucks, big-haired women and giant sprawling apartment complexes, cities of concrete. This was far from the part of Houston I'd chosen to live in that was near downtown, a part of the city called Montrose, which was synonymous with bohemian.

Jimmy and Dayna would show up often at my office door, looking like any of the other patients who dropped by and visited during the day. Always, I thought, my brother was to be a test of my character. I was, after all, in public relations for a mental health institute. There should be no stigma, I told myself, as he ambled into the building looking as if he'd slept in his clothes. Dayna was pretty and olive skinned. But she was constantly fidgeting in a way that seemed to be posturing. She always looked like she had a plum in her mouth, which gave her a perpetual pout that seemed purposeful, snobby, and somewhat sexy. Often she wore a hat, some new trendy hat that she wore jauntily. And she almost always wore high heels, which made her balance precarious. She'd turn up her heel to examine its tip, or run her hands down her sides, patting her belt before rearranging the tilt of her hat as if she were looking at herself in a mirror. She was stylish but off kilter.

My brother had to duck into room. He was six feet six. Sometimes I sensed he'd like to be inconspicuous, but he was too big and his voice too booming and his confusion too palpable. What, he seemed to be wondering in a cloud around his head, have I gotten into? To his surprise, he had acquired an entourage. Jimmy, who had been a loner his whole life, now led a colorful group down the hallway and into my office where he'd peek in and say, "Well, well. Look at my sister. The professional." Then, as usual, he'd crack himself up, guffawing at his own joke as Dayna stood behind him, checking the heel of her shoe, looking down at her pink nails, puffing out her cheeks in her squirrel-cheeked pout.

They needed to borrow money because their car was broken down. Or they were being evicted because Dayna put a hole in the wall with the alarm clock. There was always trouble, and I began to realize Jimmy wanted out, wanted to go home.

Then Dayna got pregnant.

By the time Jamie was three months old, I was threatening to hire lawyers. I was ready, I told my mother over the phone every other day, to take action if she didn't come to town and do something. No one, I said, was minding the baby.

One day when Jimmy and Dayna came to my office, they were trailed by an old woman who was carrying Jamie in her arms. She stood in the hallway while Jimmy came into the office and asked for five hundred dollars. I stood behind my typewriter and looked at the group: Jimmy was disheveled, Dayna's hair was piled and sprayed on top of her head like a drag queen's, and the woman looked like someone's frail grandmother. My office was small and felt claustrophobic as the group squeezed in, the little old lady seeming to be trying to tell me a secret from her place behind my brother and Dayna.

I needed to get them out of my office and out of earshot of my boss, who was next door and getting irritated with their many visits and calls. Coming from around my desk, I herded them out by flapping my hands in a shooing motion. I'll meet you all at the snack bar, I said to Jimmy, hustling them partway down the hall. But the old woman wouldn't be bustled away. Instead, she grabbed my arm and pulled me aside and into my office, closing the door before I knew what was happening. She hurriedly began to unwrap Jamie's diaper as if she were opening a bag filled with jewels that she couldn't wait to show me.

"Look, look," she whispered hoarsely to me as I stared at Jamie's genitals. Then she folded him over her shoulder. Lit by the fluorescent lights, Jamie's backside seemed to glow. "Look, look, they don't do anything about it," she said as I stared at the raw red skin. The windowless room became a tight box as I stared at Jamie's bottom, which was covered with sores.

All the time she was talking as if pressed for time. She told me that she had been down on her luck, had been going, she said, door to door in my brother's neighborhood asking for money. When she came to Jimmy's door, he had hired her. Now in a strange twist, she found herself having to take care of them—and the baby.

"They take my social security check," she whispered as she rediapered Jamie. She said she wouldn't leave them because she was worried about Jamie. She was rushing through the story before Jimmy and Dayna got suspicious and came back for her. Her sense of urgency was contagious. I began to feel my chest tighten with the first signs of an approaching asthma attack.

"Do something," she said, looking at me as if she was sure I could.

The next week a woman called. She said she ran a day care center and that Jimmy and Dayna had left their baby there overnight.

"Jesus," I said, staring at the layout of the newsletter on my desk.

"And it's not the first time," she said, hanging up. The dial tone was a blank buzz that jammed the rhythm of my thoughts.

A week later their apartment manager called. She told me Jimmy and Dayna had been heard fighting—first in the apartment, then in the parking lot. The manager said Dayna had run up to a woman walking by—"A total stranger!" she shouted to me indignantly—and asked her to take Jamie. In fact, Dayna had begun pushing him into the woman's arms before the woman had time to comprehend the demand. She'd stood holding Jamie as Dayna jumped in her car and sped off. Had Jimmy gone back in the apartment? I wondered. Had he run after Dayna and forgotten that someone had his son? The manager said the woman had brought Jamie to her office. "Could you come and pick up this baby?" she asked as if he were a pet I'd lost and she'd found. I looked again at my desk. There were three or four manuscripts waiting to be edited. The titles were comforting: "Benzodiazepine-Binding in Brain: Receptors in Search of a Ligan;" "Personality of the Opiate Addict;" "Facilitation of Human Learning: A Developmental Strategy." I loved poring over the manuscripts and inserting commas, correcting grammar, looking for flawed logic. I could untangle sentences as if they were hopelessly knotted necklaces. I could explain to a group of visiting high school students the history of mental health in the state of Texas. I'd learned about domestic violence, heroin addiction, senile dementia, migraines, schizophrenia, the latest drugs for treatment of all types of mental disorders. But a baby. A baby seemed beyond my abilities. What would I do with a baby?

I thought Jamie should be put up for adoption. And I knew that only Mother could convince Jimmy to do this. To get through to Jimmy one always had to go through her. When I'd called some lawyers to ask questions about gaining custody, I knew I was bluffing in order to put pressure on Mother to get involved.

Mother had always turned a blind eye to Jimmy's behavior. Their love was fed and warped by the sense of their own failures toward each other. Jimmy learned to play on her guilt—to call in what I think they both saw as a debt accrued by her failure to protect him from our father.

I wouldn't let up. I called her and cajoled or screamed or cried so often that she couldn't ignore me. I wanted her to get down to Houston and rescue this baby. I was desperate to keep my focus on my goals, believing that a professional life, a career, was to be my only salvation, was to save me from the unexpected, a category into which babies fell. I was in the midst of saving myself and didn't think I could save Jamie, too. Sensing that Jamie's life was in jeopardy, I called Mother one morning, and said, "Do something!" with such force that she did.

~:~

We stole him. That's how Dayna and her mother tell it. My mother tells a different story. She says that she and Jan went to Houston "to help out." She'd tried, Mother said, to teach Dayna how to sterilize bottles. How to powder and diaper, how to burp and rock and coo. But according to Mother, Dayna wasn't interested. She just wanted to know where Jimmy was, wanted to continue how they had been before a baby disrupted their routine disruption. Jamie's crib, wedged in the corner of the living room surrounded by unpacked boxes, wasn't center stage.

When Mother tried to feed Jamie, the milky liquid leaked from the corners of his mouth and pooled by his ears. She tried again. Jamie, it seemed, didn't know how to eat. I'd always thought eating was like breathing, not something to be learned. Later doctors would explain: too many different nipples, no routine, not held enough. Much later doctors would speak of "maternal deprivation" and its effects.

Jamie was lumpish, slow to respond to holding or to smiles. I remember looking down at him and imagining grabbing him and running and running and running through the futuristic-looking petrochemical plants where they lived. Not a place for babies. I would not pick up the baby for fear I'd never put him down.

While Dayna was at the doctor's office, Mother and Jimmy had some time alone, just enough time for Jimmy to break down and say he was "really tired of being married." Jimmy was exhausted, teetering on the edge, about to fly apart. Instead he flew away. Jimmy left with Jan and Mother. They bolted with the baby.

They called me from the La Quinta near my apartment. There was no real plan, just a sort of maternal imperative that had Mother and Jan in its grip: *Save the baby!* I don't remember where my brother was—it seemed a matriarchal circle. Perhaps he was outside smoking. The Santa Fe motif in the La Quinta made the swaddled child in the middle of the bed look like a papoose. I remember that I wanted to take him up into my arms, pat him on the back, let the warmth of baby seep into the fold of my arm, but I knew that he would always be a package deal, that he would always be my brother's son. To take him would be to take on my brother forever. Take him home, I told Jan. Take him away. And I drove home, to my own life, a life in infancy, cobbled together, precarious thing that it was at the time.

Leaving Dayna started a chain of events from which we are still feeling the aftershocks.

My mother's favorite saying—"If it's not one thing it's another"—described the succession of events: Dayna was hospitalized. She checked herself into the locked ward of the institute where I worked. My name, which was, of course, her name, was written in giant letters on the admissions blackboard: RECKNAGEL. In the following weeks, my father pulled strings to get Dayna and Jimmy a quick divorce. After that they went their separate ways. My brother started driving an eighteen wheeler. Dayna went into the armed service and was trained to be an MP, until she was discharged "for medical reasons." I heard stories. Jimmy backed his truck into a farmer's fence and didn't know that when he took off he took miles of fence with him. After that his insurance was higher than his paycheck.

For a while he lived at home with our parents until Daddy came home one afternoon and saw that Jimmy's car was parked in front of the mailbox. Daddy had told him not to park there—had told him "repeatedly." My mother told it this way: "Enough is enough," my father said. "Get out," he said. The line had been crossed and recrossed so many times that I've often wondered why this line at this time? I've thought about Daddy driving up to the house and seeing Jimmy's car. Years later some friend of my father's said he'd seen my father sometimes drive up to the house, slow down, see Jimmy's car and then leave. What I know for certain is that Jimmy and Mother had settled into their old ways of playing cards at the kitchen table during the day, playing Yahtzee at night. My father, whose identity revolved around the work he'd done, couldn't, I think, bear the sight of Jimmy sitting day after day playing cards. Always the sight of Jimmy had made my father tighten with anger—probably terrible sadness balled up into more palatable rage. "Get out," he'd told Jimmy that afternoon as Mother begged him not to send him away. Mother told me she got down on her knees. She told me that she begged. But Jimmy left. He got in the car, or so the story goes, and just drove night and day. Somewhere he stopped—Phoenix, I think, or Flagstaff, Arizona—and worked for a while in a bookstore. Then he drove again, drove until he hit the Pacific Ocean. Then he turned around and came back south, stopping in Austin to stay with my mother's mother on his way home, perhaps to use Mamaw as a mediator to negotiate the terms of his return.

Dayna met my brother in Austin. The story goes that while at Mamaw's, Dayna washed her underwear and laid it out to dry on Mamaw's mahogany hope chest. When Mamaw discovered the raised white stains that curdled the deep rich satin finish of the beloved antique, she called Mother. "Enough," she said. Dayna went home to her parents and Jimmy went back to his.

❦

I didn't know Jimmy and Dayna were back together until the day I saw them in the hospital where my father lay in a coma. They had kept their reunion a secret. It was 1980—four years since I'd last seen them. I'd heard Dayna was still angry, as was her mother, at the part I played four years before in taking Jamie and talking Dayna into committing herself. They have always considered me the mastermind of a plan that was really an improvisational arrangement. Jamie's destiny unfolded by happenstance. For a few months in 1977 he'd stayed with my mother. Then when he was four months old, my father had a lawyer draw up papers that granted Dayna's parents custody. The conditions were that Jimmy and Dayna could visit with Jamie but were not to take him from the grandparents' home. According to Mother, according to Gail, the Robertses began asking Bobby and Gail to baby-sit. Over time the grand-parents' role dwindled as Gail and Bobby's grew until it just seemed that one day Jamie was living at Gail and Bobby's.

At the hospital where my father lay hooked up to life support, the elevator door opened as if it were a curtain and this was the beginning of a play. There they stood, Jimmy and Dayna. Before we could find words, recover ourselves enough to speak, I got on the elevator and they went down the hall to see Daddy, who was, although we didn't know it then, dying. He'd been brought in by ambulance from another town near where he'd been found on the side of the road, next to his car, crumpled over, on all fours. The first day, the doctors had said not to worry. We'll run tests, they'd said. Gallstones. Nothing serious. Then they'd done exploratory surgery, discovering collapsed arteries. Gangrene had destroyed a large portion of his intestines. During surgery, he'd gone into a coma.

Moments before I'd been surprised to see my brother and Dayna—together—I'd been hovering in the doorjamb of my father's room in the ICU, too scared to go in, too scared to leave. I'd watched the breathing machine pump my father's chest full, then deflate it as if he were a bellows. I'd rocked between the door and the room, heel to toe, rocking in time with the machine, in time with his breaths, the sharp mechanical intake and release. A bellow, I'd thought, a long loud cry from an animal. A bellow, I'd repeated to myself in time with the machine, his breaths. I'd thought of our name, Reck, the family of, nagel, nails, derived from the vocation of the blacksmith. German blacksmith somewhere in his past, our past. "Your genes," my pulmonary doctor had said once. "They are used to snow. No mold. Everything frozen till spring." "Your point of origin," he'd said, cocking his head as if looking way back behind my head, way back into the past of my genes. "Most likely east Berlin," he concluded, closing my folder. A blacksmith blowing a fire to life. A life on fire. I looked at my father, his chest lurching upward, then falling dramatically, and I felt tears break like ice from my eyes, and I turned and ran.

I ran from intensive care to the elevator and that is where I bumped into my brother and his ex-wife. My first thought was that if my father saw Dayna, if he happened to flicker his eyes open, come out of his coma, the sight of her would be the end of him. He had tried to will her away, this iron-willed man who had started out with nothing. Yet he had underestimated her, had not attended to the fine print of her personality, her anger, though he knew she was always in the background, waiting for us to let down our guard, waiting, it seems, to get even.

From the hospital, I ran out into the Shreveport twilight, where my father's partner for thirty years, friend for forty, grabbed me and patted my back with stiff karate chops of consolation. Bob Adair was a short, freckled man who seemed perpetually red from complexion, high-blood pressure, or scotch. I'm not sure which, perhaps all three. A block away his white Cadillac roared, the motor running to keep on the air-conditioning for two white toy poodles that skipped from the backseat to the front like circus animals hurdling a hoop.

"I loved him," he said, pulling me toward him, weeping into my shoulder. "I loved him."

⌣⁚∾

My father, who had been an only child, never spoke of his childhood. The few facts about him came from Mother. I know he was born in New Orleans in 1915. His grandfather ran a "picture show," a movie theater there, and my father's dad played the drums at intermission. Later, Pappy, as we called my grandfather, worked for the Southern Pacific Railroad, and eventually moved his family from New Orleans to Victoria, Texas, where the Germans, which he was, still greeted each other with "*Guten Tag,*" made potato pancakes and thick red sausages, and drank beer for breakfast, lunch, and dinner, or so my mother claimed. Drank beer in *Biergärten*. My mother didn't like beer. We visited Pappy and "the stepmother," who my father didn't like, a few days each summer but the visits were stilted. The stepmother would make small talk and fetch iced tea for Daddy, who I knew preferred beer. Pappy would wheeze—he had emphysema—and rotate his right shoulder in a nervous tic and ask my father a few questions. Daddy made him nervous. Victoria was not far from good fishing spots: Port Arkansas, Port Lavaca, Rockport. Fishing villages along the Texas coast. And we were on our way there, really, just passing through on our way to going fishing.

My father's mother—who I never met, who died of a heart attack before I was born—loved to fly-fish. According to my mother, she cared more for elaborate colorful flies than she did for earbobs. My mother said she could stand all day in rubber hip boots in the cold stream and fish. Against doctor's orders, my mother explained, which were given because of an enlarged heart. Gail was only six when my father's mother died. I knew my mother could not fathom a woman risking her life to fish. My father loved to fish. Almost every family vacation I can remember was spent next to water, preferably with a bridge where crabs would congregate.

I only remember once eating seafood at home. I was seven. June bugs dive-bombed the screen door as my mother scraped the skins of shrimp and crayfish that looked like orange calluses from one plate to another, making a pile that she put in newspaper. I'd collected the soggy newspapers that had been spread on the picnic table outside and brought inside the catsup, lemon wedges and Tabasco. "Weeks," my mother said to herself, looking angry, folding the newspaper tighter and tighter around the refuse. "Weeks," she said again to the pile of empty shells. "It will take weeks to get this smell out," she said to me when I came inside. I stared out at the backyard and breathed in the thick spicy smell of shrimp boil. My father was surrounded by five men who were making him laugh. The fine art of making him laugh took me time to master, but I did.

❖

As a boy, my father played tennis. He was dead before I ever realized how odd it was for a young man in the small Texas town to take up tennis, which was once considered a gentleman's sport. In 1936 he went to college, moving to Austin to attend University of Texas, where, (again I know this only through my mother), he lived in a boardinghouse. I have a small photograph of my father as a student that I've pored over with a magnifying glass. He is at his desk in the boardinghouse. He has a beautiful 1940s-style movie star face and is dressed in baggy trousers and suspenders and a white shirt. There is a photograph tacked on the wall, a Hollywood pinup photo of a woman in a bathing suit.

My mother met my father at a dance. "Oh, how we danced," she always said, wistfully. My mother had wanted to be a dancer—if it had not been for the Depression, if she had not had to go to work instead of college. I saw them dance only three or four times. Once at Jan's wedding—a huge affair—and at Mother and Dad's thirtieth wedding anniversary.

Daddy had played tennis for UT. "People would point and stare at your daddy," Mother told Jimmy and me as we looked over old pictures. "They thought he was out in his underwear!" His trophies lined the guest bedroom mantle in the old house. I loved the tiny golden men, their arms in an upswing, stopped in perpetuity just at the point where the ball was approaching. All of the tension in the anticipation.

There are no pictures of my father washing dishes in the boarding-house—which he did, along with tutoring calculus—to pay for college.

He studied petroleum engineering. No one knew what petroleum engineers were either, my mother explained to us as we culled through the tiny sepia photographs of our father in the Texas Panhandle, the oil derricks dotting the empty flat landscape like pen-and-ink drawings.

"Cold," my mother said. "You have no idea." She hated the time she lived in the Panhandle—the snow, the tornadoes, the thunderstorms. She told me that lightning rolled in giant balls across the landscape. To this day she is terrified of lightning and hides in the closet if the sky starts to roil with thunderheads. There she was, she'd explain as we looked at the boxes and boxes of photographs, "in the middle of no-where" with a new baby. Daddy was "out in the field," making his way through one field after another, looking and interpreting graphs of seismology for Sohio, the company he worked for in those early years of the oil business.

My father's sudden illness, coma, and death worked like a magnet, pulling everyone toward Shreveport, back to each other, before we flew so far apart. Leo's children, they called us. The bankers and lawyers and accountants; the ones who told us he had millions of dollars, which came as quite a surprise, and that he'd left it all in trust, which was also a surprise.

We had not lived an extravagant lifestyle. We lived in a ramshackle mansion that people couldn't define. And neither could I. When the curtains tore in my parents' bedroom, they stayed that way. The rip in the bedspread of their room seemed permanent and perfect. The house and my family were falling into disrepair and I found no dissonance.

My father declared I had to go to a state university when I'd tentatively tossed out the idea that Chapel Hill sounded exciting to me, the one place I'd heard of—I don't know how. The school counselor had never had one meeting with me. Later I'd learned I'd been written off years before. A record—of all sorts—had been passed down over the years. A thick record of transgressions.

As a family we'd gone on vacations to lakes and seashores. There hadn't been furs and jewels and trips to Vegas until the last five years of his life. I'd never, ever thought of us as wealthy. There was old money in Shreveport belonging to families whose children went to boarding schools in the East and whose daughters came out at debutante balls at Shreveport Country Club. *They* were wealthy.

To hear that our father was very wealthy in one breath and then to be told it was out of our reach with the next made my thoughts speed backward to resee everything in the new light. Then I had to jump forward into a future I might have had with the money but now would have with only the idea of it.

܀܀

Jamie was four years old when my father died. He had been three months old when he first arrived in Shreveport to be shuffled from one household to another, staying first with my father and mother, then with Dayna's parents, the Robertses; both sets initially delighted to hold and cuddle a baby.

Initially Jamie stayed at Gail and Bobby's one weekend, then another. Then maybe he had a cold and shouldn't be moved. Or there was a birthday party on their block. Or it was my birthday. Gail counted on both sets of grandparents going on with their lives. There was gradual phasing out, a weaning of Jamie from the grandparents. Gail—after her teenage marriage and divorce—had married Bobby, who had been a high school football star, who was sweet, who was willing to take care of her, who went to work in the oil fields for my father. They had not been able to have children of their own. Bobby had adopted Scott and Stacy.

They were in their midforties when they took Jamie into their lives, but they'd already raised children and lived and worked and partied hard in the small town of Many, Louisiana, that was mainly a few stores and a church surrounded by vast tracts of oil fields. Bobby supervised my father's drilling in Many.

Bobby is a good man. The kind of man who knows about weather and which bushes in the woods are poisonous and when hunting season begins. The kind of man who knows which brand of oil to use in cars, lawn mowers, motorcycles, trucks, and boats. Who knows about heaters and air-conditioners, coolants, coals, which wood burns with the least smoke. Who knows how to clean up every kind of mess: deer blood, the blood of friends who have had fingers whipped away by the chain that wraps around pipe, the oil spilled on driveways. But who are at a loss about the mess a family can make—the kind of mess Bobby found himself in when he took Jamie into his home.

Gail had my father's huge, luminous brown eyes, but she always kept them hidden behind sunglasses. She had his hearty laugh. Her hands were beautiful—like an artist's, I'd thought when I was a girl, or maybe a model's. She'd been a model for a year or two after her divorce from

Hoy, her first husband. I could tell, even though I was only five or so, that Mother loved that Gail was learning to be a model. Mother framed the photographs—glossy prints of Gail posing next to bus stop signs. Mr. Lynn's Studio "finished" girls, my mother told me. But Gail was always to prefer the earthy to the elite. She felt at home with men who hunted deer on weekends, cooked chili, worked with their hands, and with women who canned vegetables, could tell a good dirty joke, and hold their whiskey.

Gail's children had, as Mother often said, "robbed her of her childhood." Scott and Stacy—those thieves who stole Gail's "best years"—never said a bad word about Jamie, who became a permanent resident in Gail and Bobby's home when Scott was eighteen, Stacy sixteen. Scott had quit college after his first semester at University of Southern Louisiana and gone to work in the oil fields. Stacy, who had dropped out of high school, went to beauty school for a while and worked for a photographer for a while. Then someone told her mother that she was dancing at a little juke joint across the bridge in Bossier City. Sometime after the juke joint and before she married a driller named Chuck, she married a welder and wrecked the Corvette he'd bought on time. He had the marriage annulled and went back to Michigan. Scott married a pretty girl who ran a barbecue stand on the side of the highway where he went for lunch.

Scott and Stacy, it seemed to me, took Jamie in stride, but their strides were weaving and wobbling. They seemed adrift and they drank.

To Gail and Bobby, Jamie was what in Louisiana we call lagniappe, a little something special on the side, a surprise. He was Gail's chance to choose to mother, and she turned her attention with full force onto him. She doted.

Gail and Bobby put in a swimming pool and poured a double-wide drive for a new RV. They wanted to take Jamie places, to show him things, to show him off. They went to Destin and Dodge City, Eureka Springs and Nashville. "Where America lives," Gail said, in a jab at Mother. "You can have all that crap," Gail would say, spreading her graceful hands out in front of her. "That crap" was Lincoln Towncars, memberships in the country club, bridge clubs, garden clubs. "The right this, the right that," Gail would chant dismissively. Bobby, Gail, and Jamie were off to see America. Jamie returned from the trips with rattlesnake belts, shell mobiles, and a dark tan. There were placemats and floppy hats from Florida.

Jamie had the Recknagels' big brown eyes, black hair, and olive skin. He flourished in the light of Bobby and Gail's attention. As an infant, then a toddler, then a boy, Jamie had brought our family together, giving us a sense of family unity; we'd gone into the burning house and brought someone out. He gave us reason to celebrate. It was circular, the way our joy came back to us through his joy.

Jimmy, we'd thought, had gone on with his life, and Jamie was getting one.

I went to Shreveport for every birthday. For every Christmas. I'd felt I'd helped him escape at three months old when he was so weak he couldn't lift his head, make a fist, take hold of a finger.

"Come see Jamie!" they'd all say to me on the phone. "You can't believe what he'd doing now!" It was only talking or swimming or diving, first-time stuff, but we—the foster parents all—felt so proud. "Look what a fine boy he is," we'd repeat to each other. Maybe *he* will go to college. Maybe *he* will run the oil company. This was, perhaps, the boy my father had wanted. We snapped photo after photo of daddy holding him, gazing proudly on him. We would rally round the hope of Jamie.

Oil prices were at an all-time high. My father's oil company expanded into several companies: Smackover Drilling. Discovery Oil. Bailey Drilling. His business was bearing fruit and he was bearing gifts: We got fat checks at Christmas and birthdays.

Mother got jewelry.

She'd hold each new gift up in front of her nose and smile sweetly. "Who wants this when I die?" she'd say, swinging a diamond necklace as if she were hypnotizing herself and us. "Put in your order now," she'd say in a little-girl singsongy voice. She was giddy on jewelry. "I don't want any of that damn crap," Gail would snap, laughing and talking and drinking behind the kitchen counter as we all sat around her claw-foot oak table from where we could see the new recreation room, carpeted with indoor-outdoor green turf, and out the sliding glass door that looked onto the pool. And behind the pool, a two-story replica of an oil derrick.

"You and your high-and-mighty jewels," Gail would say, bursting Mother's balloon. The gifts of pearls and diamonds and emeralds were, Mother said, "just as good as money in the bank."

"You could use it to pay for the hemorrhoid operation," Mother purred to Gail the night of the diamond bracelet, making us all laugh so hard we didn't notice that Daddy had left the room.

These gifts made us all talk—behind Mother's back. What's going on with all the jewels? We asked each other, ourselves. Was there, as was beginning to rumored, another woman? After all these years? We talked. We drank. We spent his money.

I took a boyfriend from graduate school home with me. Gail served him an iced-tea tumbler of bourbon. I saw him take a gulp of what he thought was tea and watched him wince, almost gag, and swallow. The whole family was there, hugging, laughing, talking over each other. I saw Pete's confusion, and then I watched as he put his ice tea tumbler of bourbon on what he thought was a corner table but was actually the head of Gail's old poodle, Charlie Brown. Pete and Charlie Brown looked back at us with wide, innocent eyes. Seeing us through Pete's eyes was to see complete chaos masquerading as closeness. Perhaps if we made enough noise, laughed long and hard enough, we could make it funny, convince ourselves how hilarious we were, how full of life and love. Pete vomited in the middle of the night. A virus, he suspected. I knew he had caught sight of something that had made him sick.

For six years there were stacks of Polaroid pictures to be passed around. Gail with her beautiful bright red fake nails, holding a cigarette, and always, always, the drink, would smile proudly—her goofy, drunken, lopsided grin—as she held each one: Jamie at the Grand Ole Opry. Jamie in the center of a flock of seagulls. Jamie at a chili cook-off.

Some of these would be used as evidence in court. Gail's perpetual iced-tea tumbler of Old Charter and Coke, the proof my brother's lawyers' presented to take Jamie away. The ice tinkling in a glass was the background music for the tragedy of losing Jamie.

⌇⫶⫶

The custody suit seemed to come the day after Daddy's funeral. Actually, it took two years for the case to come to trial. The Robertses vs. the Aldridges. Jimmy vs. Gail. For those two years there was talk, a tremendous amount of talk. Talk, talk, talk. We sat at Mother's kitchen table. Or in Gail's new den. We analyzed, we strategized, we went over the past with a fine-tooth comb. It seems to me now that we were all talking at once. Our hands would be flying around, our gestures growing wilder and wilder with each visit to Gail or Mother's built-in bar. Whoever would get up to freshen her drink would relinquish the floor, rise up for a breather as she scooped ice from the ice maker, sloshed bourbon into a glass and stirred by turning the glass in little circles. Then I might take my place in the circle and begin again as Gail got up and repeated the drink-making ritual. Mother, Stacy, Gail, Jan, and I were the matriarchal circle that sat as if around a campfire and went over the old days, endlessly. There was a deep comfort in this womanly circling of wagons.

The court case was the dueling of dysfunctions. The alcoholics vs. the mentally ill. Each family member was called on to declare his or her loyalties, which exposed the alliances that threaded their way through the family. I remember feeling astonished and betrayed when Jan's husband, Mike, decided not to take sides. He refused to testify, as did Jan. Such a decision was beyond my comprehension. At that point we were in what seemed a scripted drama—the cameras were rolling, we each had our part to play. What, I thought later, would have happened if I'd stepped back and refused my part? Our grievances and wounds from childhood tainted our testimonies. When each one of us took the stand, the lawyers were clearly frustrated with the rambling stories. To each of us, Jamie was a symbol. He was more and less than the actual boy whose fate was being contemplated.

"They used their money to get their way," Dayna's mother said tearfully on the stand at the custody trial. "Pulled strings," she said, dabbing the mascara from under her eyes. "Just like Nazis."

June Roberts, who had run a beauty parlor for years, began her side of the story the same way each time: "Those Recknagels," she'd say to whoever would listen. "They think they're something else."

I would say for a laugh to anyone who would listen that I sure hoped we were something else.

It was war, a real feud, *Tobacco Road, Giant, The Sound and the Fury.* Hair-pulling, tongue-lashing, vengeance-lusting hatred spurred us all into a frenzy. June Roberts thought she would show us. Take us down a notch.

She did.

June Roberts and her husband, Bill, sued Gail and Bobby for custody of Jamie. The Aldridges were certain that the Robertses intended to give Jamie to his biological parents if they won the suit.

I hated the Robertses with all my heart.

I watched my mother on the stand from outside the courtroom through the small window in the heavy door. Because I was to be called to testify, I couldn't be in the room. I cannot remember any of us speaking of what Mother said in court. For years I assumed she walked a fine line and tried not to take sides between her children. I suppose I knew that she had taken Gail and Bobby's side since Jimmy didn't contact her for several years after the trial. (I *do* remember the inevitable reunion that came later, the secret phone calls Jimmy made without Dayna's knowledge, the cards, the steady creeping back to the way they were.) But her actual words, I never knew; I never asked. *Who would want to know?* I thought when friends would ask.

Recently I reread my mother's deposition, thinking it was necessary to check my memory with the public document even though my resistance to opening the dreadful yellowed plastic folder was immense. Now I realize that the family had decided to delete from our collective memory our mother's part in the trial. Mothers, I believe we all thought to ourselves, are not meant to bear witness against their own children. I could not read the deposition from front to back. I could only look all around in it. I was scared to open up the book that looked on the page like a screenplay—all dialogue. There was no room in the legal system for putting all the lives in context.

Why, the lawyer for my brother asked her, did she not think her son fit to raise his own child?

Mother began to talk of Jimmy's hearing loss. "When he sleeps," she said, "nothing can wake him. He can't hear an alarm clock; he can't hear the telephone. He can't hear anything."

"So," the lawyer said, "you believe a deaf person should not have children?"

In the deposition there is a pause after this question, which the court reporter indicated by typing three hyphens. The question made me stop, too, as surprised as she must have been at the lawyer's trap. I imagined her pulling her purse close to her chest and fiddling with her rings as she gathered her thoughts before answering.

"Well, let me think where to begin on this," she said. "I think Jimmy and Dayna have difficulty in running their own lives without a child. They have judgment problems. And that poor little boy is so attached to Bobby and Gail. And I can't understand why they would want to uproot him, as much as he loves Bobby and Gail, and as much as they love him, as good a home as they have given him. . . . And Jimmy and Dayna fight and fuss so much."

Suddenly Jimmy's lawyer had opened a trap door. "When you say fight," he asked, "are we talking about fist fights?"

"Fists, yes. They have fought with fists," my mother said.

After this spate of questions about who told whom and were there any witnesses, my mother spoke simply, but her sentence cut through the legalese and left one pure thing in the room, on the page. "I'm afraid for the child," she said. And it was as if I'd heard her say it. All the regret of the years of Jamie's life doubled back and punched me in the gut and left me making small, regretful sounds to myself.

The document was filled with terrible questions and bittersweet answers; questions and answers about my brother's breakdown, his childhood, his school records. "He was always a good boy," she said at one point. After I closed the bound transcript that for years had been in a box in the back of Bobby and Gail's hall closet, I sat still and stunned. As far as I could remember, Gail had never said that Mother had done the unimaginable—spoken out with strength and courage, fought for what was best for Jamie, all the while knowing that she probably would lose Jimmy's love. I'd heard that the lawyers had tiptoed around Mother during their questioning, treating her as if she were fragile. In the deposition, she doesn't seem fragile, only sad and determined.

Sometimes during the trial, Randall, my former lover, who was clerking for a judge in the next courtroom, would take me to lunch. I remember red beans and rice and Randall's small diamond earring. He had studied poetry at LSU before going to law school. No one in Shreveport wore an earring, and certainly not to court. I remember how comforted I was by his earring, twinkling like a wink, a connection to my other life in Houston that grew unreal when I was in Shreveport. I remember looking up to see the Robertses and Jimmy and Dayna filing into the café where I was eating with Randall during court recess. They had banded together, locking Jimmy within their circle of family. I told Randall that June looked like country come to the city, all decked out for court as if for a cocktail party. "Jesus," I said, "white shoes! In September!"

"They're doing this for the money," I hissed to Randall, who wiped his mustache with the white napkin instead of having to answer. "Pure and simple," I said. I was so sure of everything then. So sure and so stupid and so wrong.

There are more versions of the story than there are family members. Today I can see the way the pieces of our stories could be fitted together to make the puzzle of us suddenly become a picture. I have put the pieces together time after time, turning one this way and then that, trying to see what each of us saw. I see now that Jimmy felt he had to wait until his father—*our* father—was gone before he could reclaim Jamie. Fatherhood had slipped through Jimmy's fingers before he'd realized what had happened. My father had been so quick with the finagling— one day Jimmy was married, the next he wasn't; one day he was a father, the next he wasn't. It was Oedipal, I told my friends, all my brother's manhood taken just as his father had taken his boyhood and turned it black. And then when Daddy died, Jimmy came to life, to town, to reclaim what had been his—his balls, his child, and the money that the child would get because all the money had been purposely, pointedly put out of his reach.

The way the Robertses saw it, the rich and conniving Recknagel family had swept in and whisked away three-month-old Jamie and left their poor daughter, Dayna, alone and bereft in Houston. Seeing us through their eyes is not a pretty picture. Nouveau riche. We were putting on airs. Gail and Bobby in their new RV. Me with my newly minted Ph.D. Mother and her rings. Bejeweled. We were bedazzled by the money. Full of self-righteousness. We were a tribe, protecting our possessions, our pride.

Gail's piece of the puzzle had the sharpest edges. Gail believed that the Robertses had pressured Dayna to reunite with Jimmy and sue for Jamie. Whether or not what she believed was true, she believed that what they really wanted was for Dayna to get the money Jamie was to inherit. The thought of Jamie as a pawn made Gail thrash about in fury, made her prepared to kill to keep her child. She was wild with grief; she was the wolf losing her pup.

Jimmy's stories changed. Sometimes he said that if only Gail and Bobby had quit drinking he would have stopped the suit. There were times during the trial when Mother felt that if she could just talk to him something could be resolved. But his new family formed a wall between him and us. In the court hallways or in the parking lot, each of us had moments of catching his eyes. He seemed, to us, to be under a spell, to be kidnapped and convinced that now he was a part of *them*, a valued member of a new and loving family.

And Dayna? Is she evil? my friends asked. No, I always said. Dayna had first gone to a special school when she was fourteen. When she was sixteen, she met my brother. They shared the same psychiatrist in Shreveport, as well as a past of taking batteries of tests for this or that failure to perform in school, in life. My brother decided, probably after their first conversation, to be her caretaker. My brother was and still is everything to her; the ground that shifts constantly beneath her is bearable if he is there. I have no idea what she thought about the custody suit. In her deposition, she said, "I love Jamie. God, I love him. I want to teach him to be moral. I want to teach him right from wrong. I want to teach him not to lie. I want to teach him to love God."

My opinion? I think Jimmy wanted Jamie because he was his son. But he didn't understand that the child would initially be homesick and heartbroken. He didn't realize how angry that would make Dayna, how much she would resent Jamie's sadness. Dayna punished Jamie for loving the people that she had grown to hate. Jimmy was forced to choose between Dayna and Jamie, whose warfare started within the week of the transfer and lasted until the day Jamie left their home.

Each story generates another. And another.

‿∶∾

"Our side" sat in the parking lot of the courthouse in Gail and Bobby's RV that still smelled of vacations—suntan lotion and tortilla chips. We could imagine we were fishing except for the view out the window of acres of cotton fields stiff with dried brown stalks. In high school my friends and I had gathered at the edge of cotton fields like these where we'd build fires and drink beer. A cleared cotton field almost always has at least one huge pecan or oak, dramatic in the farmer's decision to spare it and leave its silhouette spreading and hovering in the empty space. Day after court day it seemed all the woods were razed from the surrounding fields, as if nothing had been spared.

Stacked on the faux wood table were dog-eared depositions that contained the testimonies of Jimmy, Dayna, her parents, social workers, psychiatrists, pediatricians, psychologists, neighbors, and even the delivery boy from Thrifty Liquor. Gail had scrawled curses and exclamation marks in the margins—"Bullshit!" "Lies!" We had passed them around for months as if they were the latest best-sellers, potboilers. Mother, never a reader, kept copies next to the chaise lounge in her bedroom where she'd read a few pages each night before bed. Some of the pages still smelled of her Pond's cold cream. I was teaching my first class of freshman and would read the depositions when I was supposed to be reading *Hamlet*.

Gail's son, Scott, took the stand early in the trial. Dressed in cowboy boots and a white shirt, looking like John Travolta in *Urban Cowboy*, Scott, who was shy, cute, and twenty-three, settled in the chair as if he were slowly putting his weight down on a bull in a holding pen and was waiting for the chute to open.

The first question from Jimmy's lawyer almost threw him:

"Have you ever seen your mother's head in her plate?"

There was a moment in which Scott's face flew open with innocence and surprise.

"Yes," he said, his large brown eyes suddenly the eyes of Scotty, the little boy I'd thought my baby doll when Gail brought him home from the hospital. "My baby," I'd said to the neighbors.

"Did she ever scramble eggs—shell and all—for you?"

"Yes, sir," Scott said with a husky voice.

"Have you ever seen her fall down?"

"Yes, sir," he answered with a boyish grin as if he were a child know-ing he was really gonna get it when he got home.

These were the stories from Scott's childhood. They were old stories, secrets a family of an alcoholic keep hidden from everyone else until they don't seem true anymore, seem more like something one heard faintly a long time ago, or came from a book read during a bout with the flu, feverish hallucinatory secrets never meant to be spoken out loud under oath in front of one's mother.

That night Scott was arrested for DWI, and the arrest appeared in the morning paper.

✌·≀

Gail and I had struck a bargain before the trial. I'd promised to lie if she'd promise to quit drinking. It was something understood, never spoken.

I'd gone to her house to talk about my testimony a month before the trial. I knocked on the door, and when she didn't answer, I walked around the house, stepped through ligustrum, knocked on windows, cupped my hands and yelled, "Gail." Always I'd thought I could save her. Finally, after all these years of hoping, playing out imagined dramatic confrontations, I had something she needed badly enough that she couldn't lock me out. Or so I thought. If I told the truth about her drinking, she'd lose Jamie for sure. If I lied, she had a chance. This, I thought, was finally my card to play. Roaming around her house in the hot summer sun, cicadas whirring like miniature buzz saws, the three Pomeranians inside yapping, I felt like a child without a key, the house a fortress, closed.

I went across the street and asked the woman who came to the door, dishtowel in hand, if I could use her phone. In the dark hallway, I found the phone and called Gail. The phone rang twenty times, then thirty, as I imagined Gail waiting for me to give up. I crouched like a child playing jacks in the hall, looked down at the grain in the wood, watched drops of sweat from my forehead turn the wood dark. I touched each drop and drew a circle of sweat. Finally, Gail answered.

"I have to talk to you," I said.

"Talk," she said.

"Will you get help for your drinking?"

In the silence I felt the blood rushing to my eardrums, sensed the blackmail sink in, heard her mind calculating, scheming, and finally, trapped.

During all the years of Gail's drinking, we'd only spoken of her problem once, one Christmas Eve at a bar when I was home from college. I'd taken an intro psychology course and thought I was newly informed, older, wiser. We were at the Cub, a place she'd taken me since I was little—all of us piled in the backseat of Mother's car—Jimmy, Scott, Stacy, me. Customers drove in and parked and honked—at night you flicked the lights—and a bent-over old black man dressed in black pants and a starched white shirt came out and took the drink order. The cars were lined up for their bourbon and Cokes as if we were at a hamburger drive-in.

That night inside the Cub I'd taken a sip of my drink, turned to her and asked if she knew she was an alcoholic. At LSU, my boyfriend, Pike, had threatened more than once to tear the phone from the wall because of Gail's calls. I'd stay on the phone for hours, listening to her ramble and rage at our mother and father.

There was no place to where Gail would point during the late night calls, only a gestalt—Mother let her down, let *us* down from the beginning. We laid out our mother's sins on a regular basis—the vagueness about Mother that left us feeling unacknowledged, unknown, only people in relation to her, not distinct individuals who had had different sets of problems growing up. I got in trouble; therefore I was like Gail.

As far back as I can remember my mother has said that girls turned on each other. When I was in my thirties, I learned that Mother's best girlfriend had taken away her high school beau. "You can't trust them," she had always said, meaning girls and women. "Was I *them*?" I'd always wondered.

"Men don't like to be beat at games," she told Jan when she started playing tennis in her teens.

"Why do you want to look so different?" she asked me with such sorrow that I was shocked when I was fifteen and transforming myself into a hippie chick. Her pronouncements boiled our complications down to the simplest common denominators. Gail's rage at Mother was masked by the alcohol, or transformed chemically into something bearable. We would dissect the behavior of our mother and father, of Jan, who we didn't understand and who didn't understand us. Of Jimmy who kept us in gossip all the time. But to speak of the drinking—the memory loss, the bones broken from falls—was against Gail's rules, even the family's rules. For broaching the subject, Gail didn't speak to me for a year.

But this time—thirteen years later—Gail needed me. I could hear the neighbor washing dishes in the kitchen, knew she was puttering and listening as I began to cry, my tears mixing with the sweat and my runny nose, as I begged Gail to stop drinking. It was that day, on the floor of the hallway, in an unair-conditioned, thin-walled hardscrabble tract house—the kind Gail had moved into when she married her first husband, then the second, the kind she even preferred and stayed in after the inheritance—that I made the pact with Gail. Not explicitly, but understood: I'd lie on the stand if she'd quit drinking. I'd left the neighbor's house with new hope, got in my car, turned the air-conditioning on high, and looked at my face in the rearview mirror and smiled. Gail would be saved, I thought. I rejoiced and even let out a few victory whoops, drumming the steering wheel with the pent-up energy of having struck such a good deal.

I kept my part of the deal. She didn't.

When I took the oath, I raised my right hand and lost my breath. I felt my brother's eyes on me and watched him feel betrayed as I described his childhood, his first breakdown, his second. I tried to tell the roomful of people about Jamie, but words couldn't paint the picture I needed to show; all words seemed too dry and clinical. I needed metaphor, analogy. But the lawyers kept interrupting to tell me to keep my answers simple. A yes or no would do, my brother's lawyer said time and time again as I tried to testify in story form. All the faces of the drama stood out as if spotlighted as I spoke to the room. I could read the expressions: Gail's face was stoic as was Bobby's—as if they were holding their heads onto their necks only by a matter of will. If the surface cracked, if the anger and righteousness didn't reinforce the planes of their faces, then, I knew, their heads might just blow right off. Mother looked as if she were caught in a repetitive replay that was a mental mantra: Isn't this a shame. That is probably as far as her mind would let her go. Any further and her heart might give out. Our lawyer's face looked out of place. He didn't, Gail said, "know shit from Shinola" about custody law. He was a junior lawyer in the firm my father always used for oil-related legal work. My brother's lawyer's face was fat and greasy, which made him stand out as the villain. I stared at him throughout my testimony, sneered my testimony at him. I didn't look at my brother, who I believed I was betraying.

"Have you ever seen your sister fall down?"
"No."
"Have you ever witnessed your sister's face in her dinner plate?"
"No."
"Do you recall your sister scrambling eggs along with the shells?"
"No."
As if we were still children playing a game of Yahtzee in the old kitchen, I'd taken sides. Always they had all wanted me to choose sides. This time I chose Gail.

I had edited several books and articles about mental illness. *Violence and the Violent Individual. The Kinetics of Psychiatric Drugs.* I'd been a social worker in a geriatric clinic. I was getting a Ph.D. in literature from

Rice University; my specialty was southern literature with an emphasis on Faulkner. I'd been in therapy for the last five years, had dated a family therapist! Credentialed and credible, or so it looked on paper, I was the sole witness of what Jimmy and Dayna had done to Jamie—or not done—when he was an infant. The old lady who had lived with them couldn't be located. Neither could the landlady at the apartment or the woman from the day care center. People had scattered. Gone on with their lives.

I knew if Dayna and Jimmy got custody that Jamie might not survive. Hypothetical, the lawyers said. Who can predict the future? Jimmy's lawyer asked the judge, holding his short arms up in the air as if to indicate it was all to be placed in the hands of a higher power. I believed I could foretell the future. So I perjured myself in court. Each question about Gail's drinking I dismissed quickly as if ridiculous. I was persuasive, I heard. But not persuasive enough. In the next ten years, I berated myself. I thought maybe if I'd been more eloquent, been a better liar, I could have prevented what happened to Jamie. Maybe if I'd lied and said I'd seen Dayna put Tabasco on Jamie's tongue when he was an infant, maybe they wouldn't have been able to gain custody and Dayna wouldn't have gone on to do that to him and worse.

∾∾

After the weeks of testimony the trial was over, and we would have to wait for the ruling. On the last day of the trial, I saw Gail and Bobby come out of the side door of the courthouse, heads down, as Bobby guided Gail with a grip on her matchstick-thin arm. They seemed to be burrowing to their RV. Across the huge hot parking lot, I saw Jimmy and Dayna get in their car.

I walked toward them, dodging car mirrors, stepping as if sleepwalking past parking meters that stood like an army of grinning robots. Jimmy's car stopped in the middle of the lot, and I saw him put his head down on the steering wheel. I knew the form and shape and sounds of Jimmy's crying. In his attempt to win Jamie, he'd lost his family.

I ran to his car and reached my hand in to touch his shoulder. I glanced back across the expanse of the lot and saw that my sister, Jan, was waving her arms as if she were doing jumping jacks. Then I saw her hands flapping as if warning that two things were about to collide. In that slow-motion moment her actions didn't add up to make sense. What Jan could see was Dayna, who had jumped from the passenger seat, run around the car, and was about to leap on my back. A deputy who raced from the front steps of the courthouse grabbed her and pulled her away as she yelled, "Lies! Everything you said was lies!"

༜

Six months later the judge gave his ruling. He argued that Jimmy and Dayna deserved a chance to be parents. He said that all the evidence was only hypothetical, based on what they *might* do if they had custody. In the judge's eyes, the way Gail's two children—Scott and Stacy—had turned out didn't bode well for Jamie's future. Stacy, who wasn't called to testify, had been in trouble—drinking, dancing, divorcing. Scott had been in two alcohol rehabs.

Dayna's parents won custody of Jamie, and as planned, gave him to Jimmy and Dayna.

Gail and Bobby hired a private detective to watch over him, but the first night the detective had a heart attack and died while hiding behind a Dumpster at Jimmy and Dayna's apartment complex. There were ambulances and police—the detective's cover blown—and Jimmy and Dayna decided to get out of town. Within the week, Jamie was off with Jimmy and Dayna, embarking on a ten-year odyssey through four states, twenty-six schools, a boarding school, two mental hospitals, and one group home.

༜

At first, after the verdict, I tried to imagine what it was like for Jamie. It was the least I could do. I'd imagine myself at six years old, and then put myself in his place. "You have to stop dwelling on it," my mother would tell me. "You have to get on with your life," my boyfriend, Pete, would say late at night after he'd find me sitting on the sill of the window in the guest bedroom of the house I'd bought after my father died. I'd be looking out, wishing there was something to be done. To be six years old and uprooted, taken away from all you have known—places, people, pets—is, finally, unimaginable.

When the little girl fell into the well in west Texas, I kept a vigil in front of the TV. When a child was reported whisked away from her front yard, the supermarket, the farm road near her house, wherever children are picked up and taken away, I'd stare at the faces of the parents—note the way the mothers' faces fell apart in front of the cameras, chins quivering, while the fathers would be stoic, their mouths cracks in concrete. Gail and Bobby, I thought. These stories were their stories. But which stories grab the world's attention? Which stories get on *60 Minutes* and *Dateline*? If the story is too complicated then people quickly lose interest. In the first versions of my story, many readers said—"Too confusing." "I'm lost." Or "Could you clear up the genealogy?" One agent, who had asked to see my manuscript, called after finishing it and asked if I'd consider taking out "all the family stuff." "Could you," he asked, "just stick to the story of you and Jamie?"

In telling this story, I've struggled to show confusion without confusing.

7

a decade
of disasters

Losing Jamie, right on the heels of losing my father, almost did me in. Even after all these years I can't put logical form to what was felt. When I lecture students on Faulkner, I describe the way his words capture the dark and subterranean hum and buzz of the brain, the place where thoughts simmer before rising into words and consciousness. It was from this place that I keened, cried, howled for Jamie. My fierce love for Jamie, I believe, was a volatile, primitive brew. There was no justice in the world, I thought. If a child can be ripped up and away from all he's known into the unknown, then we are all at risk.

Without my father, the family seemed to spin· like an unpredictable tropical storm.

The day Mother called and told me the judge's verdict, I felt he'd sentenced me personally to the Land of the Helpless, the limbo land where one waits and waits and waits. I plotted and planned revenge, but

I couldn't settle on the place to lay down my blame that brimmed over and mixed with guilt. The world had shifted and blame slipped and slid into different slots daily, weekly, monthly, yearly. Some days I blamed it all on my father, or the money we didn't inherit, then the money we did; then I'd blame my brother, then Dayna. Sometimes I'd rage against Gail, then against alcohol before turning my wrath on the judge, the judicial system, Louisiana. Then I'd begin the process all over again.

Often I blamed myself. I touched my secret like a sore: I thought I should have taken Jamie when he was just a baby.

My life, I thought, had been a self-indulgence that had cost Jamie. Why had I not filed for custody when he was three months old? Instead of taking charge, I'd called home: "Come get this baby!" I'd cried to my mother. I was busy.

Now that he was in his parents' custody, recriminations ate up the nights, night after night. The only thing that ever settled was what I thought was the truth of me: I was not fit to be a mother.

I had a recurring nightmare: Jamie floated downstream like Moses but without the basket. He bobbed down the river that runs through the Texas Hill Country where I'd gone to summer camp as a child. Next to him swims a dog—my weimaraner that had recently been diagnosed with cancer. Gail is on a bridge and she yells down to him, "Jamie, pay attention. Marsha is here." As the years went by, others joined Jamie in the rush of water that took them away, out of my reach. Stacy, Gail's daughter, sometimes floated by, jaundiced and skeletal.

I bought a dog, an Airedale, and named her Rosie. The first weeks I owned her I almost took her back. At night I'd dream that she grew bigger and bigger until I couldn't get her out of the front door. I'd awake amazed that she was a normal-sized puppy, so enormous had the responsibility for her grown in my imagination overnight.

Gail kept Jamie's room the way he'd left it, the Dr. Seuss books, toy guns and stuffed animals spread about as if he'd just run out of the room. Sears' portraits lined the hallway walls: Jamie from three months old to six years posed behind the constant backdrop of blue, blue skies.

Gail, who couldn't bear to sleep in the house where Jamie had lived, began sleeping in the RV, an orange extension cord strung between the house and the house on wheels.

The courts eventually granted them visitation—one weekend a month. I'd picture Bobby driving through nights that smelled like giant green leaves to get to Jamie in Mississippi. Bobby of the red neck, the skin on his neck like lizard hide from working for twenty years in the oil fields. Bobby with the yep and nope answers to any question. Bobby became ferocious in his determination to stay in touch with Jamie. He blew out tires in the middle of August nights in the middle of Mississippi. He begged friends for use of their private planes. His tight-lipped, deep-voiced sounding of the name "Jamie" was as tender as the way the moonlight fell on the marshes that he drove past on his way to get Jamie. But Jimmy and Dayna kept moving, always placing Jamie a little further out of Bobby and Gail's reach.

Bobby had a heart attack, a quadruple bypass, and then went bankrupt, almost all at the same time. Cornered and confused, Bobby's world collapsed.

Over time, Jamie became a family myth who existed in a netherland, a place from where letters were returned unopened, the melodramatic "Return to Sender" written across the envelope.

Often in those early days friends would say, in an attempt at consolation, "Everything happens for a reason." I'd sneered at such remarks, feeling they were wishful thinking, solace for the weak. My strength was bred of anger and fed by thoughts of revenge, a shaky foundation that crumbled many times over the next ten years.

⌇

The year after we lost Jamie I had a laparoscopy. After the procedure I was told that my chance for having children was slim. The doctor had shot dye through my tubes to see if I could conceive. Scar tissue from the IUD I'd had inserted when I was in my early twenties was blocking both fallopian tubes. Yet the news that I might not be able to have children didn't then register with me as calamitous but more as if a difficult decision had been made for me.

Not long after we lost Jamie, I broke up with Pete, after he told me one time too many that I should get on with my life. I told him he should get on with his without me. I told him that we had nothing in common, that he had never lost anything. He hadn't lost Jamie. Pete was a golden boy from sunny California. In my mind, I aligned myself with the swampy areas of Louisiana, with mystery and magic and madness. Louisiana was where boys didn't fare as well as they must in California.

⌒⌒

In the first spring without Jamie, in 1984, I talked my mother into going with me to a Florida health spa, which, I suppose, I considered the contemporary version of a sanatorium. I'd read *Magic Mountain*. I felt I needed a rest—sun, water, fresh air. Stepping into our hotel room was like entering a Georgia O'Keeffe painting; it was all swirling ocher and violet. There was a vaginal conch shell theme on the bedspreads and furniture and at every turn I was greeted by my own reflection in the mirrors that were in the suite, in the dining room, the locker room, and, of course, in the workout room. Although the youngest and thinnest of the women at the spa, I was not the picture of health.

For ten days I was surrounded by full-bodied women of all shapes. As I undressed in the locker room, I looked at the women, the wedges and flaps of skin in lumps and clumps, some soft and padded, others taut but entrenched on thighs, flesh in half-moons beneath dark navels, leathery abdomens with lightning bolts of paler stretch marks. Like a palm reader, I read their bellies: there are many children in your past; and grandchildren in your future. As well as beach houses and cruises and the French Riviera. Cocktails and diamonds. Golf and tennis. Suddenly, not happily, I was prescient.

At the spa, large naked women stood like statues of fertility goddesses in front of the whirlpools. Tucking hair into a bathing caps, they then descended into the frothing bath as if going into the primordial deep. I was usually huddled in a corner of the pool, replaying the events of the last months the way the victim of an accident goes over the details of it endlessly as if trying to change the outcome. I would come to learn the words for the ways the mind deals with grief and sorrow: repetition compulsion, ritualistic thinking. Sometimes during indoor aerobics I fantasized jumping up and down until I jumped out of my skin, flying like Peter Pan above the sack of self. In my fantasy, I would look down at my shadow with no desire for the fictional seamstress to put us back together again.

The shiny spa brochures had promised rejuvenation and renewal. I signed up for the herbal wrappings that purportedly leached toxins from the body.

I had rough sea salt scrub-downs from head to foot. I lay on the metal table in the tiled room with three drains in the floor and was buffed by serious loofah-gloved girls who rubbed down bodies day after day.

I wanted to be touched by strangers.

I lay on the table as a woman with her hair pulled back so tight it gave her face a nonsurgical facelift took one of my arms and stepped backward until the socket cup made a pop. With my eyes closed, I felt her hands move over old wounds. In the sixth grade Tommy Jett threw a pocketknife that lodged in my right foot and stuck straight up as if in earth. We were playing a game of chicken, standing spread-eagle across from each other and taking turns tossing the knife across toward the other's foot. After the knife stuck straight up in my foot, Tommy, with great care and nervous hands, mixed dirt and water to spread mud across the puncture hole. The way the Indians did it, he said, looking up at me while holding my bleeding foot and smearing mud. On the masseuse's table I remembered consolation.

Tommy's tender touch full of mud and blood and later the half-moon scar, had left more of a mark in my memory than the peck of a kiss he'd given me in the downstairs closet one Saturday.

I went over each wound, touching them in memory as the masseuse touched me.

On my shinbone there is a scar the size of a quarter. I'd been riding a three-seated bicycle that Donny Nurdin and I had taken from the porch of a mansion on Gilbert Avenue. When we sped through an avenue and through a stop sign, a car slammed into me. As I flew up and over the intersection, the handlebar of the bike punctured my leg, the handle having no plastic over the metal tube, which shot into my leg and out, carrying with it a tidy three-inch piece of me. "Can't stitch this one up," the doctor had said, moving in for a closer look. "Nothing to stitch. Not a damn thing," he said as if to himself, looking down into the hole as if it were a well.

My hospital bed had a trapeze for me to lift myself up. I had a cast on my right leg from toes to hip and one from my right shoulder to my knuckles. Yet still I managed to turn my back on my father when he told me he planned to sue the boy driving the bicycle. He tried to explain about insurance, assuring me that he was suing the insurance company, not Donny's parents. This turning away from him and toward my beaded and bangled hippie friends was just the beginning of the rotation, the wheeling and reeling away from him and his way of fixing things. "We can fix this," my father said to me that day in the hospital, but I knew he couldn't.

One scar I had etched onto myself. It was after a family dinner, and I was about fourteen. That afternoon I'd drunk a quart of beer—chugged the bottle in a contest at someone's house after school. Throughout dinner I'd stared at my numbed hand, willing it to hold the fork and put food to mouth to plate. My heart was racing with the fear that the numbness might travel up my arm and to my lungs, then to my brain. Perhaps, I thought with panic, I'm dying inch by inch from alcohol poisoning. After dinner, my mother stood with her back to me, her dishtowel flicking into corners like the tongue of a lizard, the dishwasher providing white noise. Then numbness was taking parts of me, minute by minute, and before much longer, I believed, I would be gone. As she did her nightly routine, I slipped out the screen door and sat on the concrete step where I took hold of my own right arm with my left and began to push the top of my forearm up and down on the concrete pavement. I scrubbed my arm just like my mother was scrubbing the pots and pans. I scrubbed my arm until the skin from wrist to elbow was scrubbed away. The next day I was left with a dun sticky burn. It was comforting, the next day, to feel the sting, the raw sensation of raw flesh to air.

On the masseuse's table, I went back over the past, one scar at a time, as if to remind myself that all that remained was a faint shadow of what had been felt. I considered the possibility that someday the loss of Jamie would be a recollection, faded like an old photograph. I resisted this negation. Yet I longed for the release.

The masseuse whispered a spiritual message to me as she finished, something like be good to yourself and listen to your heart, and I tried, but both seemed muffled and foreign, the message and my heart. After she tiptoed out and closed the door, I felt my breasts, and mimicking her hands I searched my body, trying to see how I felt to her, how I felt to me.

On the third night at the spa, my mother and I had an argument in our hotel room. She was sitting on the edge of her bed, setting the alarm clock, and I was in the next bed staring at the ceiling when she said she was setting the clock for six-thirty. Each morning for the last three I'd gotten up with her for seven o'clock breakfast. Looking over at her with the clock in her hand, her hair in a net, the Pond's glistening on her face, I said, "I can't." I needed to sleep, I said. And then her mouth set in the way it does when she comes against the wall of me. "I just won't eat breakfast then," she said, and set the clock down—hard—on the bedside table. "Look," I said, "This is my vacation too." In one movement, she pulled the covers up to her chin, turned off the table lamp, and said, "No wonder you've never had children." All night the sentence reverberated in my head. No wonder. No children. Not fit. To have children. Side by side with my mother. Mother and daughter.

The next day Mother had a heart attack at the breakfast table— alone. I was in a nine o'clock aerobics class when the spa nurse came into the gym to find me. When she opened the mirrored door in the gym, I was in the middle of a set of leg lifts, weights buckled with Velcro around my ankles. I had the sudden conviction that the nurse was going to shoot me just the way it happened in *The World According to Garp.* She walked up to me and her mouth was open, and I couldn't hear her words over the disco beat, but I felt them ricocheting like bullets off the mirrored walls where I had just lifted the reflection of my leg. I bent down to unbuckle the weights that hung like sacks of coins around my socks.

My mother didn't die. She returned from the health spa in a wheelchair, which I pushed through the airport. I was shell-shocked. Skinny and numb. I felt as if I'd left the real me in Florida and returned with one of the many reflections of me I'd studied in the many mirrors of the spa.

⤚∻

Soon after we returned from the health spa, a friend urged me to see a psychiatrist. I felt insulted that she thought that grief was something that could be treated and cured. I had grown proud of the stamina of my sorrow.

At the psychiatrist's office, I noted with cynicism, which was my new and not very attractive demeanor, the Mexican tiles, the primitive artifacts resembling Freud's collection, the faded oriental carpet, the metal and leather chairs.

I remember the patterns of the sun coming through the floor to

ceiling windows that looked out onto a tangled garden of palms and
vines, the ground silky with pine needles.

I stared out at the fronds, studying the shapes of shadows as I spoke
to Dr. C., who had walked in quickly as if he were always running late.

Sitting down, he crossed his legs and made a place on his lap for a
legal pad. "What's going on?" he asked.

It was such a simple question.

His brown eyes, kind eyes, sparked as he watched me think.

"What's going on?" I asked him. "Well," I said, bringing together my
palms that had grown cold and clammy. "I'm depressed."

He looked up as if encouraging me to elaborate.

"Well," I said, "I've come into a lot of money. And I don't know what
to do with it."

"What would you like to do with it?" he asked.

"Give it all away," I said.

I didn't know, couldn't have known then, that I would spend a large
portion of my inheritance on analysis, paying for time in that room,
with that man, four times a week for seven years.

In the summer of 1983—before analysis, before I quit telling stories
to anyone but Dr. C.—I'd compulsively told the unfolding saga of Jimmy
and Dayna and the custody suit to fellow graduate students at the lunch
table at the campus cafeteria. There would be five people at the table,
then the numbers would grow to ten, then twelve, as people pulled up
chairs, drawn by the laughter coming from our table as I told the latest
installment of the progress of the trial. Weary, rumpled students who'd
sat in library carrels all morning reading novels, poetry, and impenetrable
literary theory would be hunched over tuna sandwiches, munching on
chips, happy to hear true-life goings-on. I'd always told on my family.
Using them for laughs was my revenge. Turning them into comic routines took the edge off the stories, made them mine, made them—my
family, the stories—manageable.

On the first visit to Dr. C. I didn't tell my story for a laugh. I told it
with a flat here-you-take-this-and-hold-it-for-a-while tone.

I told him that my father—for complicated reasons I'd get into later—had left all of his money in a trust. I told him that my mother had reversed this part of the will and that what I needed more than therapy was a money manager. I told him the most recent news, the day-to-day crises that had kept the subterranean roots of my problems at bay. I told him that Mrs. Reed, the mother of my ex-boyfriend Pike, had moved in with me after the suicide of her son. She had, I explained, left her husband in Shreveport and moved to Houston, where Pike lived—with another woman. I spoke of Pikes's dead brother, Richie, and gave a tangled genealogy that Dr. C. scribbled down with lines and arrows shooting across the page. He flipped the page when I told him about Afrim, a Yugoslavian I'd known from graduate school who had also recently moved in with me.

Dr. C.'s eyebrows shot up.

Afrim, I explained, had come to Houston from Yugoslavia for a kidney transplant. He'd called me after the hospital had removed his kidneys and then refused to put him on a transplant list until some problem was cleared up about money and the Yugoslavian government. "Marsha," he'd said on the phone, "you have always been my friend."

Mrs. Reed always called Afrim "Our friend," mispronouncing his name in a way that gave the whole story a dark ironic twist. Our friend, who I'd barely known in graduate school, was now living at my condo with Mrs. Reed.

"And Pike?" Dr. C. asked.

We, I explained, shared custody of a dog, a weimaraner named Luther, that had recently had his cancerous prostate removed at Texas A&M. A big gray dog. A fine man, I said. Luther.

I told Dr. C. that for months Afrim, with no kidneys, and Mrs. Reed, suffering the loss of a son, and Luther, my beloved dog with cancer, had all lived with me in my two-bedroom condominium.

And then my father's lawyers said buy a house. They said for tax reasons. And I said, "I have prelims for grad school. I have to find a topic for a dissertation." But then I drove by the only house I'd ever consider. I'd written of the house in my journal—circa 1976. When the bankers and lawyers said buy, I balked, but then drove by the Marshall house and there was a sign—For Sale.

I'd just bought the house and left Afrim and Mrs. Reed in the condo. "What else," I asked Dr. C., the room, and myself, "could I do?"

Dr. C. closed his notebook, indicating time had run out.

"When can you see me again?" he asked.

When I'd called to make the appointment, he'd told me he had no room for new patients, but that he'd talk to me and then recommend another psychiatrist. I'd heard about Dr. C. since working at the mental health institute. He was supposed to be brilliant but always booked, the doctor of the stars, the analyst of training analysts, the psychiatrist who other psychiatrists called for help for themselves or to consult about their own patients.

Dr. C. had determined I was a keeper! As I drove out of the parking lot, I had a momentary flash of hope. But then the familiar despair set in. I didn't believe that there was any cure for my sadness.

For a month I'd driven Mrs. Reed all over town so she could check out various support groups. She qualified for numerous types: parents who have lost children to violence, Al-Anon, newly divorced. I'd wait in the car until she returned from each foray into group therapy: "Those people are sick, Marsha," she'd say to me as I drove to the condo where Afrim was cutting out pictures from magazines of American luxury cars and taping them to the wall over his bed. I'd roll my eyes at how self-deluded she was in thinking she wasn't one of "those people." But I too had been thinking that the craziness surrounding me was out there, not, as I was to begin to see, inside me and radiating outward.

And to my shame, Jamie was a figure disappearing on the horizon, like a closing dramatic shot of a movie, his back becoming a dark smudge I could hardly make out.

Little concrete memory remains for me of the early days of analysis; there is only the sense of trying to fight my way out of ever-expanding chaos.

Dr. C.'s first advice was to clear the deck. "You will," he said, "eventually just begin doing things that you want to do, adding to the list as time goes by. But for now, do nothing."

Do nothing. To do nothing I had to go home and grip the sides of my bed and—what?—hold on to the rocking ship of my world. Waiting. Waiting until it was safe to come out. I remembered the crisis hotline at TRIMS. The criterion. A danger to self and others. I was, I realized to my horror and sadness, both.

First, I stopped mediating the fights between Mrs. Reed and Afrim; and the fights between the hospital and Afrim; and the fights between the Yugoslavian embassy and Afrim. I slept a great deal of the time— night and day. I'd wake to scribble down my memories of dreams to take to Dr. C.

I could still do something, I thought. Still offer something. Here, Dr. C., I have a dream for you.

For two years, it seemed as if all I did was go from my bed at home to the couch at the analyst's office, from one refuge to another, spinning out the memories and narratives of a lifetime. Yet when I check the dates and see what that year held, I see I was also researching and writing a dissertation. During the first two years of analysis, I was immersed in the life stories of Lillian Hellman, my dissertation topic. I read *An Unfinished Woman, Pentimento, Scoundrel Time* and *Maybe* over and over, traced the way Hellman retold pivotal moments in her past, discovered how in each retelling she added a twist, a refrain, a variation, maybe slight, maybe wildly different. She was the company I kept as I tried to figure out how to change my future by seeing my past from a different perspective. I wanted to take myself out of the role my family had bestowed on me, a role I'd gladly embraced: the storyteller, the comic, the accident-prone raconteur. To be a court jester is to be foolishly wise, to be on the outside but not far enough away not to be controlled by the inner workings of the kingdom.

I recorded my dreams, which were often nightmares: Jamie just out of reach as he floats down the river. Or Jamie stowed under my seat at the movie theater. I go off and leave him but then run back to get him. Jamie in the branches of a tree. Look, look, he cries. No hands. And to my horror he really has no hands!

For a long time I imagined I saw people everywhere who were missing limbs, arms or legs. An elevator door closed just as I spotted a man in the far left corner who had no hand. A woman lifted out of sight by an escalator stood on one leg like a heron. A child with no arms ran down the aisle of the grocery store and turned a corner before I could tell if it was a game, if her arms were tucked beneath her coat. Dr. C. thought that I'd mapped the feeling of the loss of my father and Jamie onto others. He spoke of bodily integrity and the way I felt mine had been threatened by the loss of two people integral to me, to my identity, to my idea of myself. I'd experienced the death of my father as if my own limbs had been torn away from me.

Torn asunder, I thought. Our family. Jamie torn away. One loss—of my father—followed quickly by the second loss, Jamie. I think that the loss of my father and of the boy I'd seen as a surrogate son and brother—Jamie—seared some basic wiring that made connections impossible, at least for a long while. My wiring seared, then sealed.

In psychoanalysis I learned to read myself like a novel back to myself. And gradually I began to make sense to myself.

What else can I say that I learned from psychoanalysis that won't sound like the boring details of a stranger's dream? I learned my family wasn't funny. When I finally stopped laughing at my family's high jinks and melodramas, I cried daily for a year. I learned that if you attend to the leak in the faucet, then the ceiling of the foyer won't fall in—as it had in my new house. Such foresight was different for me and went against the grain of my family's way of doing things. If the ceiling didn't fall in on them, then they couldn't bemoan their bad luck and also, there wouldn't be a hilarious story to tell. Some stories, I decided, were worth forgoing.

I can't remember my father ever telling a story.

He was a blank slate.

During analysis and research for my dissertation, I learned about silence and stories. The way one uses both for power and control. I learned the psychological definitions, learned about transitional objects, what one chooses, the bear or blanket, to fill the gap between mother and other. Maternal longing, father hunger, projection, rejection, all slipped off my tongue, slid into conversation with ease. I mastered the terminology of toil and trouble, and could choose the right quotation from Shakespeare that could sum it up in Renaissance, in rhyme.

I roamed around the rooms of my new, empty house and watched where the morning and evening light fell. There was a sunroom and a small garden hemmed in by a town house, giving the space, I believed, the feel of a Parisian pension. The two-story stucco house looked like a smaller version of the old house in Shreveport. Vines crawled into the windows and curled inside as if gesturing the rest to come on in. I'd taken only a few pieces of furniture from my condo—my double bed, the single bed from my childhood, and the antique secretary, a lovely mahogany desk given to me by my father when I graduated from college. I had decided I would furnish the house with one beloved object at a time, choosing as carefully what would fill the house as what would refill my life.

I had the inside of the house painted white—museum white, according to the color samples I spread out in front of me in the paint shop. No fuchsia, no bisque, no robin's-egg blue, I told the clerk. I wanted to cast the shadow of myself onto the blank pages of my new home.

For the first time in my life I began to feel the tightness in my stomach release. I had not been able to save my sister from her alcoholism. I had not been able to save my brother from my father. I had not been able to save Jamie from my brother. These were admissions I made and tried to reconcile. I carried my own life carefully as if it were sand in my palm. I trusted Dr. C.'s vision of my future, dimly forming day by day in the quiet room that smelled of his aftershave and other people's perfume. I trusted that the hours would go by, and I would get better. It was just about all I trusted.

∿

My ten years, the ones that paralleled Jamie's ten with his parents, came into focus only after Jamie came to stay. Over those years, I wrote my dissertation on Hellman and her now notorious memoirs. She'd lied in her memoirs, I argued, to fill in the blank that had been her mother. I'd discovered a pattern in her life that she joked about in the works. She tripped and fell so often that I began to suspect these accidents were equivalent to slips of the tongue. I noticed that she wrote of falling just when she was on the verge of an important revelation about herself and the way she was leading her life. I'd also stumbled through life. Over the years, I'd broken an arm, a leg, a foot (twice) a finger (same one twice) a toe (three times). I'd just begun to understand my tendency to fall down or backward—from fear of what lay ahead—in collusion with a family who valued dramatic incident, when I saw the same pattern in Hellman. In my excitement over discovered identification, I read voraciously about separation-individuation and object relations. Winnicott. Melanie Klein. Lacan. Foucault. Chodorow. I couldn't get enough of theories. When my dissertation director met for my Ph.D. orals, she held my manuscript in her hands, then set it down on the table and stared at it with a delightful smile. She was a Shakespearian scholar who had done psychoanalytic training in Chicago, and I had wanted to impress her. "How did you figure this out?" she asked. It was one of the happiest days of my life.

With her blessing and encouragement, I applied and was accepted into the Houston Psychoanalytic Institute with my dissertation as evidence of a background and interest in psychoanalysis. But within the first weeks at the institute I complained to friends about the room (no windows), the teachers and other trainees (workaholics), the hours (seven on Saturday mornings), the food (doughnuts and coffee). What

I really didn't like was the way the psychoanalysts boiled down the complexity of humans into diagnoses. I couldn't stand the way my mind began to shift into diagnostic gear when a friend shared some heartache, some gossip, a dream. People I met at cocktail parties became obsessive-compulsives with borderline tendencies or, more often, narcissists. As my language changed, I felt a strange transformation in myself and the world. I wanted my words back, the world of words. "I miss all the adjectives," I moaned to my literary friends.

I began writing a novel.

One afternoon we—the three other trainees at the institute and I—sat across from each other at the large conference table in the room with no windows. There were two psychiatrists, a psychologist, and me. The three of them were usually checking day planners, looking down at their beepers, excusing themselves to make a telephone call. They were very busy. But this day the teacher was late, and we were making a little casual small talk between us, talking about the common occurrence of flying in dreams.

"I'd love to fly," I said, imagining the feel of gliding through waves of air.

"You would," a fellow trainee said with such derision that I felt burned, my imaginary wings singed away.

She was a woman who had gone to medical school before women were a familiar sight, a woman who had white skin and red hair that she covered in the rain with a scarf tied in a '50s style, a woman who had looked at me with scorn from the day I walked into the room. But within a month of training she had stopped looking or speaking to me. I'd concluded that either I bothered her or she couldn't be bothered with me.

And suddenly we were speaking.

"Who wouldn't want to fly?" I asked.

"I wouldn't," she said.

Her feet were to stay firmly planted on the ground.

At that moment I wanted to rid myself of the weight of the room that was heavy with the sense of responsibility these people carried—or imagined they carried—on their backs.

I resigned a month later.

Sometimes I felt I was always looking over my shoulder, trying to see the past as I ran into my future. Obsessed, my friends would have said of me. Preoccupied, I'd have said, about the way I lived and relived the past in my present, looking for clues, trying to connect the dots, find the themes. Maybe I was preparing the way, laying the groundwork, doing my homework, gathering strength for what was gaining on me. I was always glancing behind me, sensing him there, biding his time until he was ready, Jamie. Yet when he came, I was far from ready.

8

if nights
could talk,
stars would sing

In the spring of 1993, I received a letter of acceptance to a writers' retreat. Free room and board for the month of July in Montauk, Long Island. The year before I'd published a short story in a literary journal and one day a call came from an editor with a New York publishing house who had read the story and wondered if there was a novel behind it. Not yet, I told her. After her call, I began writing in earnest. I wrote several more stories that I sent off in my application for the retreat. I wanted the time to string the pieces together into the coherency of a book. When I'd heard from a friend about Edward Albee's barn, which housed six artists a month, I'd thought it might be the place to begin. My fantasy was that my novel would take shape, that my life would take shape, out of town, in the country, away from anyone I knew, or who knew me.

Jamie arrived the same spring as the acceptance letter. At the time, I didn't see the two as opposed to each other, didn't see an either/or situation between my writing and Jamie. I must have sensed a change in the air pressure. There was, I see now, a choice hanging there—in the air. But I pushed the uneasiness to the margins of my mind. This was where Jamie had resided for so many years—on the periphery. The fact of him had not settled into consciousness. To me, Jamie was temporary. Writing was permanent. Like teeth.

My plan for the summer, before Jamie arrived, had been to have my house renovated while I was at the writers' retreat. I felt that there was about to be a change—in fact, I was almost giddy with plans for change. I'd told Kelly, an interior designer I'd met at the park where I took the dogs, that I wanted all the white walls in the house painted shades of green. I told him, "Bring the green of the outside in." In the month before I left for Montauk, Kelly would fly in the door with cappuccinos and scones and an armful of paint chips and fabric swatches, which he'd fling over chairs and sofas as if throwing flower petals to the wind. He also swooped up Jamie in his enthusiasm, refusing to act as if there were anything unusual about Jamie's menacing looks. "You," Kelly said, draping his arm up and over Jamie's huge shoulders, "could be an artistic consultant of sorts." Pushing and leading Jamie out the back door, Kelly would point at the garden. "What do you think? A pile of rocks right there in the center. *À la naturel.* Like your aunt?" Or, "I know," he'd say, pretending there was a conversation going on that wasn't: "What about a bricked path?" "You agree?" "Oh, yes, you are right, so right."

He'd jump into his BMW, honk and wave before turning his attention toward Fire, his Dalmatian that always rode shotgun. He often rang me up on his cellular phone as he sped away from the curb, delivering what had been his mantra since he'd gone into remission from cancer: "Girl-friend, everything is going to be copacetic." I didn't know what that meant but it sounded good.

July and Montauk seemed a long way off and surely when the time came, I thought, arrangements for Jamie would be made. Even the words I used were vague—arrangements would be made.

Jimmy and Dayna were sidetracked in their momentum to fight for Jamie. They'd driven to Shreveport to try to find him, checked into a hotel, and then gone to the racetrack, where they'd lost so much money they couldn't pay their hotel bill. They had to stay in the hotel until they won enough money to leave. They were no longer an immediate threat.

Even though I'd agreed to adopt Jamie, I don't think I believed I would really end up with him. Certainly, I thought, it would play out like before: Gail and Bobby would come and get him. Gail would come and tell me what to do. These were my thoughts, half-formed and then shoved aside in all of the excitement of the prospect of new colorful rooms and the new writing career. I told friends I was on the cusp of new beginnings. I went to a psychic. I called Athena Starwomen. Change was prophesized. I envisioned agents, editors, publication. I foresaw literary soirees in my new refurbished living room. Jamie, I thought, was really only a momentary cross to bear.

I told friends that Jamie's sleep patterns made it impossible for him to live with me. But perhaps it was my sleep patterns. I'd lived alone for years and Jamie's schedule—sleeping from four in the morning into early afternoon—had kept me awake in New Orleans and then in Houston. All through the nights he listened to his Walkman, smoked cigarettes, and remained wrapped in an armor of privacy that he seemed to defy me to invade. Or maybe the truth was that I was scared to know what was going on behind those fierce black eyes. What would he be in my home? A guest? A visiting relative? A surrogate son? We fumbled around each other awkwardly, not sure what each expected of the other.

I set him up in my neighbor's garage apartment and offered to pay him to help Kelly with the house renovation. His first job was to rip off the backyard deck. Initially he went at the deck with wild fury. As he worked, I watched him from the kitchen window. He was misery in human form. With his hair, he hid the face that could humanize him. Next to him worked an architectural graduate student who Kelly had hired to replace the deck in my backyard. It was an awful coincidence that the student's name was Dana, and equally awful that Dana was a perfectionist who looked like a male model from a Guess ad. A couple of worlds were colliding before my eyes. Dana had dated Ashley Judd before she was a movie star. Dana had gone to a prep school, then to Williams College, now he was at architecture school at Rice University. Jamie had dropped out of the eighth grade. He could have been an extra in a film about children of the street. The director might have told him to tone it down a bit.

I'd bite my fingernails as I watched from one window after another—worrying that Jamie might keel over from the exertion, watching the muscle in Dana's jaw clench and unclench as if all his impatience was a knot he chewed in the corner of his mouth. I saw Jamie dig the shovel into the ground and saw his loose and lazy motion that sent a slow-motion brown arc of dirt into Dana's face. I turned away from the window.

Watching him, I felt convinced Jamie had now been replaced by a creature who bore no resemblance to the boy I'd pictured and mourned over the years. I wanted to flee from the sight of him. It was a cruel trick from a fairy tale. I imagined him as a stone placed in my pocket that would surely sink me, me of the stony heart. *Too late,* I said inside myself. *Too late,* I wanted to say to him. *Too late for you, Jamie. Too late for us.*

Like magnets being turned by supercilious gods, we were drawn to each other yet repelled by each other. I backpedaled furiously from a boy who believed that his only power was to appall and repel. He must have spent the last ten years practicing being repugnant. He had it down.

I never considered not going to the writer's retreat because of Jamie. As my new life was spreading out before my eyes—new house, new life—Jamie'd stomped his combat boots across the middle of the arc of it.

"If I had this house," he said, "I'd paint everything in it black."

"I bet you would," I said, already tired of his black view of everything.

"I like black hair best of all too," he said. "Straight, oriental black hair." He looked straight ahead and blew out a plume of smoke.

"Your hair is nice," I said, lying, since it was a greasy, matted mess.

"I hate it," he said. It wasn't straight enough for him.

His hair was dark, dark brown with the slightest natural wave.

"Well, whatever," I said.

"For instance," he said. "If I had your hair, I'd shave my head."

My hair is wavy and its exact color hard to pin down. Sometimes in the sun it seems red, in the summer almost blond. Actually I am fond of my hair.

"Nothing personal," he said, before sucking deeply on his cigarette.

Before I left for Montauk I made more elaborate plans for the two dogs than I did for Jamie. I didn't know he was deciding about me as fast and furiously as I was deciding about him. I packed a trunk to be sent to Montauk that was full of dog-eared manuscripts, versions of stories, dozens of old journals, a quilt, scarves, gauzy skirts, postcards and books. I was leaving town.

I took a taxi to the airport to fly to New York, waving to Jamie who gloomily perched like a vulture on the curb.

Bobby and Gail were to drive down and pick him up. Like a giant chess piece. "Good-bye, good-bye," I trilled, light-headed at the prospect of escaping from Jamie, who had sweated and lurched through tearing up the deck, who'd grumbled and groused about the heat, the minimum wage, the dogs underfoot. Good-bye, Jamie.

⁓

I flew to New York City from where I took a bus to Montauk, arriving in the small whaling town with my computer and suitcase. A tanned, bleached blond dressed in an old Hawaiian shirt jumped out of a car and said he was the town's taxi service. "Could this be it?" he asked as he let me out at the end of a dirt road that led to an old huge barn that looked deserted.

As I walked into the quietness of the barn, which smelled like the old washhouse from my childhood, I was ready to write, ready to open up the stories of my family to the light of day. My second-story room had wooden floors and screened windows that looked out into a thick meadow full of yellow flowers, brambles, and vines. Set loose from darkness Jamie had brought to my life, I felt free. My family had always outrun my ability to transcribe them on the page. In my small room near the ocean, I floated through the days, the ballast of the past two months tossed away, and the stories flowed onto the computer screen.

As I wrote I was surprised to find myself writing *to* someone.

Perhaps it was the seaside town full of fisherman; the hardware stores full of fishing gear; the markets full of fresh fish; the smell of the sea, where my father always took us for vacations. I remembered bending over a wharf as a child, the smell of creosote faint, as I watched him pull up the crab net, water pouring out of the basket, crab legs clacking like dominoes as they reached for something familiar, their bearings. He dropped the contraption near our feet and cursed absentmindedly as he untangled the crabs from the trap. *Dear Daddy,* I began as I sat typing in my room in Montauk. I circled back and cast the invisible net of memory, pulling it to me, finding it full.

Dear Dead Daddy.

What I began turned into over a hundred letters to my father, who had been dead ten years. *You wouldn't believe,* I wrote to him, *what has happened. What has happened to us since you've been gone. And you'll never believe who is back.*

Jamie.

Your Jamie.

Our Jamie.

As a child I'd written notes to my father. From the time I learned to write I stopped passing the phone to Mother when the driller called for my father from the well site. If he wasn't home, I wanted to be the one to take the messages. I would search for a pencil and once I had it gripped tightly I'd write the message on notepaper. I remember the heavy black phone receiver and the way it clunked back in its cradle when I hung up. "This morning, drill bit broke," the man on the other end of the phone might have said. Until I learned "real" writing, I wrote my father notes in a child's fat letters. "Found salt water. Have to plug." Or, "The core samples are full of sand." They had sent down the pig or were burning off the gas. They needed more pipe or they had perforated into sand. I loved to transcribe the foreign language of the oil fields called in by the drillers and roughnecks. "One wrong word could mean millions," my father once warned me when he couldn't decipher a message. After that the world seemed alive, had a core, was worth millions, and was somewhere outside, far away from our house.

In Montauk, I felt again that world—the field—where my father had often gone and sometimes taken me. There was the quiet of the night in which I could gather together the pile of facts that were like hundreds of puzzle pieces in my lap. *Who were you?* I asked my father. *Did you,* I'd often wondered and now asked, *make your fortune on the backs of black men paid low wages? What would you think of Saddam Hussein? A country lit on fire, burning, burning their own resources. What we all use to get from here to there gone up in flames.*

This letter to you, I wrote, *is a labor of love.*

You believed in work, were your work, made me work—for you, for me. To labor at something you love. That's what you taught me.

    Mother had said, "You're the writer," when she handed me the notes she'd made for your obituary, which I wrote. Who were you? I wondered then as I wrote the dates, the facts of your career in the oil business. Sohio. Panhandle. Smackover Drilling. Gas fields. Oil companies. Survived by. Who were you? I asked myself in Montauk. If everyone says I'm so much like you and no one knew you, then who am I? I've acquired the vocabulary of self-definition. But I worry about what comes first, me or the words? I say them to myself in a chant. Reciprocity. Another one: Echolocation. The word for what the dolphin does to measure the distance between himself and others, himself and objects. The eloquence of an echo. The dolphin knows his location by relation.

I wrote the thank-you notes. Thank you so much, I wrote to a hundred people, thank you so very, very much for the dozens and dozens of roses, your favorite flower. Father Rose, Father Thorn.

My words are a pile of stones by my side; on your side another kind of accumulation—the money, the wells that came in, the respect that followed, hard currency.

I now have words that settle in my stomach late at night, the ones I think I could have used to make you listen to me. That's what I want to do: awake you, shake you, words thrown like pebbles on a windowpane. I want to tell you my stories of the night. I can tell them funny. I can tell them sad. Which do you want?

The first year I was in Houston I worked in a downtown bar called the Greenroom. As the day workers drove away from town, I'd be going against the tide. I'd walk the five blocks from the parking lot, past the Pennzoil building where I'd check myself in the huge black glass panes before entering the smoky dark pub. The walls were brick and old black-and-white photographs of the Texas oil boom days hung on them. These photos seemed static compared to the thought of you. Your smile was looser, wider than the frozen grins on the photo faces. "My daddy," I told the bartender one night, "is an oilman." I loved the sound of the sentence. My daddy is an oilman. My bartender was a cocaine dealer.

At the end of each night in the bar, I'd gather the candle and ashtrays from the glass-top tables, then use hot water to loosen the candles until they popped out of the holders. Then I would insert fresh white ones for the next night. While I did this on one side of a small utility room, the bartender worked on the other, quietly dividing his money into neat piles of fives and tens and twenties. It was an orderly life.

I always wore bright red lipstick and 1940s dresses from resale shops. I drank burgundy from a giant green bottle with sediment on the bottom. I took Valium. I hoarded them in tiny enameled pill boxes like Mamaw used for headache powders. I watched myself in the mirror behind the bar as if I were an exotic fish swimming in a tank.

These are the things I never told you when I called home, often from the pay phone in the bar.

On New Year's Eve I was reprimanded for kissing the customers. (There is a name for this: echopraxia, the abnormal repetition of the actions of others.) That night I roused a man passed out on the couch who had a braid down to his waist and dark brown eyes. He was a cook in an all-night health food café where musicians, waitresses, and bartenders went after hours for espresso and whole wheat pancakes. I took him home with me and he stayed three years. He had two pairs of jeans, three shirts, and a pair of huaraches. His hair always smelled like bacon.

One hostess at the bar looked like me. Or I looked like her. It was this confusion between us, and between others about us that got us off on the wrong foot. And that we had slept with the same moody, angel-faced singer who was the rage that summer and the next. The hostess committed suicide. Three years later the angel-faced singer's partner— who played the blues, who had wire-rimmed glasses and a beard and the beginning of a belly—was murdered. He was shot by a parolee who had heard he had dope in his house. He was murdered in his farmhouse in Magnolia, Texas, where he rode horses, grew tomatoes, and canned vegetables with his girlfriend, who was also murdered. I'd kissed him twice, both times right after he'd just stepped down from the stage. I kissed him twice and he is dead. There is no connection except in my mind, in my life.

All of this, I knew then, would have given you a heart attack.

A heart attack of the gut, that is what the doctors said about your quick death. Self-combustion. In Dickens's Bleak House, *a character spontaneously combusts, leaving residue of charred smudges, bits of smoking hair and fabric. It is always a matter of what is left.*

Since you died:

Bobby won the World Championship Chili Cook-off. He was on Good Morning America. *He didn't have much to say. The network flew Mother and me to New York to celebrate.*

I earned a Ph.D. and at the same time fell in love with a married man, a writer who was visiting my university for a semester. He looked like he would be most comfortable holding a golf club—instead of me, I mean. He said he was going to leave his wife but he didn't. My hairdresser said, "They never do," as he cut off four inches of my hair. "Cut," I'd demanded of him, because Jack had written me a letter that said he often thought of my hair whipping in the wind. I wrote him back that memory was false. That my hair was not how he remembered it at all.

When I showed Mother one of his books, she turned it over to look at his picture, and said, "He looks just like your daddy."

Jan got divorced. Her husband had an affair with a secretary. You had known her. You would have been surprised. You would have done that head-shaking thing you always did when disappointed or disgusted. Shaking your head as if the bad news would fly off like water from a dog's coat.

Gail and Bobby lost Jamie.

Gail and Bobby almost lost their minds.

We all did.

And then Jamie escaped and came back—home.

The stories are like a giant ball of string. They can branch off in any direction, depending on which string I pull. But it always seems to go back to you. I can't decide what to call you after all these pages. Whether to call you "my father," which sounds too much like "art in heaven." And I can't call you Daddy, although I always did, but now that makes me too small, you too big. Dad sounds as if I have a sweater around my neck and am bounding down some steps swinging a tennis racket. It has to be "my father" as in respect and fear, the possessive that implies the other side, the "my daughter." The place from where I stand, the place from where I write. I tell my students that death doesn't end a relationship. There is a constant conversation, an evolving understanding as each year the dead one is not, he is, because now you have reached the age he was or he would have been. The gaps are filled in and fleshed out. From across the span of death, I see what you must have seen: a gaggle, a bunch, a brood, a bother. I spent years watching you watch us. I was locked in "us" and unable to reach across the chaos to you. My father.

One afternoon, exhausted, I pushed my chair away from the desk, and both the computer and chair cracked suddenly, and then the screen went blank.

Two weeks of my writing were gone.

I'd met a chef, a black man from Jamaica, who had come to pick me up to take me to dinner just as my work vanished. When I went downstairs to meet him, I threw my arms around his neck and began to sob, explaining that everything was gone.

In his Caribbean lilt, he whispered, "Oh, now. Oh, now. It's all still there." He wiped my face as if I were a child and held me by the shoulders, and said, "Go on back up there." His face was beautiful, the brown eyes calm. He smelled of summer and cologne, strong and sweet. I wanted to stay nuzzled in his neck, hear his words full of care, his beautiful accent.

"No," I cried, "it's gone, it's gone."

"Not so," he said. He tapped me on the temple, and said, "It's still right here."

"Gone!" I cried, with such force that he must have understood what all was missing.

"Go back upstairs," he said firmly, practically turning me toward the stairs. "It will come, baby. It will come."

He was right.

As I heard his car pull out of the gravel, rocks hitting his hubcaps, the dust filling the air, I was already back in the story. Again, as if by automatic writing, the sentences scrolled down the screen.

There is a story I often tell about a dog. I told the story to Jack the writer the first night I met him. I saw him fall in love with the story. Not long after he fell in love with me.

I was on the side of the house with my arms full of newspapers to put in the garbage when I saw him. He was trotting down the other side of the street. As if he owned the street, I thought. "Hey," I called "What do you think you're doing?" He looked around as if to say, "Who, me?" "Come over here," I said. And I saw him decide, saw him make the decision to cross over the street and into my life.

When he approached me, I bent down on my knees, put my face level with his muzzle and spoke to him softly. I called him Mr. Man. "What are you up to?" I whispered in his ear, which was as large as my palm and felt like satin. Later I'd call him My Mr. Man. He wore a collar that made me know there was some heavy-metal asshole in his past.

This dog turned out to belong to the owner of a tattoo parlor ten blocks from me, a grizzly bear of a man covered in tattoos who days later came pounding on my door to demand his dog back. Some friends of his—who had been in the process of stealing my neighbor's water hose—had seen the dog in my yard and reported back to the tattoo artist.

"I want my dawg," he shouted at my unopened door, his hands in fists on his hips.

The house suddenly was surrounded by men stepping over my hedge to peer through my windows, their bracelets and key chains jangling as they stalked the house in big black boots in broad daylight. A neighbor called the police while I held the dog around the neck and made promises to him. "I'll never give you back," I told him. I didn't think to call the police myself, instead I called Pike and told his secretary there was an emergency, and when she said he was in a meeting, I told her to get him. "Men are after me," I said. "Just tell him that," I said. "Men are after me."

This is the way I always tell the story.

There was a dog and his name was Harlow.

I thought he would have been tattooed. But he wasn't. After I learned where he came from, I looked all over his body, touched him, spoke to him as I glided my palm across the shine of him, thinking where I would have chosen to mark him if I were an artist with needle and ink. But the only marks were dozens of puncture holes around his neck, some scarred, some scabbed, that came from the dogs his owner had him fight. Harlow wore a necklace of abuse.

Pike came to my house within the hour of my call. He stood outside and talked to the police, who told him I should give the dog back. "Even though possession is nine-tenths of the law," the policeman said, "it doesn't seem worth tangling with these guys." Pike, who was dressed in a Brooks Brothers blue suit, bent his ear toward the policeman and looked down at the street and nodded his head in sharp punctuations of agreement. Later Pike will tell me the policeman said that "these guys" were bad characters, had records, were too dangerous to stir up. "Like lifting up a rock," he'd said to Pike, "and out they crawl."

When the police and the tattoo guy and his skinny, scary sidekicks dispersed, Pike came in to talk to me. He cleared his throat and spoke sternly: "Marsha," he said. I knew he thought I'd gone too far. "Marsha," he repeated again in the voice of a father. "Give the damn dog back." I searched his face for the boy I'd known, but all signs of the hippie he'd once been—long lank blond hair to his shoulders, bell-bottom jeans, a cocky walk—were gone.

"No way," I said. I knew this dog was a test, one given to me by the universe, perhaps my second chance to rescue. The thoughts and images of Jamie filled my mind. When the judge gave his ruling in 1984, ordering Jamie be given to his parents, I should have fled with him, I thought. Picked him up and run to Mexico, I thought. That is the way you do it.

Pike broke my thought in two with his biting sarcasm. He shouted at me: "Do you want to go underground for this dog? Sell your house? Change your identity?" The veins stood out in his neck. He was, I thought, a distinguished-looking man, had grown into one while I wasn't paying attention. Such an air of authority bristled around him. You— Daddy—would like him now. Oh, how he wanted to grow up to be you. And how I grieved that you didn't see in him who I saw.

"Yes," I'd cried to Pike as he peppered me with questions. "Yes," I answered to anything he said to me as I hugged Harlow, pulling the mass of him toward me until from head to haunch his body touched mine. "Yes," I said to Pike.

"You're fucking crazy," he yelled, getting into his car and peeling off to return to his job, leaving me alone with the dog. My other dog, Rosie the Airedale, paced nervously in the house. Harlow—and I—had pushed her to the edge of our world from where she sat and watched us.

After Pike left my house, I'd called the tattoo parlor. Pike had muttered that I could probably pull it off. "Fuck," he'd said, shaking his head the way you used to. "You'll probably get him to give you the damn dog. You are your father's daughter."

The owner of the Black Dragon Tattoo Parlor was named Ralph Cottongin. My heart had raced as I dialed the number and listened to the ringing. "This," Pike had said, pacing and angry, "must be some damn maternal thing."

Whatever my motives were, the ones I understood, the ones I didn't, I was convinced that I had to convince Ralph Cottongin, the illustrated man, to sell me his bad dog or I'd have to run away with Harlow. I knew I would not—could not—give the dog back.

"Hi," I said when Cottongin answered. "I'm the woman who has your dog."

"Listen, woman," Cottongin said, "I want my damn dog back."

My hand white-knuckled the phone as I imagined the phone like a toy at Cottongin's ear. I rushed him with information. I told him that his dog had heartworms, an advanced case, that he wouldn't live long no matter who had him. And the cure was expensive. I told him that the vet had taken from a shelf the plastic replica of a dog heart, then from out of another cabinet he brought a giant jar that looked filled with a dead octopus that had long tentacles yellowed and tangled and terrible. "Heartworms," he'd said, holding the jar up in front of me. "They will eventually suffocate him," he'd said. "He will suffer a long, slow, horrible death." I told Cottongin all of this.

"Jesus, woman," Cottongin said, and then there was only breathing for almost a minute, and I felt I heard him thinking. After an intake of breath, he began talking. He told me that his wife had left him, that his tattoo parlor had been broken into and all his tattoo guns stolen "and now you," he said.

I had come at the end of a very bad month.

Then there was another long pause before he said there might be a way to work things out. During the silence, I wondered about myself. What, I asked myself, my heart beating in my ears, would I do to keep the dog?

Cottongin said he'd sell me the dog.

When I walked up the two wooden steps into the small shack that looked out onto the busy intersection of Westheimer, a strip of clubs and resale shops and sex shops, I thought about who might see me entering the black Dragon Tattoo Parlor, the name spilling out of the mouth of a big dragon painted on the whole side of the building. I had put on a short black skirt and a tight T-shirt. My lips were painted bright red. My hair loose and wild. I didn't want to leave anything to chance. I didn't want him to think I thought my money could buy me anything. I didn't want him to think I was a yuppie who always had the cash in hand. Cottongin, who wore a leather vest and no shirt, walked over while wiping his hand on a paper towel before he extended the blue-black ink-stained hand to me. His hair fell loose and gray to his shoulders, which were covered with tattoos. We shook hands.

"I love the dog," Cottongin said. "Slept with him right in there," he said, pointing to a backroom, "every night since the wife split."

I gave him the money and he gave me a receipt on his business card. "Received: Harlow. $500."

"I can't believe he came to you," Cottongin said, shaking his head as I walked out the door.

In Montauk, I had pictures of Harlow thumbtacked to the wall next to my desk beside a picture of me with the roughneck Johnny. Scattered across a table were twenty or more family photos, which I'd shuffle and shift as if they were tarot cards. Often I fell into my single bed, holding one in my hand, closing my eyes, trying to find my way back to the point—my mother would say I was looking for the fault line—where nothing was ever the same again—for me. Or to find the place at which it could have been different.

> *I had to have Harlow put down. He bit three people, three citations from the city. I'd tried for a year to protect people from Harlow, Harlow from people. Harlow wouldn't let anyone near me—he'd go for the throat.*
>
> *Rescued dogs get like this, the vet explained.*
>
> *I had to face the fact of Harlow: the damage done to him was irreparable. The damage done to him had spread across my life.*
>
> *"Sweet man," I told him, and his legs buckled beneath him as he went down, dead by the vet's needle.*

For months I keened, I cried, I howled for Harlow. There was no justice in the world, I thought.

In my room in Montauk, I stared at the entries of the journals I'd brought with me:

1981	My father died
1983–84	teach freshman class
	testify against my brother
	Richie kills himself
1984	Jamie gone
1987	turned in Chapter Two of dissertation
	meet Jack—writer
	Scott broke his neck
1988	Teach southern lit course
	April 21, Jack left today
	May 2, receive Ph.D.
	May 14, Pike marries Claudia

———

From the east end of Long Island where one can imagine being at the end of something big, I saw my own story with a certain clarity I'd never had before. During my time at the residency, my past finally became, to my amazement, the past. As I wrote, I listened to my neighbors in the next rooms—typing, typing. Stories were filling up the barn that Edward Albee had bought to lodge writers. I could feel them swarming overhead like barn owls, like trapped sparrows, like black bats huddling under the eaves of our lives.

I was gathering the past as the white moths fluttered against the windows, when Nestor, a painter, hollered up the barn stairwell to tell me the phone was for me. I came down the stairs and curled in an old stuffed chair in the main hallway and put the receiver to my ear. The boy who I insisted on thinking of as only passing through my life was on the other end of the line. His voice was like an electric shock. From my line to his, I felt the surprising shudder of attachment. From my hand grasping the telephone, I imagined his hand and his ear. My breath quickened. He was real.

"I can't take it," Jamie said instead of hello. "Not another night, Marsha," he said in a whisper. I had never heard him say my name before.

Worried that Gail and Bobby would overhear him, he'd taken the portable phone to their back porch, but still whispered and kept the phone cupped so that his voice sounded hushed and desperate.

"What is it?" I asked. "What's wrong?"

"Everything," he said. Bobby was fed up. Bobby had expected—and deserved—gratitude. All he got was a sixteen-year-old's bad attitude. "Mow the goddamn yard or else," he had yelled at Jamie over and over that month. The growing grass became Bobby's obsession, the battleground, every blade like one to his heart. After all he'd done, he must have thought, and the boy can't cut the grass.

I could picture it: Gail in her usual nest on the couch surrounded by the Pomeranians, her cigarettes, the channel changer, and her drink.

Jamie had been their redemption, the loss of him their hell. They were still milling around in their sadness when he came back from his own ten years of torment.

I tried to calm Jamie down, but my heart was beating so hard that I held one hand against it as I tried to think. How could I tell Gail—for Jamie—that he wanted to leave her? She still thought of him as hers. She was my big sister, my beloved big sister, my sister of the big heart. How to explain this version of Jamie to them? I'd tried once before, trotting out my psychology terms, trying to give them names to help them understand. "Marsha and all her psychology," they'd said to Jamie. They didn't believe in the unconscious.

"I want to go home, Marsha," he said. Each time he said my name I felt faint.

Home, I thought. *He is calling Houston home. My home. His home.*

Most people wouldn't see a simple telephone call as a significant sign of life, a crucial beep on the screen, but I'd glimpsed the depths of his apathy that had kept him with his parents long past the time he could have walked away. During the phone call, I felt his energy and will, and knew they were tiny tendrils poking out their new growth from where they'd been buried for half his life.

As we talked, I imagined him on Gail and Bobby's porch, the fields of cotton spreading for acres until meeting the highway where the lights glittered, merging with the stars. The small house, the one he'd lived in until he was six, was at the end of a cul-de-sac that had once been out in the country, surrounded by soybean and cotton fields, but was now being encroached upon by strip malls and more houses. Yet there was still the country feel to the area where vegetable and fruit stands were on the side of the road and pecan groves backed up to a golf course. Pickup trucks were parked in every driveway on the block, deer rifles could be seen hung in racks in the back windshields, Confederate flag decals on the bumpers. Louisiana, the Dream State, according to the license plates. For the month of July, I'd often been right back there, revisiting in memory where Jamie was, where Jamie wanted out of. I knew the pull of the place.

I'd known Jamie had been wavering about staying in Houston or going back to Shreveport.

Jamie was sixteen and spinning and no one knew where he'd stop.

That summer, the more I thought of having a teenager, the more I acted like one. But there was another part of me, the back of my mind, that wanted Jamie to give me a chance. To give me a chance to give him a chance.

When he called, I knew he'd chosen one life over another, me over them, us over them.

I told him I'd telegraph a money order so he could get on a bus, and arranged for a former student to meet him at the station. I didn't talk to Bobby and Gail because I didn't want to hear their side of the story, which I knew would be one too many sides for me to handle.

I chose to take sides. This time I took Jamie's side.

That night I searched for words to console him, and gave him the ones given to me all summer by my Caribbean lover, which, as I chanted them, seemed to echo back to me in the big barn. "Don't worry," I told him. "Everything's going to be all right." Like a lullaby, a mantra, a prayer, the words followed me as I went upstairs and turned off the computer that held my past, who I'd been before Jamie came to stay.

9

disorders of
the sleep state

Back in Houston, nothing was fine. From the upstairs window of my guest bedroom, I could see Jamie's apartment, and it seemed still and strange, as if that were the place in the fairy tale where the giant slept, having been put under the spell of evil parents. Sometimes I'd try to rouse him. I'd knock on the door, lift open the mail slot, bend down and scream into the hole.

Sometimes he'd stumble down the stairs, glowering, his brow furrowed so horribly he appeared to be wearing a fleshy Halloween mask. He'd open the door as far as the chain lock, and ask me, "What?" A flat-out, you-are-inconveniencing-me "What?" His eyes would be almost matted shut, and once, only once because I tried not to look after that, I looked down and saw that his toenails were getting so long they were curling under.

"What do you mean, 'what?'" I'd say, trembling with everything I wanted to ask him, ask anyone, ask the universe: what was I going to do? What was going to happen? What?

My first impulse when Jamie came to Houston was to get him into therapy. I subscribed to the most conventional wisdom of the mental health world. He must go over his past, I told him, if he was to get on with a future. "No therapy," he said. "No more headshrinkers." Before, during and long after the court proceedings, Jamie had been sent to psychologists for tests and talks. His private conversations always became public. In court Jimmy and Dayna's experts disputed the testimony of Gail and Bobby's experts. Once in Houston he was determined to keep his own counsel.

At night I sat in the pool of light at my kitchen table, ate takeout and drank wine. I allotted myself two glasses a night, but within the year, I was finishing a bottle. I hid the empty bottles, taking them to the recycling bin at the health food store so the neighbors wouldn't see. I usually drank after what I began to call my "sessions" with Jamie, which were the afternoons or evenings when he showed up at my door, and I'd take him with me to walk the dogs, or to dinner. At those times, fortified by wine, I'd hear myself going on and on, waxing rhapsodic about all the reasons to live. "You can be anything. An artist. A musician. We can travel. Go to Europe, to New York City." Stubbornly, sullenly he would say the only place he wanted to go was to Sedona, a town in Arizona where, according to him, the practice of witchcraft was socially acceptable. Sedona, I thought. Perfect. Covens of witches, people who had been abducted by aliens, New Agers. We could all meet together, one happy family in Sedona. My belief in the wonderful world I was laying out before him was shriveling. My world was shrinking down into a knot of worry that I tried to dissolve with Chardonnay.

"Your problem," he'd said to me as if talking to a small child as we sat one evening in my car outside his apartment. "Your problem," he said again through my deep sigh, "is that you think I'm human."

I stared across the street at my house. I wanted a glass of wine, I wanted to be in my bed watching Geraldo, the covers pulled up around my head, the dogs settled on each side. Why was it my job to convince the most depressed person I'd ever met that he was human?

I was only going on instinct, gut reaction, day to day.

"But I'm not human," he said.

I continued to stare straight ahead and watch the birds swoop down to eat the mosquitoes, their frenzied bird cries filling the quiet of evening. Maybe, I was thinking, this is all too much for me, maybe he will pull me completely under. Maybe, I was thinking, he is too far gone. Maybe he *is* hardly human.

"You're probably worrying about that sparrow over there," he said, "thinking it might be choking on a bug."

I was seriously formulating my denial when he said, "I don't care if it chokes to death or not."

I pictured sparrows gagging on bugs and felt sick to death of Jamie, felt his view of the world was filling the car, my world, with dense gray fog that would change the way I saw the birds in the evening or the sun set over the trees.

I put my hands on the steering wheel and opened and closed my fingers. "Empathy," I said. In a monotone I explained about feeling as if you *were* another person. Humans, I explained, are distinguished by their ability to care for others.

"Empathy," he repeated with sarcasm. Jamie went on to explain that he thought empathy had gone the way of tonsils. Of no discernible use, he said. In a robotic tone, he trotted out theories he'd read about altruism, how there is really no such thing, just a facade for selfishness. No one, he said, is anything but selfish.

Why, I wondered, did I want to sacrifice my life to help him?

He quoted Noam Chomsky and Huxley and Nietzsche.

He wasn't my son, I thought as he continued his argument refuting that anyone ever really acted without regard for the self. Often he talked like an anthropologist—talked as if he had been observing "us" for a long, long time and had come to certain sad conclusions.

There was no reason to love him in the face of his constant badgering

136

and pushing me away, I thought. Genes calling to genes? I wondered. I studied the outline of his face in the dark and wondered where my love for him would come from, what would be its point of origin.

Over the next five years there were so many times I didn't like him, and even times I thought I hated him.

～

The first year with Jamie I started going to a honky-tonk a few blocks from my house called the Boatyard that reminded me of Louisiana bars. There was live music, pistachio nut dispensers, two cats and a dog that roamed around inside, a dart board, and regulars. No ferns or fancy drinks.

I went one night with two former students, one in law school, the other working with computers, and we danced to the live music.

At forty-two, I kicked up my heels at the Boatyard, drank tequila and with my ex-students as audience, leaned over the bar one night and asked the bartender if he would marry me.

The bartender, Kevin, seemed to consider the proposal, his head tilted slightly as if listening to a high-pitched whistle. "No?" I asked with mock sadness as I waited for his reply, as did the ten or twelve people sitting at the bar.

"No," he said as he calmly wiped a glass dry, pushing the dishtowel with care around the edges before he put it in the slot above the bar.

"What can a girl do?" I asked, shrugging my shoulders and looking at the other patrons before I went back to dancing with the two students.

Kevin, who came home with me the following week, had a yin-yang tattoo on his bicep, wore baggy khaki shorts, and a wise-guy smile that was half self-deprecating and half tender. In my fantasies, it would be like in *Alice Doesn't Live Here Anymore:* Kevin and Jamie would bond, and Kevin and I would fall into working-class love, playing darts at night at the bar, drinking beer, going fishing, who knows what, and things would be simple and fulfilling and happy ever after.

I realized I wanted an instant husband—just add alcohol and stir.

Yet it became clearer to me, after Kevin, that a man wasn't going to come onto the scene and save me and Jamie. He had lots of advice and no children. Buck up, buckle down. That's what he thought Jamie could do. And I certainly wasn't the flirty, merry woman he'd met at the Boatyard. I was cantankerous—prickly and full of woe. I now fell into that category of women I'd heard my men friends talk about, the single mom, the inconvenience of her. I was to be alone with Jamie, just the two of us, loners who had a whole lot to learn about working in tandem. I stopped going to the bar. I began drinking alone.

⚓

I would sit at my kitchen table, drink and make lists on yellow legal pads. I'd always made lists. Most of them had been compulsive documentation of what I saw as my progress. The lists of what great books I'd read. What books I needed to read. How many students I'd taught. The jobs I'd had. The degrees I'd earned. Lists of the men I had loved, the men I had made love with, the men who meant the most. Then there were always the lists for the grocery store, pet store, dry cleaners and hardware store. These lists had lain crumpled on the floor of my car like poems: tacks, Comet, birdseed, wild and domestic. I also made lists of the bad things I'd done. The cities I've been to. The worst things I'd said to men. I used to make lists on yellow Post-its.

I moved on to yellow legal pads once Jamie came to stay. I realized I needed to order my life if I was going to organize Jamie's. I went to an office supply store and bought boxes of legal pads and Post-its in bulk.

Yellow legal pads littered the floor around my couch and bed. I went into management mode, turned on the part of me that gets things done, the part that wrote a dissertation, the side of me that my sleepy, dreamy self kept pushed aside. Because once I geared up, I was determined to check things off my list.

Adoption. Emancipation. Education.

Those were the headings on three legal pads.

Yellow Post-its were stuck to my bathroom mirror, to the front door, even to the steering wheel of my car. "GED tutoring—Mon.—8:00 A.M." "medical supply rental—C-Pap machine" "Call lawyers" "Get birth certificate" "Dentist, 3:00 Tues." "Hair?"

During that year, I often went down the block to the eighty-year-old notary, Mr. Eulenfeld. I'd met Mr. Eulenfeld when I was walking the dogs. He'd reminded me of my grandfather, my mother's father, who had been a sweet and gentle man. Mother would be speaking to him long distance and I'd hear it in her voice—her daddy was crying on the other end. After she'd hang up she'd smile and shake her head: "You can't say 'I love you,' 'I miss you,' or even 'good-bye' without him crying." My grandfather, we always said, cried coming and going, so tender was his heart. Mr. Eulenfeld was a man who seemed to have been preserved intact from the past—his office was cluttered with cheerful calendars hanging on the walls, some of which dated back to the '50s, with pictures of puppies and kittens. As I sat in his office—time out of time— I'd watch him slowly, with one finger, type the forms on his old Olivetti. He still used carbon paper for copies and the old pieces of white corrective tape to correct errors. He was, I thought, my lucky charm, an antidote to the surly, bored bureaucrats I had to deal with to get Jamie adopted, emancipated, and signed up for GED. Eustace Eulenfeld. He was right out of *To Kill a Mockingbird*. It had been about eccentrics like Eulenfeld and me and Jamie. Eulenfeld sang in a barber shop quartet. He kept his door unlocked and his money in a cigar box. I worried that Mr. Eulenfeld would get robbed. At each parting I'd tell him to please lock his door. He'd just smile and pat me on the back and tell me everything was going to be fine. I knew the door would be unlocked the next time I came with reams of paperwork for him to sign and stamp.

I kept the jottings and scribblings in a file that I labeled "Jamie Documents." The legal pads and halved envelopes with phone numbers written every which way were the closest I came to keeping a journal of the first two years with Jamie. On one legal pad—clearly from the first year with Jamie—there are names and numbers of our New Orleans lawyer and then the names and numbers of social workers and psychiatrists who had seen Jamie right before he came to Houston.

Then there are the legal pads with the GED information, names and numbers written quickly, scribbled and scratched up and around the margins, circled and starred. My lawyer had said the judge would want proof that Jamie was enrolled in GED. The catch was that he had to be emancipated to get enrolled in GED classes. I'd spend whole afternoons on the phone—four or five hours in which I'd be passed around from one robotic voice to another, with lots of Muzak in between, as I sat bearing down on my pen, scratching over the numbers with manic nervous energy as I worried about how I could get us over all the hurdles before us if this one had stopped me in my tracks. To enroll in the classes for tutoring—that was the prerequisite for taking the GED—we had to have affidavits from a judge that Jamie was emancipated and records from Jamie's past schools—there had been twenty-six in ten years. It had, I screamed over the phone at one woman in Austin from the Department of Education, been easier to get a Ph.D. than to get this kid lined up to take the GED. At that, she suddenly switched from being a robot to being alarmed, huffing at me with indignation that Jamie was a truant. He could be picked up right now, she said. "You are breaking the law."

"Come arrest me," I said, slamming down the phone.

The legal pads record the names, people in a long chain of command, supervisors of supervisors: Mrs. Erwin, Dr. Fields (by the side I'd written *"nice"*), Joe Johnson (next to his name I'd scrawled *"sweet!"*), Stephanie, Chris Thomas, Jo Smith, Carolyn Kline. Each line a memory of frustration or of hope: "GED—materials—ourselves—tutor."

At the bottom of this history of battles, I'd scrawled in bold black letters: ***"If all else fails: ?????"*** Had someone said that to me? Had that person let that sentence drift into the awful silent space of the phone wires where I was already suspecting that failure was preordained. Many days I'd bolster myself with the reminder that I'd actually earned a Ph.D.

Certainly, I'd think to myself as I circled the block with the dogs, biting my fingernails, staring into space for minutes at a time, certainly if I had managed to get a doctorate I could get Jamie signed up for GED.

I can't remember the details—the Louisiana judge finally signed a document; I paid the lawyers. Jamie was signed up for GED tutoring. Chipping away at the boulders that impeded our progress, I thought often that our situation was hopeless. I thought I didn't have it in me, didn't have the strength of character, the wherewithal, the staying power.

I'd thought it was difficult to get him signed up for GED until I tried to get him to go to the morning tutoring session. Each morning I'd go to the corner gas station, buy him a Coke and a Payday, then drive up to his apartment and honk. He would stumble toward the car, his blue jeans hanging down on his hips so that his jean cuffs, which were brown and rotted, dragged under his boots; his shoes were untied, his clothes slept in, sleep was in his eyes, and new pimples that he'd raked with his fingernails were large wounds. "Here," I'd say, handing him his Ritalin, and as he stared straight ahead, he'd stick out his hand, dirt caked in his palm lines and accept the pill. I'd gotten Ritalin bootleg from a friend. I'd think what others would think, my friends with children, all the yuppies who had done it so right, as I handed my new charge a breakfast of Coke, a Payday, and Ritalin.

My life and mood depended on whether Jamie got up in the morning or not. He slept and I seethed. Sleep had been my brother's solace. He'd spent more time in bed than up and out in the world. I remember walking past his room to the bathroom to get ready for a date. Then on my return late in the evening I would head back to the bathroom to wash my face and pass Jimmy, in the same position in the bed. That sleep had a complete stranglehold on Jamie alarmed me because I was so frightened that he was walking the somnambulist path his father had laid down. Wake up, wake up, wake up, I'd cry, butting my head against the steering wheel as I waited to see if he would appear at the door.

10

the state we're in

In the fall of 1993 I called the Baylor Sleep Lab and made an appointment to have Jamie's sleep monitored overnight. The Sleep Lab, in the middle of the Texas Medical Center, was right across the street from TRIMS, the mental health clinic where I'd worked when I was twenty-five. It was at TRIMS where I first saw Jamie, a tiny infant in the arms of an old lady concerned about his diaper rash. Now I was taking him back, sixteen years later, to where, for me, it had all started. My mind was flicking back and forth from past to present as I parked in the lot where I'd parked when I worked in the medical center, and guided Jamie toward the building where the lab was on the fourteenth floor of Baylor College of Medicine.

Jamie was to spend the night. He would be wired up to dozens of monitors and watched through a two-way mirror.

After we gave our names to the receptionist, a young technician dressed in a green scrub suit came in and took Jamie by the arm, leading him off and down a hallway. I watched Jamie and the technician walk down the hall toward the lab; I saw a successful young man leading a misfit. I felt scared for Jamie, and I also felt aligned with failure, felt that finally my family was inescapable, that their troubles would forever be my troubles.

Another technician in a scrub suit, a black woman in her thirties, came in holding a clipboard and began to ask me a series of questions. I was still thinking of the shambling bear of a boy being led away when she began the bombardment.

"What was James's date of birth?"

I couldn't remember.

"Where was he born?" she asked impatiently.

"In that part of Houston—west? What is it? Baytown? Bay City?" I was now asking her questions.

"And who exactly are you?" she asked, looking at me suspiciously, raising her eyes, finally, from the clipboard to give me a dramatic once-over. "In relation to James," she clarified after staring at my face, which was full of confusion. I wanted to tell her about seeing him in his crib, about being afraid to hold him because I knew I should run with him.

"James?" I asked, lost in the past, not recognizing the name since I always thought of him as Jamie. I was sweating and miserable and at a loss for answers. I hadn't had the answers sixteen years ago. I wasn't sure I had any now.

There were so many questions. Vaccinations. Childhood diseases. Schools. School! He hadn't finished the eight grade. Or was it the ninth?

I searched through my purse for the court order that stated Jamie was temporarily in my legal custody. She said someone "with legal authority" had to sign him in.

"I didn't raise him," I explained as I rummaged through my purse that contained dog tags, Altoids, index cards on which each student from my last term's class had written on the first day the title of their favorite book. My eye kept catching sight of girls' loopy handwriting: *Emma.*

Great Expectations. For the last six years these had been my children, these students, these smart students who were premed, prelaw, predetermined to have a successful life.

"Who did?" she asked.

"Who did what?" I asked still looking in the purse.

"Raise him," she repeated.

"No one," I mumbled down inside my purse, mainly to myself. "He was raised by wolves."

"Excuse me?" she said.

"A joke," I said. "Forget it."

I left Jamie at the lab reluctantly, feeling as if I'd dropped him off at a mental hospital, his worst fear. I knew he didn't trust that I wouldn't trick him, wouldn't commit him the way his parents had.

In the elevator I looked up at the mirrored ceiling and saw the circles under my eyes. I was aging—in many ways—at an accelerated rate, turning before my very eyes into a harried, been-up-all-night-with-the-baby new mother.

That night I didn't sleep, but instead tossed and turned in what I would later learn was a parallel to Jamie's night in the lab. When Jamie called at six that morning and said come and get him, I was dead tired, cotton mouthed, red eyed. When I arrived I was told immediately by a technician, who had clearly been impressed by the severity of Jamie's malady, that Jamie had writhed and flailed all night, had torn off the wires and suction cups repeatedly and had even reared up out of the bed and run toward the wall. I thought of a caged, terrified animal.

I didn't know what state I'd find him in, but when I saw him sitting in the waiting room he looked more alert than usual, more awake, and, in fact, he looked more rested than I did.

"Hey," I said.

"Hi," he said. "Can I go smoke a cigarette now?"

An Indian doctor dressed in a sari beneath her white coat came out of an adjacent office and asked, "Are you James's mother?"

She spoke in a whisper and was so discreet and dainty that in contrast

I was made more aware of Jamie's massiveness and my own rumpled confusion. None of these professionals could realize how loaded each of their questions were. Mother. Son. Everywhere we turned for help that first year—GED tutoring, lawyers, even the dentist—we would be asked the daunting question: What were we in relation to each other? No one could imagine how hard we were working to figure out the answer to what seemed to them such a simple question.

"No, I'm not his mother," I said, "but I'm adopting him." I looked over at Jamie, who didn't look very adoptable. People were always surprised when I said I was in the process of adopting him. To most, adoption equals babies. Jamie wasn't a baby, or a boy, or a man. He was actually all three.

In a hushed tone, the doctor began her spiel.

"James," she said, "has severe sleep apnea." She sat down, sliding around the desk to sit in a huge executive chair, holding up his chart as if she were a child and it was a giant picture book, her head disappearing behind the chart.

"Code blue three hundred times," she read. She didn't let that sink in—that he had actually come near to death three hundred times during the night—before she continued as if chanting: James, she said, must lose weight, quit smoking, stop drinking caffeine, not eat after nine at night, and sleep hooked to a C-Pap, a machine that pumps outside air into his mouth and nose through a hose connected to a face mask.

Then with a slight lilt she said, "For the rest of his life," and laid down the chart.

I let the words bounce around in my head.

"For the rest of his life." The words of Jamie's doctor spilled into the room like a necklace of beads breaking, each sound of the bead on the floor a reminder of loss, as if broken was a process that goes on and on. Jamie had told me many times—his words like cold, hard steelies—he didn't care if he lived or died. Now he might really die. I was busy reseeing everything in this new light, adjusting to this new view of the world as the doctor continued.

"Jamie is an unusual case," she said.

I looked across at Jamie. He didn't own a toothbrush. He couldn't take a shower, could only bathe for reasons I didn't know yet. He only drank Cokes. He smoked four packs of cigarettes a day. I hadn't known where to begin even before it had become life or death.

The doctor, confused, I suppose, because we weren't responding, weren't acting appropriately shocked or horrified or attentive, began to pantomime.

"The muscles," she said, grabbing her throat perhaps to grab our attention, "collapse during sleep." She rounded her lips in an O and pretended to be drinking a milkshake through a straw. Most other peoples' muscles stay rigid during sleep, she explained.

"His muscles inside the throat are like a wet paper straw," she said, and then her black brows furrowed into an X exactly where her red Indian dot, the *bendi*, was painted as she noisily sucked from the invisible straw in the invisible glass she clasped with both hands. She looked as if she were playing charades.

As Jamie and I walked out of the building, carrying Sleep Apnea Support Group pamphlets, he stopped to light a cigarette, and said. "I couldn't understand a word she said. What was she anyway, an Arab?"

I looked at him as if seeing him for the first time.

"What?" I asked, as he stood blinking in the morning light, surprised at my tone. "What are you?" I yelled, throwing down the keys and the pamphlets. "A fucking racist?"

The shock on his face was that of my brother when he was a teenager and my father would yell at him. It was a look of total innocence and ignorance. Suddenly he had the expression of a scolded child, and I saw the child who had once run through the early houses of his life—my sister's, his grandmother's—with the glee of the unpunished. I wanted to put my arms around him, tell him that I hadn't slept all night worrying about him and the strangers watching over him in the night, people who I was scared would judge him quickly and harshly for his long hair and dirty nails. I always feared that someone would hurt him with a word or a glance because they didn't see his shadow self, the little boy, the little boy who was lost and now found and now changed. But instead, just like my father, I'd yelled.

11

emancipation day

Over the next year, I grew to hate the telephone. I hated talking to people who were of no help. I hated talking to my lawyers. I hated talking to my lawyers' secretary. I hated talking to anyone in my family because I felt I had to say that everything was going just fine. And I hated that the telephone was the only line between my house and Jamie's apartment, and usually I was left holding my end and listening to the ringing and imagining the scene at the other end.

He had only let me in the apartment three times in nine months. Once, before he'd met anyone from Houston, and he was still somewhat amazed, pleased even, yet befuddled about living alone, he'd showed me how he'd fixed up the small space with the stuff I'd given him, and some things he'd found in the trash, and some things Gail and Bobby had brought down one weekend. I'd walked around the rooms—the two of them—and oohed and aahed about how great it looked. I did like it.

There was a hippie quality to the way he had arranged candles, his stone collection, his magic books. The last person who'd lived there had put glow-in-the-dark stars on the ceiling and left some Christmas lights.

The next time I saw the apartment, I had to hold my hand over my face. Near tears, I looked at and then away from one mess to another, from the kitchen sink filled with cigarette butts floating in each of the twenty waxy Coke cups to the pizza boxes littering the floor next to his bed where there were hundreds of cigarette butts. The sheets were grayish and in a wad at the end of the bed, the exposed mattressed was stained with urine. Huge clumps of paper towels soaked yellow—upchucked mucus, he told me when he saw me staring—lay in a trail from the bed to the bathroom. His toilet looked like the ones I've seen in movies about prison life. "Jesus, Jamie," I said. "Jesus." The apartment was his lair, and he was a sick animal who'd crawled away from the world to die or recuperate. How could I know which?

The day we had to be in New Orleans to meet the lawyers for the emancipation, I couldn't get him to answer the telephone. Finally I'd thrown the phone receiver on the couch where it bounced onto the floor and as I marched across the street to his apartment, I heard the ringing following me, escalating the pounding of my heart. I rapped on his door, my arms crossed as if trying to hold myself together as I paced around, my anger growing into rage. Here I was, I thought, shelling out thousands of dollars on lawyers, and he couldn't even bother to get up. Now I'd be out the plane fare.

I began to beat on the door with the palms of my hands. Then I made fists and pounded, throwing my full body weight behind the effort. I lifted up the mail slot and breathed the dank, cellarlike air, thinking of Jamie as the monster above, hissing and snoring in his lair. I could hear the phone ringing from inside and could also hear the eerie sound of the droning sleep apnea machine as I bent down and began to scream into the mail slot. First I screamed his name. Then I cursed his name. I stepped back into the street and looked up at his window where I saw half of his face appear and then disappear as if he were the Phantom of the Opera or the Hunchback of Notre Dame. He was watching me. He was watching me lose my mind.

On the drive to the airport we didn't speak, and we didn't speak on the airplane. I sat down quickly next to two other passengers, which left him no option but to sit behind me. I needed to steady myself, I knew, because losing control the way I had at his front door frightened me and left me limp and woozy. While on the packed plane, I studied the palms of my hands that were already bruising bluish from hitting the door. I'd never hit anyone with my hands, but there had been times lately when I wanted to hit Jamie, and these were strange and sickening feelings. Halfway to New Orleans, Jamie leaned forward and tapped me on the shoulder, bringing his face next to mine. "Could we," he asked in his husky, sleepy voice, "go to the Mystic Curio when we get to New Orleans?"

"Yeah, sure," I said, still wrapped tight in my anger. My mouth was dry from the adrenaline of my explosion of violence earlier, and I was obsessively making up various speeches I'd deliver to Jamie later, after I'd cooled down. I was spending a whole lot of money, I would tell him. There was the flight to New Orleans. The hotel room. The lawyer. I was stewing in self-righteous anger, beside myself with self-pity when he tapped me on the shoulder again. "What is it, Jamie?" I said through gritted teeth.

"Your breath smells terrible. What did you eat?"

"Jesus," I said to myself, heated humiliation prickling my neck and face. Lately I'd begun to talk to myself as if all of this was really happening to another person who was watching and commenting and sympathetically appalled for this poor woman—me. Me of the foul breath. Me the new dragon lady who spewed flames of gall and venom. I turned around in my seat and stared at him. His big face was pale and luminous, full like a balloon, his expression one of simple curiosity.

"You've never had bad breath before," he said sweetly, blinking brown limpid eyes at me. We were packed tight into a small plane, my elbow had knocked against the woman next to me when I turned around, and a man in a business suit who sat next to Jamie was trying so hard to act as if he hadn't overheard anything that he looked crazed. Because of the man's self-consciousness, mine vanished. I started giggling thinking of the two of us, the two for the road, two addled and bumbling travelers, one full of herself and the other out of it.

"What are you laughing at?" he asked, smiling a smile only perceptible to me.

"You asshole," I said, slugging his shoulder, making sure I didn't get close enough for him to catch another whiff of my breath.

Through the New Orleans airport, Jamie shambled behind me, his jean cuffs catching in the heels of his boots, his breathing machine slung over his shoulder.

I heard myself telling him to hurry up, come on, get in the taxi, not even recognizing my voice that sounded like a schoolmarm's voice, scolding, instructing. I was a camp counselor, a drill sergeant, a cheerleader. Everyone I'd ever rebelled against. All these new voices were unrecognizable to me, sometimes taking me so by surprise that I thought when I looked in the mirror I'd see my third grade teacher, Mrs. Porter, or maybe my old swim team coach, Walter. I'd never realized these people resided in me and now they'd woken up and taken on the task of getting Jamie from here to there. Shape up or ship out, they hollered. No one ever promised you a rose garden, they simpered. Life's not a bowl of cherries, they concluded.

⚬⟂⚬

After we'd settled into our hotel, I called our lawyer, and we made plans for driving the next morning to Baton Rouge for the court hearing. Jamie was to be declared an adult, emancipated, have all legal ties with his parents severed. When I'd gained temporary legal custody the week before, my sister, Jan, had sent a bouquet of flowers and blue balloons with white lettering that read: "It's a boy!" The card read: "Congratulations!" It was signed from Mother, Jan and her daughter, Jenifer, and Gail. I'd stood in my foyer and looked at the card for a long time. Big-hearted,

151

wrong-headed, I thought. My family—fond of forging ahead. Even though at the time I'd felt uneasy with the acknowledgement, there were many times during the next six years I wished someone in the family would send their good wishes. Jan was always there—but her children, the very fact of their health and happiness—made it hard for me to call her and compare notes. I didn't feel as if I were raising a teenager. I felt more as though the wild boy of Avignon had scuttled in the side door and was still quivering and cowering in the back room of my life.

In a deep visceral response to not ever having had a child, I wanted to adopt him. I wanted him to be mine. But I'd been advised by psychologists and lawyers alike that once I'd adopted Jamie I should emancipate him. One psychiatrist said, "No Recknagel should ever hold power over this boy again."

༈

The next day Mark McTernan, our Richard Dreyfuss look-alike lawyer, picked us up in his van. The road between the two cities was one I'd been on hundreds of times. When Pike and I were in college in Baton Rouge, we had often driven to New Orleans and back in a night. All the possibilities that I was newly realizing would be buzzing in my head along with the whisky, the dark of the Louisiana highway unfurling like a ribbon. We'd go hear music, eat a ham and cheese po'boy at a place we'd found, I'd get my hair cut—like Jane Fonda's in *Klute,* I'd ask the hairdresser. At LSU I'd been shaken awake by the words of my poetry teacher who jumped around the room, his small hands clutching the paperback book of poetry from which he yelled at us, spit the poems out as if angry, growling out the poems of the Beats and of Roethke, Berryman, Dickey. Poetry, to my surprise, wasn't the stuff of rainbows, antebellum trees dripping moss on old gravestones. Real poetry, this teacher taught us, showed us, was full of explosions. Poetry could unsettle and maybe undo. I was coming undone in college. I was on mission to dismantle the southern myths I'd chafed under for nineteen years.

The corseted consciousness that had left me straining, yearning, lonely, and frustrated for so long.

Mark drove north to Baton Rouge. On the side of the road, trees were strangled by kudzu, the vine imported to Louisiana to help control some pest but which had taken over the state and done considerable damage to the wetlands. The landscape dripped and glistened, bubbled with what was underneath, the water moccasins, turtles, and alligators. Shacks and power lines and trees had been turned into sculptures of green by the kudzu, which transformed the world into a fanciful topiary. The scene was beautiful unless you knew the truth, knew everything was being choked to death by the vines. Always the deception of the kudzu had fascinated me. To me it represented Louisiana, the way the state glittered and beguiled, its tendrils becoming ties impossible to break. I'd left Louisiana, I told Mark, because of racism, political corruption, the stifling social scene. And, I thought as I watched the green shapes fly by and tried to keep up with Mark's conversation, because of my family. They were just like kudzu, I realized. Not what they seemed.

Mark was telling me that he and his wife were renovating an old house near Tulane, his children were toddlers, and a handful. Life was full and messy, and though he was proud to bursting with it all, he was cranky with the wear and tear of domesticity. He was a family man, and it showed in every move he made. Nuclear family, I thought, right before my eyes. Jamie and I were a family in the making, makeshift, taking form by the shadows we cast, constructing something of our own as we talked, as we made our way down the Louisiana highway. My new family sat in the backseat, plugged into his Walkman, eyes half-closed.

I tried to make up for Jamie, who acted as if Mark didn't exist, by acting interested and interesting for two. Mark and I touched on subject after subject: crime, politics, stocks and bonds, Houston, his in-laws, who he told me lived in Baton Rouge; his father-in-law had been a professor of agriculture at LSU and was retired. We talked of break-ins, muggings, car thefts.

In midsentence, in the middle of a true-crime story, Mark turned and looked at me. He then turned the same intense gaze back to the road, hunching forward and squinting, holding the steering wheel tightly. He bobbed a couple of times in the seat as if testing a diving board before leaping.

"Your brother had one condition," he said. Mark looked at the road, then at me, his head whipping back and forth.

"A condition?" I asked.

"For his cooperation," Mark said. He looked at me again as if making an assessment.

"Well?" I asked.

He spoke the words as if reading them: "They specifically requested that you be kept out of sight. They said specifically that if they see you, the deal's off."

There was suddenly a blank space where there had been potential for more small talk. My whole life became the line in the road, the route I'd somehow got started on and now had to keep traveling, one that led away from the people I'd loved. I saw them in my mind as tiny figures on the side of the road, some waving, some frowning, some turning their eyes away from the sight of me. There was Gail and Bobby, who seemed to be cheering us on as if we were in a parade. I saw Mother, whose bewilderment showed in her vacant expression. I saw my brother, my baby brother, Jimmy, receding to a speck as I sped by in the van with the lawyer and Jamie. I felt light, as if something essential was gone, had been sapped from me in an instant. I felt the wind blow through the gaping rough-edged tear inside of me. I saw them all left behind.

My heart broke on the outskirts of Baton Rouge.

The sun came through the windshield, falling into my lap and across my upper arm, touching me like hot hands. Always, I realized, my victories had been salt in my brother's wounds.

I am my brother's enemy, I thought. *I am not my brother's keeper. Not now. Not ever again. Not like it was once was, when I was a sister, a good sister. I am my brother's enemy,* I said to myself, rocking to the rhythm of the statement, adjusting to the solemnity of the fact. *My brother must hate me,* I thought. My brother hates me, I understood.

I made myself remember what he had done, what he had let happen to his son. That way I could learn to hate him, too.

For ten years, my brother and Dayna, who were childlike themselves, had hurt a child, had hurt Jamie, had turned him into the somnolent creature in the backseat. A week before, as Jamie and I had stood before a deli and peered inside the glass at the choices, he'd nervously looked at the food, then at me before he asked the question: "Sometime could you explain to me about what's normal?"

He was looking down, seeming to be ashamed. I wasn't sure what the question referred to. We had argued about food. Searching through my refrigerator, he'd gripe about the guacamole or hummus or tabouli. Often when we went out to eat, we'd go to my choice, then to his favorite—to a health food restaurant, then to Whataburger.

"Portions," he continued. "What do people—regular people—eat?" he asked. "I mean," he said, staring straight ahead, "how much at one time? And how often?" I tried not to stare at him openmouthed so I wouldn't scare away other questions. How much to sleep and when? How much to eat and when? Even how many movies to rent at one time was a question for him. He'd told me his parents usually rented six movies at a time, which they would watch all in one sitting, usually from midnight until dawn. Jamie, it turned out, didn't know about proportion of any sort.

Sitting over our lunch that day, I told him that maybe we had found a use for me. "Why not," I proposed, "consider me a consultant." We had had trouble clarifying my role—he didn't want to think of me as family. But I couldn't say I was a friend, either. "You've managed to fit in," he said, "without selling out." That was a great compliment. Jamie was realizing that perhaps he'd found another alien—but one who had mixed with the natives long enough to know their ways. He didn't, it turned out, want to appear foolish or to startle or amaze with what he didn't know. He was like someone who was hiding the fact that he'd never learned to read. He'd never learned to read the "normal" world.

One night a few months before the court proceeding the whole ten-year
ordeal poured out of him, came out in a rush of prose not slowed by
any punctuation except some exclamation marks. Mark had suggested
Jamie come to his own defense, express his desires in his own words.
Jamie began that very afternoon. He wrote as if there were a deadline,
as if this would be the first and last time he would ever deal with this
again. Jamie started writing around noon one day, and was still sitting
at my computer when I left for dinner that night. He wrote in my study,
his hair cascading onto the keys. He wrote in the dark, all through the
night, while I slept. I'd get up to creep down the stairs and look in at
him, see his back like a solid wall filling up the room. The story spilled
out, typed quickly, two fingers at a time, the years delineated with bold
letters: **TUPELO, SAVANNAH, BATON ROUGE.** He titled his sum-
mary: **AMMUNITION.** At sunrise he left a copy of the twenty-page
history on my dining room table, crossed the street to his apartment,
and slept for two days.

Jamie never wanted to talk about what he'd written. But I had taken
the pages upstairs, and sat on my bed, turning them as if skinning myself
alive. About the first weeks after he was taken from Bobby and Gail and
returned to his parents, he wrote,

> *From the moment I got to my parents' house, I could see from the way*
> *they screamed, fought, threw things, treated their house, pets, . . . etc that*
> *they were not normal as most people. The first place we lived was in*
> *Shreveport in an apartment close to where Bobby and Gail live today. I*
> *still get almost nauseated just looking at it. I remember the day I left*
> *my surrogate home forever. I got out of the car with my bags and my*
> *Aunt Gail kept promising I would be back with her within a week. (that*
> *never came about) but little kid I was, I kept hoping in spite of my*
> *situation. My memory is fuzzy about that time, but I remember them*
> *{Jimmy and Dayna} constantly arguing about who had more authority*

over money, each other and least importantly me, the one thing they had fought for so desperately, they now cared very little for. I guess it was just a way at getting back at all the people that have had power over him {Jimmy} at that age. He was in a rage of anger all the time, so was my mother. She would walk around in a daze, talking to herself crazily, muttering things like "I can't believe he's not going to punish Jamie!!! Guess I'll have to do it!!! So she would usually have me go get her weapon of choice, sometimes a switch, sometimes a belt, a coat hanger, but painful enough to get her anger out at me, Jimmy and the world. Sometimes I would cry hard to begin with so she would stop beating me sooner. I'm mad that they didn't leave any scars because then there would be solid evidence. They threatened to beat me with a razor strap. Although I had no idea what a razor strap was, but it sounded pretty painful. One day when she was hitting me I started crying, she started laughing she started calling me a "baby girl" and took my clothes off, put me in a shiny blue dress, threw me outside and locked the door.

When I read what Jamie wrote, I thought I couldn't live with the information. My whole body shuddered. I tried to get the images out of me as if trying to shed clothes that were on fire.

He wrote,

My hope of returning to my home died slowly, but surely. My hope for life faded. I went into a deep sort of depression, if that is possible for a kid that age. I used to sit in my room in the corner, sort of like a trapped animal. Nowhere to go, nowhere to hide. My life was meaningless at the time and over the years I've thought about ending it, but as always, that animalistic, instinctive part of me came out, and my will to survive overcomes, always has, always will.

I would put the pages down, close my eyes and try to breathe more slowly. Then I'd gather the courage to read on. He wrote,

By the time I was placed in Parkland Hospital, I was completely emo-
tionless, much like a machine, (come to think of it I was like a word
processor). I took in data from the outside world, processed it, filtered it
of all emotion, refined and revised it, and then spit out a reply. A ma-
chine. Machines had brought me up—TVs, radios, video games. I was
no longer human, but a carcass, a shell with no purpose in particular.
Long before I became hardhearted, I had often wondered whether I was
an experiment. A research to find out how much you could torture some-
one before they snap. I decided to give them—experiment or no—a run
for their money.

Jamie wrote about sleeping under his bed for the first two years he
was returned to them. He wrote about his mother's weekly rampages in
which she'd come into his room, topple over shelves, ransack his room.
"I don't have to worry anymore about people plundering into my things
all the time," he wrote.

His mother loved tape recorders. He wrote about her hiding one in
his room periodically. "I'll catch you in your lies," she'd said, walking in
an exaggerated way to emphasize her stealth. "Just you wait." She would
cackle and prance around the room like the witch in *The Wizard of Oz*.
After neighbors called social services, a woman came out to the house.
Jamie wrote,

"When the lady had left the house Dayna came in the room and
picked up the tape recorder hidden in the plant, looked at me, winked
and snickered the way she always does. And then walked down the hall
droning out, 'I got you now, babe, got ya now!' " The social worker had
asked repeatedly, "Are you sure you're all right?" seemingly puzzled at
his firm declaration that all was well. "Fine," he'd said. "Everything is
just fine."

To Jamie, the arrival of a social worker—alerted by neighbors—meant
more trouble: another move, a new school, beginning again.

Jamie wrote about being seven and watching Dayna in the door of
the bathroom as she brushed her hair. "Stop watching me," she

screamed, turning and hitting him in the face with the brush. "You pervert—watching me!" she'd shout, convinced he wanted her for more than a mother.

"I know," she once told my mother, "about Jimmy and Marsha."

"What are you saying, Dayna?" Mother asked.

"They had celestial relations," she said.

"Celestial relations?" Mother had asked.

Mother called me and asked what those were.

"Oh, Mother," I groaned. I'd heard from my brother when he lived in Houston that Dayna had made such a charge. "She means incestuous relations," I told Mother, whose quiet on the other end of the line indicated she didn't really know what that was either.

Driving down the highway to Baton Rouge, I kept thinking about Jamie and the blue dress. From his words, I saw him as he stood at the window of the suburban tract house on the edge of town in Baton Rouge, a neighborhood where each house looked the same, except at Jimmy and Dayna's house there was a seven-year-old boy standing outside in a blue dress. "Oh, so now you want in?" I imagined Dayna saying in the voice of the Wicked Witch of the West.

I pictured Jamie going from window to window, tripping over the hem, his hands splayed against the screens, wanting, as he had not wanted before, to go in. I thought about the blue dress on the ride to Baton Rouge so I could be made stronger by hate.

When Mark turned in to a parking lot blocks from the courthouse, I looked around, wondering where I'd wait. Downtown Baton Rouge was empty and the day had turned gray and cold. Mark began inching his van down one aisle after another, slowly searching for a parking place. I saw a man with gray hair and beard opening his car trunk and reaching in to take something out. The man turned his head toward me, and looked right into my eyes.

What beautiful eyes, I thought. What beautiful eyes that big man has. Familiar eyes.

He was my brother.

But he couldn't be my brother, I thought. This man is middle-aged. My mind churned sluggishly through the information before my eyes. I realized that I'd freeze-framed my brother into images that were like photographs: Jimmy at six, at twelve, at seventeen, at twenty. I had missed the years in which his hair had gone white, his girth widened, a manliness emerged.

"Oh, my God," I said in a whisper as I held on to the seat so I didn't pitch forward from dizziness onto the dashboard.

Mark stepped on the gas, driving out of the parking lot, apologizing profusely. Jamie, who was still lost in his music, fell sideways as Mark peeled out of the lot.

"What's going on?" he asked, pulling his earplugs out.

"It's Jimmy," I said. "Jimmy, your dad."

"Who cares?" he said, replacing the earplugs.

Mark was zipping down one street and then another. He had begun to mutter to himself.

My enemy, I thought. My brother who'd loved chocolate milk and Chips Ahoy! cookies. My brother who'd loved *The Three Stooges,* and lemons with salt, and drums and guitars and lawnmowers and filling stations and the people who worked in them. My brother who'd had skinny legs, hound dog eyes, and a huge laugh that came from his belly. My brother who loved dogs. And movies. And card games. Any game. He had been my mother's favorite. Her damaged baby boy. I loved my brother. Yet I loved Jamie. I didn't know how to fit those two parts of a puzzle together in one mind.

⌒

While Jamie was in court, I sat in a conference room and drank cup after cup of bad coffee and read old copies of *Redbook* and *Good House-keeping.* When Jamie returned with Mark, who was patting him as if he'd done a good job, he was emancipated. I shook his hand, then hugged him awkwardly, his arms remaining loose at his sides as my head bumped off his chest. I shook Mark's hand. There was the taste of stale coffee in my mouth. Jamie had just faced his parents and had a lawyer request that he be released legally from them. The break was swift and out of my sight. Jamie would never speak of those five minutes—how he felt, what his parents looked like, where he stood, how far from them.

A clerk came in and whispered to Mark, who excused himself, saying he had to sign some more papers. "Meet me down at the street," he said.

As Jamie and I headed toward the elevator we saw two people standing in front of it. The woman, who had on more makeup than Tammy Faye Baker, was taking a huge drag on a cigarette, her cheeks sucked in until they were hollow. Dayna, Jamie's mother, Jamie's ex-mother, was standing ten feet from us. Seeing my brother again, I was surprised by how much he now looked like my grandfather, Papaw, Mother's father. He just stood and stared before he began hitting the elevator button with his palm, wanting, I could tell, for the opening of the door to save all of us from each other.

Dayna narrowed her eyes as if trying to get us into focus. I began to back up slowly, keeping my eyes on her, my arm outstretched across Jamie's chest.

She lurched into movement. By instinct I bolted away as she started chasing me. Like in a cartoon, I was stopping at crossroads of hallways, deciding, then taking off. "I'm sorry, someone's after me," I said to a secretary as, gasping for breath, I ducked into her office. I crouched down behind a filing cabinet and tried to melt into the wall, pulling my purse across my chest as if for protection. When Dayna seemed to have left I finally got up, brushed off my dress, shouldered my purse and apologized to the secretary who'd never said a word, I felt as if I'd been emancipated. Nothing, I thought, could humiliate me anymore. Jamie and I both were free.

I found my seemingly unflappable lawyer standing in the hall, pale and uncertain. Jamie stood like Lurch beside him, no curiosity, no response, just waiting to be commanded: go here, turn there. Mark asked me if I thought we ought to take the stairs.

On our way out of town, Mark pulled in to a gas station and filled up, but when he tried to start the van, it sputtered, then died. No, I thought to myself, no. I have to get back to New Orleans. I needed to be far away from the city where I'd been victorious, where I'd put another nail into my brother's coffin. I'd consoled myself through the day by thinking that in only three hours I would be in New Orleans, how I'd soon be listening to music in the 544 Club with its small, wooden dance floor lit from overhead by a string of Christmas lights. Night, I'd told myself, would inevitably come, it always did. Soon I would lay down my day, order a scotch, and let all the sorrow come back to me folded into the lyrics and turned into the low growling notes played by the blues band on the corner of St. Ann's and Bourbon.

The mechanic walked over to Mark with the look of a surgeon delivering bad news. Hours, he said. It would take hours to fix the van.

Jamie paced around the front of the station, smoking with such force that I could hear him inhale. Mark called his father-in-law, the retired agriculture professor, who decided to come over. He'd take us on a tour of campus, he told Mark.

Before Mark's father-in-law arrived, Jamie went into the station and asked one of the attendants for a phone book. "What do you want with the phone book? I asked.

He mumbled that he had a girlfriend who lived there.

"Girlfriend?" I asked.

"From the mental hospital," he said.

Great, I thought.

I left Jamie poring over the phone book and went outside just as Mark's father-in-law swung into the lot in a huge white Lincoln Continental. He stepped out in all his retired glory—a pinstriped jumpsuit, his hair white and combed back with a military finesse. "Let's go to Sears," he said, clapping his hands as if we were his troops. I called for Jamie to come on and get in the car. As I held the door open, he ripped a page from the phone book and stuffed it in his pocket.

"My God," I screamed as if I'd caught him peeing in public or something equally unbelievable and uncivilized.

The father-in-law managed to ignore Jamie's existence in the same way Jamie had acted as if Mark were invisible. While navigating through traffic as if driving a yacht, he spoke straight ahead and in sonorous tones to his captive audience. As he sailed through the streets in his cool and quiet car, he launched into a harangue against environmentalists. "See those trees?" he asked. "They make more carbon dioxide then all the cars in the city." Mark laughed a too-hearty laugh. Jamie looked at me as if I'd agreed with the evil white man that trees were the enemy.

We did a quick drive-through of the LSU campus and then went to Sears. In the parking lot, the three of us emerged bedraggled while the father-in-law hopped out and rattled his keys and strode ahead as we followed. He needed to buy a bucket, he said. As I watched him troop off, he became every know-it-all, late-middle-aged white man I'd ever known. He was my father. And I blamed him for everything. As we followed him up one aisle and down another, I blamed him for the Vietnam War, for Reagan, for the demise of the rain forests, for my brother's sadness.

I watched him as he took hold of the sides of different buckets and containers as if checking the teeth of a horse. He was the bankers who kept my money locked away in a trust I couldn't touch. He picked out his bucket, shelled out the money for a clerk he never looked at, and walked away, expecting that we would follow him like ducklings, or like a pack of dogs behind the Alpha dog, and he was right. He never looked over his shoulder to see if we were following. We were.

Once back at the gas station, I went into the rest room and stared at myself in the mirror. My brother had seen this face that was reflected back to me. What had he seen? Was I as much of a surprise to him as he to me? Would I ever see him face-to-face again?

I washed my face and put on lipstick. I bought a package of M&M's from the vending machine and sat down next to Jamie in one of the '60s orange plastic chairs.

"Why'd you take the page from the phone book?" I asked him as I looked inside the package. I'd learned if I wanted any information from Jamie it was best to act as if I didn't want it too much.

Jamie began speaking to me of Karen, the girl he'd met in the locked ward of Parkland, the first girl he'd ever called a girlfriend. He'd torn out the page with all the listings of her last name. He planned to call each number.

"The bones in her back?" he said with a question. "What are they called?"

"Shoulder blades," I said.

"Yeah," he said. "Her shoulder blades stuck out from her hospital gown. And when she bent over, you could see her chest. It was like a cadaver's."

I couldn't think of anything but the sight he'd given me.

"What was the matter?" I asked.

"Eating disorder," he explained with the briskness of a doctor inured to disease. "Just bones," he said, shaking his head and taking a deep drag off his cigarette. Then he laughed and looked at me a little sheepishly, a little proudly. "She was bony to sleep with."

She had black spiky hair and a tattoo—not homemade like the one on his ankle but a nice one, he said, from a tattoo parlor.

"She was real fucked up," he said.

He told me she had been sexually abused.

I looked out the window at the five o'clock Baton Rouge traffic, and nodded my head, trying to imagine the day room of the hospital, Karen and Jamie talking as patients shuffled by and a TV blared. Jamie told me that he had made love to her night after night in the locked ward of the hospital on a twin bed in a real cold room. I tried to picture Jamie, big and broad shouldered and the skin-and-bones abused girl sharing a small bed as nurses padded in and out, checking to make sure no one killed themselves.

"You could hear people screaming up and down the halls all night," he said.

"Yeah," I said, I knew about that from the hospital I'd worked in. I knew about how unearthly a scream can be in the quiet of the late-night shift, the shadowy hallways lit blue as the insomniacs paced up and down in blue hospital gowns.

In the mornings, he said, he would wake himself convulsing, so cold that his teeth would chatter like dominos clicking.

"She held me," he said. Karen would rub his numb arms and face back to life. His face would be hard as plastic, and when she massaged it, he could hear it crackle. Afterward he'd stand for thirty minutes under the hot shower, trying to warm himself. It was the sleep apnea and oxygen deprivation that had made him turn blue, stop breathing, throw his back up into a back bend, wet the bed. "How could they not know?" I asked him. I meant about the sleep disorder, but Jamie thought I meant about him sleeping with Karen. That was the one thing in his life up until then that he thought worth telling, that he thought was good.

"But the nurses," I repeated. "Didn't they ever hear you trying to breathe?" He had been in the hospital for ten months, then in one in New Orleans for one month, and then later at a home for boys in Denton, Texas, for a couple of months. No one had remarked on his sleeping problem.

"Sometimes," he said, looking at the end of the cigarette, "sometimes I thought I was an experiment." He told me how over the years he thought that someone had put a computer chip in him when he was an infant, and that he was being monitored for how much a person could take.

"I'm plastic," he said. "You could light a match to me, and I'd melt like a plastic spoon in flames."

"Jamie, what do you mean? I asked, although I was scared for him to elaborate.

"Here," he said, putting his big bear hand to his chest. "Nothing. I feel nothing."

"You will," I promised. "Really, you will. I swear it."

"No, Marsha," he said. My little shreds of wisdom and lame assurances seemed nothing compared to the certainty in his voice.

The truth was that I didn't know if he could get better. Each day I had to try to convince myself as well as him that he could find a heart and ultimately a life for himself.

All day I'd been thinking about being back in New Orleans—alone— where maybe I could get hold of myself and remember that I had had a life before Jamie. But then Jamie had given me a look inside, a view from where he was, who he was, and I'd felt myself straining hard to see what he was showing me, what he had seen. As I made myself look, let the pictures seep in, he grew quiet. I looked over to see his head hanging way down as he studied the concrete floor. "Hey," I said. He raised his face to me. With my index finger I tucked each side of his long black hair behind an ear. I'd reached up to his face in the gesture of the mother who picks up a child who's fallen from his trike, a movement of the hand that promises things will be better. I then held the package of M&M's in the air with a tilt of my head and he nodded. I poured the last of the M&M's into his open hand.

12

for those who wait

The first year Jamie came to Houston I often took him to a park six blocks from my house. I walked him there the way I walked the dogs, in hopes that an outing in the air would do him good. He complained constantly about the sun, claimed he couldn't think straight in daylight hours. I thought it was just a matter of readjusting his internal clock. "Come out and play," I'd holler up at his window. I'd try to be non-chalant because if he sensed I wanted him to do something, he'd balk. He groused but shambled along beside me, keeping his head down as if to prove the sun hurt his eyes. Often Rosie's leash would get wrapped around his leg. "Don't be mean," I'd say as he'd untangle himself and mutter about stupid Rose.

I'd spent countless hours in this park. I'd gone there without a dog to mourn the loss of my father. That season I'd watched the dog owners from a gray-slatted bench where sometimes I'd laid my cheek against the cool metal rail. It was the flip side of good memory, cold and hard. In the fall of 1981, I'd come to know the dogs and each one's particular way of bounding or running or racing through the world. There was a leaping black poodle shorn down to a bootblack finish. There was a huge chocolate Lab that lumbered, punch-drunk like an old fighter—gentle, dumb, strong. I'd seen the fig tree tricked into producing early fruit only to be struck down by a last, late frost. I'd seen twenty years' growth of bamboo become, in an unprecedented freeze, a giant dried arrangement around the reflecting pond. Lightning had struck an oak, stripping the bark as if it were fruit peel pared by a knife.

I'd made friends there. I'd fallen in love there.

I'd walked Jamie to the park with a purpose, a plan, a hope that he would also find something there. The open green space was between an ecumenical chapel and an art museum. Perhaps, I thought, Jamie would enter the chapel or go to the museum. Maybe he'd be inspired to paint murals, or to become a street artist, another Basquiat. Or maybe he would meet someone in the park who would sense his potential and offer him a job. Even a part-time job would be fine. Maybe he would discover a love for dogs and decide to be a veterinarian. Or a veterinarian's assistant. Things happen, I thought. Something will happen, and then things will be different.

ᴗ:ᴦ

"Is he a sociopath?" I'd asked the psychiatrist, John Stocks, who had treated Jamie at the New Orleans hospital. On the day Jamie and I had arrived in New Orleans to hire a lawyer, I had looked him up and when I called he'd said to come over. Dr. Stocks and I had sat in his sun-filled house, the wooden floors worn to a richness like doeskin. In a strange coincidence, I'd met John Stocks at a cocktail party in Houston the year before. The night of the party I'd told him about Jamie—who I'd just heard had been committed to a hospital in Baton Rouge. It seemed to me a miracle that Jamie fell into his care when he was transferred to a hospital in New Orleans.

Sitting in Dr. Stock's living room, I'd stared at the sun patterns on the floor and held my breath while waiting for the answer to my question: sociopath. Or salvageable? Dr. Stocks, who had a goatee like Freud's and wore a paisley ascot under his white shirt, had shaken his head. "No, no, not a sociopath," he said.

I'd taken a deep breath and sunk back into his old couch. I could hear shrieks of children playing in Audubon Park coming through the open windows.

"Really?" I'd asked, incredulously.

"Really," he said. "But he's pretty pissed."

I sat and looked around the room. Yes, I'd thought, Jamie is pretty angry. His anger, like radiation, seeking out the soft parts of me, burning them down to an essence.

"Not unscathed," Stocks said. "Not by any means. But he does have a conscience."

Jamie, it appeared, was not malignant.

"That's a good thing," I'd said, talking mainly to myself.

I'd always thought he had to have a conscience or I had to let him go. That has been my worry, my terrible fear, that he would be beyond help. One to throw back.

It's funny to think now that *my* conscience was what made me keep him because I was told that *he* had a conscience. Could I have lived with myself if I'd turned my back on him?

"And very smart," he'd added. "He could go to college. He could be anything. He could be a psychologist. He's very analytical."

Smart, analytical, and a boy with a conscience. There were times in the next six years when I'd unwrap those lines in my mind and rub them during bad times for good luck.

I was embarrassed to be ashamed of Jamie, but I was. At first when we started to go to the park together, I searched my friends' eyes for any hint that they were exchanging looks, smirking, or whispering. It was the same feeling I'd had when my brother would enter the sunroom where all my friends would gather on weekends. My mother had always told me, "Be sweet." It's about the only moral directive I ever received from her, but it was hard enough. If someone wasn't sweet to my brother, he or she had to go, even if it was Andy, who'd just moved to Shreveport from Florida, who had streaked blond surfer hair and blue eyes, and who I thought I loved. The year my brother became a Jesus freak, he'd once walked into the sunroom, where the lights were dimmed and couples were burrowing into the couch to make out, and methodically begun to pass out Jesus pamphlets as if he were a priest giving a blessing. Andy tossed his long hair back with his hand, his trademark gesture, and in his nasally voice began to sing, "Jesus loves us, yes, he does." Like a crisp fall leaf under a magnifying glass, my little love for him dried up, turned to ashes I could taste in my mouth. He had to go.

Jamie'd never enter the group of dog owners standing by the big oak in the center of the park, or sit on a bench. Instead he'd plop on the grass where he'd soon be whipped by a frenzy of tails as the dogs circled and pushed their noses up under his tangled hair to snort and sniff at the back of his neck. A beagle lifted his leg on Jamie's wide back. And then the other dogs came to investigate.

He'd put his big arms around the neck of the testy rottweiler, and I'd hold my breath, waiting for the dog to take a chunk of cheek. But the dog would begin to lick, broad bands of tongue searching out Jamie's ear, then diving up over his shoulder. One huge Lab would circle his lap as if making a bed before coming to rest as a bundle, his big friendly head lolling on Jamie's knee, looking out at the rest of us as if he'd found the best spot in the park. Jamie's voice, taking on a tenderness I'd never heard, baby-talked the dogs, kept up a murmuring patter as he took both hands and cupped a muzzle, lifted it up to look the dog in the eyes.

I'd told him not to look them in the eyes. "They consider it a challenge," I explained in the same voice I told him to make eye contact with people when he spoke. But he didn't listen, and no dog bit him and no person at the park revealed himself a snob. He'd mumble answers to questions and when I'd complain, he'd say, "I can't talk small talk." Or if he ignored a hand extended after an introduction, I'd stiffen, the muscles in my shoulders holding myself back for the constant scolding taking place silently in the back of my mind. "How can you buy into that society bullshit?" he'd ask me. There was no sense repeating the ridiculous Archie Bunker rhetoric that even I couldn't believe came out of my mouth—like that I had to buy into the bullshit so that I could make a living so that he could sleep the livelong day.

Though Jamie acted as if he were oblivious to his surroundings, he was really anything but. As if on constant alert for betrayal, he'd gather information; he'd rifle through my mail, read each Post-it on my refrigerator, and pick up conversations a room away. He read faces and tone of voice in seconds and could detect an "asshole," "a shrink," or a someone recently out of a mental hospital from across a room. He'd had years of practice. As a boy he'd watch his mother—the tiny flicker of muscle spasms in the jaw foretold a seizure, a certain narrowing of her eyes alerted him that she might turn on him with accusations—of theft, of lying, of conspiring. To live with someone who acts paranoid makes one paranoid. The way to be inconspicuous is to pretend the rest of the world doesn't exist—since you are trying to pretend not to exist. That was one of Jamie's problems—a failure to fully exist.

It was months before I told someone in the park part of the story, explaining that Jamie was my nephew, was the son of my brother, who had met his wife, Jamie's mother, in a mental hospital when they were teenagers. The evening he'd overheard me say I was his aunt, he waited until we were halfway home before he said, "I don't think of you as my aunt."

"I've been an aunt as long as I can remember," I told him, laughing, thinking about Scotty, born to Gail when I was six.

I'd beamed when the owner of Café Artiste, the place Jamie and I went for coffee near the park, asked us, "Brother and sister?" I wanted any connection, the weave of some relation to hold us in its web.

"I don't think of you as family," Jamie said again, more firmly.

"But that's reality," I argued. I noticed Jamie's stride had become more purposeful, the way it did when he was walking on through to the other side of his thoughts, stomping on my arguments before they arose.

"If I think of you as family, I'll have to hate you," he said, not breaking his stride.

I tried hard not to explain Jamie or apologize for his behavior or his appearance. One afternoon, a perky girl bounced into the park like a young golden retriever. She was making the rounds, meeting the dog owners, excited to have found what she called "the doggie park." There'd been a feature article in the newspaper, which happened about once a year, and when it did, there'd be an influx of newcomers. When she went over to Jamie, I held my breath in the same way I'd done with the rottweiler. I positioned myself closer to them and pretended to listen as two dog owners talked about the flea problem—garlic powder in the food?—while I really was eavesdropping on Jamie. I wanted to know how he sounded when I wasn't listening. I needed clues as much as he did.

"I'm a solitary practitioner of anything mystically speaking," I heard him tell her. She must have asked him what he did.

I saw her head bobbing with more questions.

"I practice Wicca," he said, looking serious and studious at the ground. "Though I'm not a Wiccan, technically speaking."

"A Wiccan?" she asked, tilting her head, and pulling on the cuff of her cutoffs.

"That's white witchcraft," he explained, putting his cigarette out in the dirt and fumbling for another. "Totally different from black magic."

"What sign are you?" she asked as I drifted away and back to my friends.

On the walk home, he asked the question he'd asked me many times since he'd been in Houston: "Why are girls only interested in astrology?"

"Horoscopes," he said, inhaling on his cigarette as if with his whole body. I thought he was going to let loose of the smoke as if cleaning his system of all silliness. "Fluff stuff," he said. "Why always fluff stuff?"

Women utterly perplexed Jamie. He had read voraciously since he was a child, and he was full of theories. His formal education had been practically nonexistent, but he had educated himself, which made his knowledge patchy. He knew a lot about some things and nothing at all about others, such as history. Growing up, he'd had time on his hands—no friends, little adult guidance, moving from city to city. Books had been a constant. He had thought about language and gender and power. He valued reason above all else. The main woman in his life—his mother—had been unreasonable, often irrational. Naturally Jamie had generalized and concluded women were unreasonable.

My role, I thought, was to show him a different kind of woman. Yet along came a ditzy girl in the park who confirmed his opinion. Women, I explained to Jamie, do feel linked to the stars and the journey of the planets. "You know," I said, "the moon, menstruation, all that."

"But," he argued, "that's boiling down matriarchal goddess-centered religions to the triteness of, 'Will I have a date next Friday?' "

"I know, I know, Jamie," I said, finding myself caught in an argument I didn't even believe myself. Why, I wondered silently, is it mainly women consulting palm readers, fortune-tellers, and horoscopes. Why do *we* call the horoscope hotlines?

"Why do they act so bubbleheaded?" he asked me as I was mulling over the same question. "Women," Jamie said, shaking his head in the age-old gesture indicating our unfathomable nature.

I hated that Jamie only had disdain for girls and wished I could argue better in their defense.

In my teens I'd been a bubblehead. I'd worked hard to be levelheaded. I was embarrassed when caught by Jamie in stereotypical behavior.

"God, I'm fat," I'd once moaned on a walk.

His quick glance told me of my shallowness.

Feminist theories in graduate school, reading hundreds of books by women, and psychoanalysis had all helped me break old habits. In my twenties, I'd played up the southern drawl, unconscious of the subliminal messages I was sending. Over the years, I'd tried to rid myself of southern belle-ism and chafed under any teasing about my accent. I'd once asked a classroom full of students to critique themselves according to demographics. The English Department was under the sway of deconstructionists' theories, and I was a zealous convert. I did the assignment with the students, looking at myself from a critical postmodern distance: I wore guess-my-weight ensembles, with black camisoles, two earrings to an ear and comfortable footwear. Or cowboy boots. I'd been called strong and independent—by those who loved me. I'd been called many other things as well: Stubborn. Willful. Ball-breaker. A fucking pain in the ass. No day at the beach.

After Jamie's entrance into my life, self-definition became important. For me, for him. I needed to have a good grasp of who I was because I found the "me" he often threw back at me was some wild-eyed raving maniac, a knee-jerk liberal on good days, a shrew on bad days, and certainly, as Jamie had made clear, a freak about personal hygiene.

I began to brace myself for what might come out of his mouth that might wound.

Everything about me was under inspection. And I discovered over time that I cared deeply about his good opinion.

One afternoon, as we walked through the campus quadrangle, he said, "A puff of wind could blow you away."

"What do you mean, Jamie?" I asked, looking down at my dress, trying to see what he saw.

"Someone could just run by and pick you up like a twig and take off!"

I didn't feel like a twig. I thought about arguing but just kept walking, worried that I was shrinking away, becoming a skinny, persnickety spinster.

Later that night as I took off my clothes for bed, I pinched the flesh at my sides and wondered if I was getting too gaunt.

"No," a friend, who is also a psychologist, said when I told her about the exchange. "He just wants you to be really substantial." She thought Jamie was worried I wasn't solid enough to hold him to the ground. Or maybe, she said, it was the fear that if he turned his back I might disappear—blown off the earth by a gust of wind, kidnapped, snatched up by strangers and displaced—as he had once been.

Staying grounded in the face of Jamie's constant testing was hard enough. "To see if you'll bounce back," my psychologist friend had explained as the reason behind the constant criticism. And sometimes the world got flipped upside down by outsiders, by someone whose benign remark would send me into a panic, make me question my decisions, my motives, my entire life, long after the remark had been tossed off and forgotten by whoever had uttered it.

I always remembered the day at the beginning of the fall semester, the first year with Jamie, when I was going up the stairs to the department, I found myself in step with a professor near retirement who for the last several years had seemed somewhat lost, his eyes blinking behind thick glasses at the academic world that must have seemed as though it had changed overnight while he was sleeping. Ibsen, his field, was out. Toni Morrison was in.

In his patrician voice that could make one think—if you were in the United States—that he was British, he said, "Well, Marsha. How are you?"

"Well, it's been kind of rough. I've taken on a bit of a problem teenager, who was an abused child," I said, surprised the minute the sentence was out of my mouth.

"Well, Marsha," he said without skipping a beat, "I hope he doesn't murder you in your sleep. I've heard that can happen with those kids."

I couldn't speak. I opened the stairwell door and walked through, leaving him to catch the door before it slammed shut on him.

Why would I take this on? Did I know what I was getting into? What I would go through? A friend at a cocktail party had smiled and said she'd heard about my "project." "Why," she said, "would you want to take on something like that?" Taking on, getting into, over my head, into trouble. The prophesies of friends and acquaintances sapped my energy, reflected back to me images of Jamie, myself and the future that I didn't want to see or couldn't if I was to "stay with it." Prepositions had plagued my life since Jamie's arrival. So I stopped seeing most of my friends except for a few, the ones who would go to dinner with me and listen. Just listen and nod and hand over a napkin when the tears began, which was inevitable.

⚮

At the park, I practiced not watching Jamie. I was, I noticed, so like my father. But I stopped my hands from brushing off the dandruff from his shirt, using a fingernail to remove a crusty pizza stain. I had never imagined how hard it would be to let someone be.

The dog people treated him with the patience they had for unsocialized dogs, the ones that were playing one minute and the next had crossed the line from playful to rabid, the growl reaching the pitch that makes the hair on the back of your neck stand on end. But Jamie knew he was the unpredictable mutt in our midst.

⚮

The dog park was four blocks from my house if you walked south. If you walked the same distance north, you'd hit Westheimer. One afternoon, I was returning a movie to the Blockbuster on the corner of Westheimer and Montrose where there was a group of kids hanging out in the small seedy strip center that housed a Subway sandwich shop, an Eckerd Drugs and an empty building that had once sold office supplies but was now a wide-open canvas for graffiti. I glanced across the street where I saw a line of kids in several shapes and sizes cutting a swath through everyone else walking down the street. They dodged and skipped but stayed in formation while following a tall stick-figure of a boy who seemed to be oblivious to the line that snaked behind him. It was clear that the flock was trying to learn to walk his walk. But none of the members could sustain the cool indifference to everything in the path. Some broke ranks, would giggle or play trapeze artist on the curb or stop and tie a shoelace. But I noticed that the boy bringing up the rear was stomping out a serious statement, looking neither left or right, as seemingly oblivious to his surroundings as the thin blade of a leader. The boy at the end of the line was Jamie.

⌣⸪

It was spring 1994.

They came one at a time. The first one, the leader I'd seen a few months before, was named Stephan. It seemed that the process was gradual and then completed overnight. One day there was just Jamie and me, and the next there was Stephan. Then there was Alex, and then Alex's girlfriend, who worked at Erotic Cabaret, a place that sold boas and white face paint and metal studs, all the regalia they needed to turn into sexy, scary vampires. There was Oha and the girl with the crazy eyes, her lashes thick with black mascara, who wore thigh-high leather boots and a fake fur coat in the summer. And there was Dorie, who was sort of normal at first, and Jenna, a groupie for the bands that played at Numbers, the main club for the Goths. The saddest, I suppose, was Cain. I came to know many of them.

I didn't understand, at first, what was happening. Much later I understood it this way: They had come for Jamie.

Cock-of-the-walk, I'd thought when I first saw Stephan, when he was walking down Westheimer, a street lined by a mismatched jumble of old houses and new storefronts, a ten-block strip that feeds directly into downtown. Glittery but also sad and worn—like the drag queens that strut past the streets' coffee shops, gay bars, and tattoo parlors—Westheimer is depressing by day and tantalizing at night. There are always a cluster of kids at the bus stops and in the Blockbuster parking lot. Many are authentic runaways but most are wannabees who come after school, who stuff their school clothes in their backpacks and put on the black, add the nose rings, and try to blend in with the real ones.

Later, after I'd gotten to know Stephan, I told Jamie I thought he looked like Kurt Cobain but Jamie said no, that he was like Lestat, the character in Anne Rice's *Interview with a Vampire*. Jamie was right. Stephan's face was more finely boned than Cobain's, and Stephan was skinnier, too skinny to be as sexy as he was in his black skintight jeans. He wore his long ashen blond hair pulled back in a ponytail until he shaved it all off except for his forelock, which his girlfriends took turns dyeing different colors. He probably sold the ponytail. I heard they went for up to three hundred dollars.

"I don't fit in there," Jamie told me when I asked him why he'd chosen the street people over the dog people.

"Why?" I'd asked over and over again one night at dinner, my head in my hands, the waiter circling the drama, scared to come near.

"I'm out of my league," he said. I'd thought that they would inspire him, but instead the writers and painters and social workers and interior decorators and computer programmers had made him more aware of the gulf between him and others.

"At least on the streets, I can be king," he said. He picked up his hamburger and smiled, adding, "Even if it is king of crap."

Sometime later in the early fall, I awoke in the night with my heart beating hard and wondered if there had been a sound, a movement that left me so frightened. I sat on the edge of the bed and listened. Rose lifted up her head from her blanket on the floor and then put it down with a thud. She'd heard nothing. Jack the lost-and-found dog kept snoring. Maybe there was nothing in the night. I tried to go back to sleep but felt something wasn't right. I got up, stepped over Rose and Jack and went to the guest bedroom to look out the window that gave a panoramic view that included my neighbor Ross's house and the roof of his garage apartment, Jamie's apartment.

At first I thought it was a moving tree branch with wispy limbs. Then I thought it was my tired eyes. I looked harder, trying to make out the shadows within shadows. Gliding down the street was a girl or boy. As it moved under the streetlight, I saw it was a couple with their arms around each other's shoulders. Perhaps they're just passing by Jamie's apartment, I thought, I hoped. I watched as they turned and disappeared; perhaps a tree had blocked my view, or a dip in the road. From my perch, there was a blind spot, which was Jamie's door and the three feet between the street and the entrance to his apartment. It was strange to see people float up the street and then suddenly disappear, sucked into the night.

From that night on I would awake and as if drawn by an intake of breath, I'd quietly take my place at the window. Rose grew used to the routine and would join me, jumping from the chair to the bed, where she'd settle and hang her paws over the bed to look with me out into the night. Each night more of them came, making a beeline for Jamie's place, which, I learned, "they," the street kids, now called Stephan's place.

"So you're the aunt," Stephan said. I'd spotted him and Jamie a block away, and decided it was time I met Stephan, so I'd pulled the car up next to them. He knelt down by my car window, holding on and bobbing.

"You don't look like an aunt," he said, smiling, tilting his head. Jamie stood behind him and watched us size each other up. Stephan's face was waxen white; his high cheekbones stood out as if he were a quick drawing of only a few stark lines, a slash across the oval that brought character to the forefront. His eyes were green and clear, and he wore mascara. The sides of his head were shorn to a baby chick fuzz while his long ponytail, sleek and peroxided white, was pulled up tight near the top of his head. When he bent to speak to me, it fell into his face, and then into the car. Hot pink tints had been blended carefully throughout.

He grasped the door with familiarity, looked me in the eyes, and said again, "Aunt Marsha," as if savoring the joke of me, the irony of us. I was studying the gargoyle on the silver ring on his pinkie as he swept my body with his gaze. For a minute, he made me feel fifteen and fluttery.

"What is it about him?" Jamie asked me later.

"What do you mean?" I asked.

"Girls love him," he said. "You were flirting with him."

"I was not!" I said, and punched him on the shoulder. "That's crazy."

I'd known a few Stephans in my life. He was like a lead singer but without a band. He didn't even need a band to have a following. That year, Stephan was in prime, full of his own power, not yet visibly stained from the outside.

It surprised me when I learned he sometimes sold himself for the price of a hamburger to the old men who cruised the streets for young boys. There was no sign, yet, of the brown spot of decay that rotted them away, these kids who lived behind convenience stores, scavenged and stole and shot up and snorted and postured.

I was used to hearing Jamie's groggy voice whenever I called his apartment, day or night. But Stephan began to answer the phone on the first ring as if expecting a call.

"Is this the aunt?" he said flirtatiously one night when I called and asked for Jamie.

"Yes, Stephan, this is the aunt," I said.

"The lovely professor aunt?" he teased.

"Right, Stephan," I said.

"Listen," he said. "I've talked to James about this, and I want to ask you something."

"What, Stephan?" I could hear thumping bass notes in the background, and I pictured the apartment that Jamie had made clear was off-limits to me.

"You're not gonna get mad, right? Now, don't get mad, all right?" he said.

I thought it was the chitchat, the kind we'd fallen into, a repartee in which we sometimes spoke of Jamie as if he were our wayward teenage son.

"What, Stephan? Is something wrong?" I asked, my Rolodex of fears beginning to spin.

"I have a proposal," he said.

"And what is that, Stephan?" I asked, thinking he wanted money, a request I'd been expecting.

"I want to go down on you. If you'll let me go down on you, I'll pay you. I'll pay you three hundred dollars," he said.

Sitting in my wicker chair, a stack of student papers in my lap, a two-story stucco house enveloping me, I wondered if this was a test that I could pass or fail.

I looked at the pots and pans hanging over the sink, the trappings of a big real life, and realized I didn't have a clue who I was dealing with, who Stephan was, what he was truly capable of. I held the phone to my ear with my shoulder as I opened the refrigerator and took out a bottle of wine and poured myself a glass.

"Are you there, Aunt Marsha?" he asked.

I took a gulp of wine, and said, "Stephan, Stephan, Stephan." Mainly I was biding time, hoping that I could find the right words to tell him that he was scaring me, that I thought he was my friend, that, in fact, I'd begun to consider him the responsible one across the street. I'd made similar misjudgments with my family. I'd be convinced Gail was crazy and Jan was sane; then I'd talk on the phone to Jan and she'd start telling me about the child who got healed of a brain tumor at her church last week, and I'd ping-pong back to Gail is sane and Jan is crazy. It took me years to realize that there isn't an easy either/or dialectic at work in the world.

"Well?" he asked, "Can I come over?"

"I don't think so, Stephan," I said, turning his offer down as if he'd asked me to a movie. "Let me speak to Jamie."

I stood and held the small wooden antique table in my kitchen. When

Jamie came to the phone, I fumbled for the words as if I were an angry fifteen-year-old whose best guy friend had sold her down the river to the other boys.

"How could you let him talk to me like that?" I asked, no longer interested in teaching a lesson or exhibiting self-control as an example. I was just a girl talking to a friend who was a guy who had turned into the betrayer.

"Like what?" Jamie asked.

"With no respect. For me."

"What do you want me to do?" he asked glumly as if he were already doing something else.

"Beat the shit out of him for one thing," I yelled.

"I thought you were a feminist," he said as if I'd disappointed him.

He put me on the defensive and just sat on the phone breathing while I tried to find some good words. Honor and integrity and self-respect sounded bankrupt. All the words that I wanted to use seemed, when put in front of him, to get leached of their essence. How could I get the right language to fit between us, to tether us together?

"Stephan could have anyone he wants," he said.

"Not me, Jamie," I said. "Not me."

They began to come to my door. First Jennifer of the wild eyes came to ask what to wear to interview for a job at the Marble Slab, a yogurt shop.

"Not a feather boa," I told her, laughing.

Oha came next. Wendy was her real name, Oha was her anarchist name, she told me. She was so overweight I didn't know which chair to offer her. Oha had asthma and no money. Her last job had been dancing, as a joke stripper, at a bachelor party.

"Oha," I said, "promise me you will never, ever do that again."

"It wasn't so bad," she said, her small brown eyes almost hidden inside her bloated face.

I felt sometimes like Oz, dispensing wisdom I didn't know I had. Or the fairy godmother with a new twist. An aunt who wasn't wicked. I worried and fretted and devised plans for saving them. I felt inept, unschooled in the martial arts of motherhood.

On New Year's Eve of 1995, Stephan came to my house with Jamie and Oha. I opened the door and Stephan held his bleeding arm out to me as if it were an offering. I stepped back and let them in. The story began right away. Stephan was explaining as I was leading them all into the kitchen. He said he and "some girl" had been playing with a knife, and she'd "dropped" the blade on the top of his hand. As I washed and bandaged his hand, I begged him to go to the emergency room. After I'd touched him, I went upstairs, out of sight, and poured Listerine over my hands and arms. I'd not wanted him to think I thought he was diseased, a pariah, a carrier of AIDS. Three weeks later his hand was operated on at Ben Taub, the charity hospital, where they attached the tendon he had severed New Year's Eve. "No big deal," he said, the next time I saw him with his arm in a sling.

One afternoon Stephan—who never again mentioned his proposition—came to tell me Cain was ripping off people in the neighborhood. Stealing from my neighbors.

"Jesus," I said. "Who is Cain?"

Cain, Stephan explained, was a legend. He'd slept for an entire year behind the Stop and Go on Westheimer. But he'd been in and out of Jamie's apartment and was also slipping in and out of my neighbors' garages, according to Stephan. "Just small stuff," Stephan said. "Power tools." Things easy to pawn, I understood.

I think Stephan had begun to develop a family feeling, liked living somewhere with an aunt across the way.

I bought Cain a bus ticket to Phoenix where he'd said he had a father or a stepfather. Jamie and Stephan weren't sure which it was.

While I waited outside the apartment for Cain to come down, I said to Jamie, "Don't let him cash it in."

"Okay, Okay," Jamie said impatiently as Cain ducked quickly into the backseat without a word. As I drove to the bus station, I kept looking at him in the rearview mirror.

"Your dad lives in Phoenix?" I asked.

"I think," he said, and touched the bill of his cap nervously.

He smelled so bad that I'd had to open all of the windows to keep from retching. The smell and the sadness. The smell of the sadness. Both had become one in my mind. I knew as I glanced again at Cain in the mirror that there was no father waiting in Phoenix.

Because I had the money, I could dispose of Cain, clean him out of the neighborhood, relocate him. I felt as if I were in some futuristic movie in which the detritus was shipped off to another planet. I didn't know what to do with Cain so I sent him away.

I was discovering that one was enough, plenty, often too much. And when I began to worry over the others, Jamie became disgruntled. They told me he'd declared me off-limits. Don't bother her, he'd told Stephan and Jennifer. She's very busy, he'd said.

I'd read about parents "losing their children to the street," but the phrase, and even the many newspaper and magazine stories, had never said much to me about the children. After two years of learning their names, hearing their stories—eyes averted with shame in the telling, or, more often, a boastful survivor pose, or just a worn-out sigh of a story— I better understood the breadth of the shorthand journalistic expression. I came to think of the street as a living, breathing entity, a snake that grew longer and slinkier and more bedazzling at night. It slept curled— like the children—by day, and then spread out its seductive wings when evening fell.

I'd never been a patient person. Like my father, I couldn't, or wouldn't, stand in lines. When there was the oil crisis in the '70s, my father bought a parking garage in downtown Shreveport because it had a gas pump in the basement. He'd been an oilman for thirty years, he'd said, and "I'll be damned if I'm gonna wait in line for gas." I thought of my family, who had no idea what was happening with Jamie, as I watched and waited through the nights. My father would not have waited. He would have had to do something. Lay down the law. "Why don't you *do* something?" he used to exhort me when he saw me reading a book. Action, not reflection, counted in this world.

Yet I decided to wait, to bide my time and watch over Jamie.

As the fall changed to winter, I watched. At first, I stayed alert, my whole body braced for the assault of what I might see. Night after night I expected the worst, working my post like a lifeguard who wants to jump in and make a save. Disaster would come, eventually, I was certain.

But as the months went by, I began to feel the terror loosen and resolve slowly into a strange peace. In the darkness of the bedroom, I felt a patience take root that I'd never felt before. And, perhaps as a result of exhaustion and desperation, yet maybe better explained as some sixth sense about Jamie's nature, I began to have hope. I began to believe that all would be well. One night I sighed and tucked the pillow under my chin and looked up into the tree branches and relaxed into the evening sojourn. I was surprised at the calm that came as I settled into overseeing, gathering my pillows and quilt and dogs.

I never talked to anyone about those nights. They were something that I sensed I had to get through alone. It was my secret and I suspected that if I shattered that solitary vigil, the whole delicate membrane I'd woven between my room and Jamie's apartment would melt. Then Jamie might float off and away from me.

The hours of sleeplessness, I came to believe, were the dues I had to pay, that I owed, were what other mothers paid. I imagined all the new mothers awake as I was awake, sharing the predawn hours with me, rocking, rocking, dreaming up a future for the one who slept in their arms. My child was out of arm's reach. Yet I could stretch my mind to hold the thought of him. If he cried, I believed I would hear him.

Stephan helped me. Looking back, I think that Stephan knew he was just passing through, but that Jamie had a chance. By saying no to Stephan about sex, I'd restored some faith in Stephan, I believe, that some adults wouldn't be scared away, no matter what some boy/child did to test them. Some of us had staying power. Some of us weren't scared. I grew to hope the best for Stephan, but still to wish him gone—not dead, no—just gone. Jamie basked in the shared glory of the shadow Stephan cast over the street people. Jamie was enchanted, under his spell.

"We're gonna make a demo," Jamie would say to me. "Stephan has contacts." There were always plans for renting studio space for recording a demo. Some agent from Warner Brothers had called.

At least, I thought, at my most optimistic, Jamie has dreams. More often I thought him delusional, out of touch with reality, and out of touch, more and more, with me.

"I need to get Jamie to a shrink," I told Stephan one night on the phone. "Will you help? Will you talk to him?"

"It's done, Aunt Marsha," he said.

Her name was Mrs. Cecilia Samish, and she introduced herself as Mrs. Samish, though she was my age. Yet the formality suited her—and me.

To get Jamie to her office was an ordeal. To get Jamie to any appointment, to wake Jamie up, took such effort that I'd spend hours preparing myself ahead of time. *Don't blow up*, I'd tell myself. *Don't say cruel things you'll regret.* Sometimes I couldn't help myself. I'd tell him that his smell was intolerable. I'd say to myself, *Don't tell him that there is sleep in his eyes*, and then two minutes later I'd hear myself saying, "Jamie, there's something in your eyes." Could he brush his teeth, wash his clothes, bathe? I learned to block out the stares of others, and over time I learned to look the other way, to talk to him without inspecting him. I'd drive up to his apartment and honk, wait for Stephan to poke his head out the window and tell me Jamie's status: dead asleep, beginning to stir, or ready to go.

Stephan would escort him down the stairs as if presenting him as exhibit A. Jamie would wobble like a drunk man, spilling rumpled and myopic into the sunlight. "Cleaned him up for you," Stephan said one day, patting Jamie on the back as if he were a head of cattle. "Sleep from his eyes. Scrubbed under his arms. Powdered the inside of his shoes. He's all yours." That was what I was most afraid of.

During most of the appointments, Jamie'd take a pillow from Mrs. Samish's couch and keep it in his lap, and as I talked his breathing would change, lapse into the rhythm of sleep. Most times he looked like he was just out of surgery and still trying to fight through the anaesthetic.

"Is this some kind of hibernation?" I asked Mrs. Samish, looking over at Jamie, whose face still had sheet creases pressed along his cheek.

"Sort of," she said, going on to explain that teenagers would sleep most of the day and be up in the night if you let them. Society's demands finally jolt them out of their nocturnal ways, she said.

I really had no power over Jamie. No legal power. He'd received about twenty thousand dollars in a trust when he was emancipated and until that was used up, he was self-sufficient. He thought that a fortune and he and Stephan ordered pizzas to be delivered every night. His money was sent to me each month by the trust fund, and I wrote the check for the rent, the sleep apnea machine, the towels and sheets and furniture, and hundreds of pizzas.

⌇

That year I never saw him wide awake but twice, once when he fell through his kitchen ceiling and once when Iceman beat him up.

One night Jamie appeared pale, panicked, and bleeding at my front door. He rushed in and began to pace in the foyer, his hands gripping the sides of his head, pulling his hair dramatically as he said over and over: "Something terrible has happened!"

I felt faint and braced myself for the worst.

The side of his face was brush-burned.

"Please," he said. "Please don't get mad."

All his street swagger had evaporated, and I thought that surely someone was dead. I'd never seen Jamie in such a state before.

"I fell through the ceiling of Ross's kitchen," he said.

For a minute, I couldn't make the correspondence between the way he was acting and what he'd just told me. I just stood speechless until I started to giggle and then to laugh.

Jamie had no skills for gauging levels of disaster. For him, falling through the ceiling had been like falling back into time. He thought he would be punished. Or maybe not. Because he played Dungeons and Dragons, his parents had committed him to a mental hospital for Satan worshipping. Their reactions were never commensurate with whatever trouble there was and neither were his. There was no hierarchy of experience.

He watched me as if waiting for me to blow up.

When I took his arm and said stupid, motherly things like, "Accidents happen," he kept watching me closely as if this were a trick.

When we walked over to his apartment to inspect the damage what I really did was inspect the apartment for any clues of what had been going on. Out of the corner of my eye I scanned for crack pipes, crack being my biggest fear. There were large amplifiers, a guitar or two, crumpled Whataburger bags, and ashtrays everywhere. But what really scared me was the nest Stephan had made for himself in the breakfast nook. He had tented the tiny room, stringing up Indian fabric on the ceiling, covering the walls from floor to ceiling with posters. Inside the tribal chieftain's tent were makeshift Mexican altars, collector's-item records, skulls of rodents, feathers, African masks, three guitars, a huge stack of porno magazines, books by Kant, Heidegger, and Nietzsche. A love nest, I thought, where he brings girl after girl. Jamie had boasted that Stephan had three and four a day some days.

There was a huge hole in Ross's ceiling where Jamie, all two hundred pounds of him, had fallen through.

"What in the hell were you doing up in the crawl space?" I asked.

"Trying to make another room," he said.

How could I stanch the flow? I wondered. How many more were coming to stay?

———

If I was ever outside in my yard when my neighbor, Ross, drove up, I'd hurry inside. I worried constantly that the time would come when he would say Jamie must go. Ross was Scottish and a pub crawler and seemed oblivious to the invasion that was taking place. I was always waiting for the call about the mugging or the theft or the bad element my nephew was attracting. Each time the phone rang, I thought our time was up.

I decided to control my own destiny, to take the initiative: I asked Ross to dinner.

As we stood in the crush of people at Ruggles, the hip restaurant he'd suggested, I wished we'd gone anywhere but to this place where all these happy couples were trilling across the room to each other and sliding sexily by us. The music and chatter made it too hard to talk so I drank one giant goblet of wine after another until Ross began to look like the love of my life. I wanted to lay my head on his shoulder and tell him that he'd saved my life. When I woke up in the middle of the night, I faintly remembered a lovely Scottish accent and a chicken dish that looked impossible to manage with a fork. Then I remembered Ross had been in my bed.

The next morning, Ross was gone when I opened my eyes, and the world I'd fallen asleep in was not the same one I woke up to. I tried to raise myself off the bed only to be assaulted by the spinning pieces of my world. Everything was falling onto everything else and every-thing had fallen out of place. The ceiling fan, the desk, and the cane settee went flying by when I turned my head. I tried to reconstruct my evening to determine how I could be so ill after four glasses of wine. I'd gone out with Ross. I'd had too much to drink. But that was nine hours ago.

I dragged myself, eyes closed, to the telephone and called my doctor. Since it was a weekend, I got his answering service. Staying sprawled on the floor, I waited for him to return my call. Brain tumor, I thought.

Aneurysm. Death. I slept awhile on the floor where Rose roamed around, circling me, periodically nudging me with her cold nose.

When the doctor called, I told him I'd gone to sleep fine—a lie— and woke up to the world spinning.

"Is it the room spinning or is it the inside of your head? he asked.

I moved my eyes around, which caused massive upheaval in the room.

"The room. I think."

"Good," he said.

He told me to get someone to take me to the emergency room.

Once there I sat for hours on the edge of a gurney with my head hanging down and panting like an overheated dog. When the doctor finally came in, he said that Sundays were hell.

I agreed.

He asked me if I'd been under a lot of stress. I looked up to smile but immediately put my head back down because there went the room, up and over and around. "Oh, God, oh, God," was all I could say in little gasps as I waited for the nausea to recede. He referred me to a neurologist and gave me a prescription for pills that knocked me out. Asleep I didn't spin. Asleep my dreams spun into nightmares, the unconscious churning out quick clips of doom.

The neurologist, whom I went to a week later, tapped me on the knees with a little hammer, made me walk toward her, close my eyes, and touch my nose with my right index finger, then my left.

"What we want to rule out is MS or brain tumor," she said.

Sitting miserable and wrapped in a gown, I nodded in agreement.

After about five minutes of putting me through the same test they give to drunk drivers, she said, "Vertigo," and snapped her chart closed as if saying, "Next."

"Isn't there anything I can do about it?" I asked, so pitifully I made myself cringe.

"Your brain will readjust, eventually," she said, and gave me a little pat on the thigh before leaving the room.

The spinning was winding down like a merry-go-round on its last lap when I went to the acupuncturist who was small, bald, brown, and Chinese. He took my whole head in his hand as if it were a melon, and I let him hold it, the muscles in my neck relaxing as I gave the mess of my mind to him.

He held my head in his hands for what seemed like a long time, before he gently released it and went out of the room. He returned with a row of needles laid out on a blue towel.

"Tired brain," he said. "You have tired brain."

He took a needle, aimed at my forehead, and stuck it right where my hair and forehead meet, where the thatch of gray always appears first, alerting me that I need to get my hair colored.

I left his office sporting one needle in my bangs and another in the crown of my head.

I took my pills and slept through the nights. I dreamed that Jamie's apartment was swelling like a tick. One night I thought I heard a chattering birdlike voice, and I thought of them roosting, dreamed they were flying now from Westheimer, on broomsticks, their black clothes becoming a long black path that others would follow.

A real bird had worked its way into my dreams. Sometimes I think I saw the three boys walking down the middle of the street, felt the cold air whistling through my windowsill, as I saw them toting a birdcage, saw it bang against his knees. But maybe I just imagined the scene because I could also just as clearly see the poor bird passed from the hands of one street person to another in freezing temperature, probably for a bag of dope.

"What is that?" I yelled at Jamie over the phone when I first heard the bird in the background.

"It's Robbie."

"Who in the hell is Robbie?" I'd asked, thinking it was another person come to stay.

"A cockatiel," he said.

Soon after, I recognized that I was transferring all my pent-up need to act, to save, to do something about Jamie onto the bird, but I couldn't stop myself. I'd go to the pet store and chat up the sales clerk, speaking to her of Robbie as if he were a Dickens character, an orphan that needed an advocate. I bought books on cockatiels and would call Jamie and read him what I'd underlined: "Cockatiels are the most fragile of all birds." The book says, I told him, no drafts, no cold rooms, and no cigarette smoke.

"Jamie," I'd begged, "please take care of the bird."

When he changed the bird's name to Israel, I thought, poor bird, a creature whose fate had somehow come under the control of a boy who had himself been just as bounced around.

The day Jamie wanted to bomb for roaches, we had our biggest fight. At the hardware store, we were looking through all the powders and sprays as Jamie told me how much he hated bugs, how he'd always hated all insects, that he wanted to nuke his place.

"But the bird, Jamie," I reminded him. "You can't set off roach bombs with the bird there."

"Marsha," he said, "it's just a bird."

I'd only felt such anger once before. That time my father was at a big cocktail party and he was talking to several men about the Vietnam War. I was in the full glory of my sense of right and wrong. I was eighteen. The war was wrong. Peace was right. My father was clearly part of the military-industrial complex. I got up in my father's face and with the fury fueled by the purest octane of teenage self-righteousness, I said to him—in front of his friends—that it was easy for him to be for the war. "Because," I almost shouted, "your son is too defective to ever be drafted."

I turned that seething hot mass of emotion full force onto Jamie.

"Just a bird!" I yelled so that all of the clerks turned and looked at me. "You, you are just like your father!" I said, articulating and flinging at him what I knew was his worst fear as well as mine.

Jamie had a history with birds, held a memory while most of the other ones had been closed off somewhere in the back of his mind. He would begin one of the few stories of his past and of his parents with: "I had a bird when I was growing up," in just the way my students would recall the corgi or German shepherd, their memories like fuzzy Alpo commercials, all sloppy kisses, groomed and gleaming dogs. "We went in Denny's one afternoon," he'd say. Evidently Jimmy, Dayna, and Jamie were on the move again, the car was packed, and the caged bird—a cockatiel—had been left outside in the August sun in Louisiana. When they returned to the car, the bird was hanging upside down and muttering. Jamie never told the story with the sense there was a moral to it, only the flat-out facts of a bird locked in a car, found swinging like a cartoon bird and speaking nonsense until it dropped to the bottom of the cage, dead. I could imagine the cartoonist's balloon above its head filled with stars and question marks and curlicued circles that implied, "Cuckoo."

In the hardware store, I started shaking the metal shelf with both hands and the poisons began tipping over and rolling to the edge. "Just a bird," I kept saying, as I held on to the shelf both for support and for the feel of something solid in my hands that wanted to flail at Jamie. "Just a bird!" I'd say again, giving the shelf a good shaking. The spray cans began to roll off the shelf and onto the floor where their tops bounced off and skittered across the cement floor. Jamie began to back up slowly as if afraid to have his back to me for fear I might jump him. Then he was gone and I was on all fours, crawling around, crying and searching for the tops of Yard Guard.

"He's made me crazy," I told Mrs. Samish at the next visit. "I wasn't crazy before," I said as I began to cry. "I spent a lot of money on not being crazy." Then I sobbed in earnest, in total capitulation. For me, it was an admission of what I had been afraid to tell anyone. "Just like them," I cried again, meaning now I was just like my family, Jamie's family, our family. Jamie sat across from me on the small plaid couch and watched me cry, periodically handing me a new Kleenex.

"The bird. Stephan. Cain," I said between howls. Jamie sat up on the edge of the couch instead of trying to disappear into it as he usually did. Finally, he sighed just like my father used to when I'd have what he called one of my "crying jags." Jamie got up to go outside to smoke.

Mrs. Samish and I sat there as I looked at the Kleenex I was crushing into a small ball. A needle was sticking out of my head.

"Marsha," she said, becoming very still, the kindness in her voice like a hand that touched the whirling globe and made it stop. "Marsha," she said again, blinking behind her big glasses but otherwise holding completely immobile. I looked up from my Kleenex and into her eyes.

"He just might die," she said.

I just stared at her. Then I looked around at the order of the room. How cool and nice it was, I thought. I looked back at her face to see if she were serious and then I held her eyes, locked mine onto hers in hopes that I could learn how to make that not ever, ever happen.

"If he dies, I'll die," I said. I was sure of it.

"They do. These kids," she explained looking very, very sad. "They come to a point—the ones who weren't cared for. And they decide. They push on and live, or go on strike and die—maybe by accident, or accidentally on purpose."

I thought about the sleep machine and how much I badgered him to sleep with it and how much he resisted. I thought about the call that would come, probably from Stephan, telling me he couldn't wake him. I saw Jamie blue. I saw him dead.

"You have to be prepared," she said.

At that moment, Jamie burst back into the room and sat down with such violence that he bounced me up from my side of the couch. I looked at him and he looked so sheepish, so surprised to have made such an entrance, that we both laughed. And then we couldn't stop. I fell over sideways and took the pillow with the elephant picture on it and hit Jamie in the stomach, pummeling him, with my head buried in the couch. My hair was wet from tears, and I felt like a child soaked by the rain and giddy with the wildness of the weather.

I'd forgotten about Mrs. Samish. I'd pushed death away. It would not come for us.

"You two have a great capacity for laughter," she said, grinning. "That's one thing."

"You have to laugh," Jamie said as if instructing Mrs. Samish.

Jamie always says that the best thing that ever happened to him was getting hit over the head.

Iceman, the drug dealer who wielded the blow, had his name tattooed across his chest.

He'd come looking for Stephan, but Jamie was the only one home when he came calling to collect money Stephan owed him.

Jamie told me only fragments of a narrative: Iceman had walked up the dark stairwell, the lightbulb having gone out a year ago, and walked in on Jamie playing his guitar. He strolled around the apartment, picking up books from the table and turning them over, putting his face up to the bird cage and whistling. He flipped open the flap of Stephan's tent, then wandered over to where Jamie sat strumming.

"Seen Stephan?" he asked.

No, Jamie'd said, then gone back to strumming.

Iceman left.

Then a few minutes later he appeared in the doorway.

Jamie had propped his guitar next to a chair.

"I think I'll take this," Iceman said, casually as he slung the guitar over his shoulder. For what Stephan owes me, he said.

"Hey," Jamie said, and followed him down the dark hallway. He was halfway down the stairs when he heard the whispers. He saw the darkness move, figures scuttling, and Jamie's heart began to beat faster. He was still trying to make out the details of the shadows—Alex? he called out. Jennifer? and then the shadows came up the stairs and were on him in a tangle of arms and legs. Hands and feet came at him, punching and kicking him until he bent to avoid the blows, holding his arms around his head. While he was down, someone reached toward his neck. Jamie felt the quick yank as the guy grabbed the magic charms he wore around his neck. Then Iceman's fist came up and around and connected with Jamie's forehead.

Coughing and crying on the phone, Jamie just kept saying my name. I ran barefoot and in my nightgown across the street and up the stairs to find him with a huge knot on his head and a black eye already swelling shut.

"He'll be back," Jamie said. "He'll get my stuff. All my stuff."

I lugged three armloads of stuff across the street from his place to mine and put Jamie to bed in the small bedroom, the one that faced the backyard, not the room from where I watched. Because I had to watch that night. Acting like lurking figures in a bad detective movie, they came, racing from tree to shadow to tree before dashing inside the shadow of his entryway. I thought I recognized Alex, a musician who was Jamie's rival for Stephan's friendship. I felt them running up his stairs as if they were climbing my spine one vertebrae at a time. I went to look at Jamie, his face like putty, his eye looking like it had been smudged with ink, and wondered whether to call the police or not. I walked back and forth from one room to another, looking out the window at the apartment, then looking at Jamie, who was out cold. Once I yelled into his ear, "Should I call the police. Should I call them on your friends?" I sat back and looked at his inert body. There was no response.

At first light, Stephan knocked on the front door, and when I let him in, he scuttled about, peering over his shoulder. "He's up there," I said, pointing to the stairs that he took two at a time.

I sat on the stairs and listened.

"Dude, I'm sorry. Oh, dude. Don't worry. We'll get him."

"No," I heard Jamie say. "No, Stephan." He sounded weary but awake and spoke like a father talking to a child who is getting carried away.

I went downstairs and into the kitchen to make coffee. I heard the front door close.

I never saw Stephan again.

Jamie and I went to the apartment to pack him up and move him to my house. At his front door, I bent down and ran my fingers through crystalline dust that had been poured in a careful line in front of his door. By now I was somewhat numb to surprises but this line we had to cross scared me. I felt like a character in a B horror movie who walks into the haunted house with deep wariness of the unknown that is about to be known.

As we walked up the stairs, Jamie pointed out to me the place where they had knocked him down.

Inside, all of the furniture had been reduced to sticks. There were feathers, glass, torn sheets, and splintered chair legs littering the floor.

Wherever I stepped it felt sandy under my feet.

Between each doorway there was the same small hill of sand as if a small animal had burrowed from door sill to door sill.

"What is this?" I asked Jamie as I examined the formations that were in the entryway of each room.

"Salt," he said matter-of-factly as he picked up shirts and rummaged through the covers on the mattress on the floor.

"Salt?" I asked, looking around for a shaker, my mind trying to piece fragments together to make sense out of the odds and ends scattered about.

"Magic," he said, grabbing some books and throwing them into a large black trash bag. "Wards off evil."

"Did you do it?" I asked.

"No," he said.

"Who did?" I asked, looking up and around to see if someone was watching me. I felt them there watching. I always will.

It was then, my question still unanswered, that a horrible screech came from the corner of the room, and I screamed. It was Robbie, the cockatiel. I lifted the unwieldy cage off the floor and held it up near the window. He was bright green and had a crayon-yellow head. There were two perfect orange circles on each side of his beak, and a feather bloomed from his head as if he were wearing a French hat. I put both arms around his cage and carried him down the stairs and across the street and into the guest bedroom where I put him in front of the window from where I'd watched the year go by.

13

food not bombs

In 1997 Jamie moved to an apartment complex called The Place. Next to the freeway and falling into disrepair, it was probably one of the few places that would take a Goth-looking nineteen year old with no references. The dreary pile of buildings seemed anywhere but the place to be. To gain entry, I had to drive up to a box, press a code, and then hope Jamie would answer and buzz me in through the huge iron gate. I can still hear his voice, feel my stomach go hollow as his sleepy, irritated "Hello?" came crackling across the intercom. I'd have to shout, "Jamie, it's me! Open the gate!" Often he would go right back to sleep, the phone off the hook, and a car or two would come up behind me. I would be locked in by the cars yet locked out of his complex. Sometimes I'd back up and drive to the side of the apartments, where I'd bang on one of his windows that looked out on an alley. I'd hear the metallic shuffle of the aluminum blinds and then I'd see his eye. He'd sometimes just let the blinds close. That meant he wasn't coming out. And I wasn't coming in.

We had reached a new level of frustration with each other.

I was furious that I'd had to pay a big lump sum to my neighbor for the damage done to his garage apartment. I wasn't sure what to expect of Jamie anymore. He had told me that he was through with the street scene but neither of us knew what would fill in the blank.

During his time with the street people, he'd acquired a great deal of computer equipment. I'd stopped asking where the various monitors and units came from—I knew I didn't want to know. At The Place, Jamie began to spend eight to twelve hours of the night on the Internet. In a sense, he was dating. I think of this time as his epistolary period, a germinating of a self that he presented to the world via chat rooms and later through his Web site. Pictures and life stories were exchanged, sometimes real-life dates set up, but mainly there was a back-and-forth, an opening to others that I'd not seen before.

He decided to apply for a job at the computer lab at Houston Community College. An old friend of mine was in charge of hiring and he gave Jamie a chance. At his job, Jamie was required to relate to students from three until nine, which woke him from his zombie-state at least three times a week. What he loved about computers, he told me more times than I could stand to hear, was that they were more reliable than people. There was nothing emotional about a computer, he said. He said this to me in a monotone as I sat in the car tired from teaching, tired from worrying about getting him to work, tired from worrying that he would not ever come to life. I sat there with my nerve endings rubbed raw, a walking live wire about to ignite out of frustration and total helplessness as he would give a discourse on technology. Such perfection, he'd say as I sat catching glimpses of my imperfect self in the side mirror of the car, seeing all the lines that had formed between my eyebrows, from my nose to mouth, the imperfections that were drawn there by worry, the heavy pencil marks of time and love.

Nothing riled Jamie, but his passivity could send me into a rage. If I cried and cursed, he'd look wounded and confused. "How could you care enough about anything to get so worked up?" he said to me in the aftermath of one of my emotional onslaughts. "Will he," I asked friends rhetorically, "ever care about anything?" Ever let himself care?

A girl named Lori had moved into his apartment. Her skin seemed painted the white of a geisha, her hair dyed the black of crows. She was sullen and sexy. Jamie would go to work covered with purple splotches all over his neck—huge, ghastly bruises caused from her painted mouth, sucking, sucking. Then another guy moved in who was in his thirties. He wore old-fashioned clothes—tight western jeans with a rodeo belt and western plaid shirts. I didn't know about him until I knocked on Jamie's door and he opened it. "Howdy, ma'am," he said, sticking his hand out for a shake. The man had on a wig that looked like the plastic hair on dolls. I stood speechless before this scarecrow who I was sure must be going through chemotherapy for cancer.

Driving Jamie to work, I said to myself, *Don't say a word. Don't ask who. Don't ask what. Keep your mouth shut.* I didn't want Jamie only to associate me with recriminations, with nagging and whining and eyes rolled to the ceiling.

I was only a few blocks from his apartment when my resolve fell through. "So, does your friend have cancer?" I asked.

"Why would you think that?" he asked irritably.

"Because of the wig," I said with what I hoped was a nonchalance.

"What wig?" Jamie asked, now too curious to be angry at my nosiness.

"The wig, the wig on his head, the fake hair propped on his head! The one that's on crooked!" I said, now hitting my hands on the steering wheel.

"You know, now that you mention it, I haven't ever seen him comb his hair," he said, looking mildly puzzled as if trying to think back on his friend's hair habits.

What I wanted to scream was why was this bewigged redneck twice Jamie's age sleeping on Jamie's couch.

The next time I went to the apartment there was a woman who

looked as if she'd stepped out of *Laverne and Shirley*. She was a good-ole-girl-down-on-her-luck waitress type who tried to bond with me about "the kids." "Oh, those kids," she said, referring to her daughter and Jamie. She was Lori's mother.

"No way, Jamie," I said when we got in the car. "She has to go."

Only after I went in and told her she had to find new lodgings did Jamie tell me that she had been arrested for shoplifting, was out on bail, had skipped her court date, and now there was a warrant for her arrest. She was using cocaine. Her daughter started using with her.

They have to go, I told Jamie.

"But you should see her clean the apartment," he whined. "They vacuum all night."

"I bet," I said.

One fall day I arrived at The Place to take him to work and saw five or six kids dressed in black draped over a beat-up car, lounging and smoking, bedraggled, pierced, tattooed, and relaxed into different stages of posturing for the public. They seemed thrown about like laundry hanging out to dry. "Who in the hell are they?" I yelled at Jamie. I thought we'd left them behind us, I said. Doomed, I thought. We are doomed to be tracked down by the grackles of the world, circling birds looking for free meals, refuge.

He told me they were different from Stephan and his crew. They were anarchists, he said. Members of Food Not Bombs.

"You'll be evicted," I told him. I pointed out it was my money, my name on the lease, my name on the line. "My name," I'd shouted. "My name!"

It was weeks before I settled down enough to hear about Food Not Bombs. Jamie was working for a collective that cooked for the homeless. He and the other black-clad kids culled Dumpsters in the back of large grocery store chains for discarded produce, which they cooked in Jamie's apartment. They distributed the home cooking on Sundays to the home-less and hungry on Westheimer.

"You don't know how to cook!" I yelled "What about a health per-mit?"

He'd looked at me as if I'd just said let them eat cake.

One afternoon, I'd gone to Café Artiste to grade papers. After I or-dered food at the counter, I wandered to a table where the Houston newspaper lay opened. On the front page was an article on Allen Parkway Village, a housing project that dated back to right after World War II, which had been a lightning rod for controversy for twenty years. Sud-denly, right on the front page, in the third paragraph, was my name. It took a few seconds for me to realize that Jamie was being quoted. Jamie Recknagel. Since 1976 I'd been the only Recknagel in this town. In the article he'd told the reporter that the residents of Allen Parkway Village wanted to stay in their community—where their church was, where the bus stop was, where their gardens were—and that they—he and the squatters—were prepared to stay for as long as it would take.

There was something about the inscription of the words. His name, his words inscribed onto the front page of a newspaper of the fourth-largest city in the United States. I was astounded and proud that he had made enough ruckus for a good cause to be recognized. That's what I valued, I realized, as I looked at Jamie's words. I just stood and shook my head, remembering when I had first had my name in print as a byline, the power I'd felt, and now, Jamie, at nineteen, had made news. And for a just cause—speaking for the poor who were being displaced.

I'd come from a family that had never spoken of charitable acts. There had been the check written for this that and the other. Lung cancer. Muscular dystrophy. But never the passion, never the front lines, the extension of self into the world of people who suffered. When I'd become aware and conscious, then involved in civil rights and the women's movement, my parents thought it was a phase. I could count on silencing a room of family members when I brought up such topics. My views were little bombs to be drenched in drink. "Another scotch, anyone?" would be my parents' way of changing the subject. My family had one main conversational topic—ourselves, our antics, our melodramas. I'd never considered that someone from my own family would ever concur with my liberal political views.

He was speaking up. It was a turning point in my feeling toward Jamie. If he cared for others, I would care for him. It was that simple and that complicated. It was a bond that finally, I believe, brought us to the brink of trust, the brink of love, into falling into friendship and respect that made all the rest, which was to come, possible.

In 1993, Allen Parkway was prime real estate for the city, just down the freeway from a downtown that was booming. Situated near what is called Freedman's Town, a section of Houston deeded to freed slaves since Emancipation, Allen Parkway was now considered too valuable to let it lie fallow. The poor would be relocated, the spokesman for the state and federal agencies said. Moved to the suburbs.

Originally it had been housing for white veterans returning from the war, and then in the '60s there had been lawsuits that cleared the way for black veterans to move in and the whites moved out. Eventually the subsidized housing on a large spread of land shaded by oaks was primarily occupied by African-Americans, who turned it into a thriving insulated community that whites were scared to enter. Later, during and after the Vietnam War, Vietnamese moved in alongside the blacks and Hispanics.

All that summer Jamie talked to me about the disenfranchised, his rhetoric reminiscent of my own in the '60s, over the war in Vietnam, on poverty.

"But," I said to him, "I thought you didn't care—about . . ." I stumbled for the words. "About much of anything," I said.

Jamie explained to me, who had not caught up with this new boy who was up everyday and walking the miles to Allen Parkway from his apartment, that it was people as individuals that stumped him. He would fight for the greater good of all people.

My face, I'm sure, was illuminated with astonishment and pleasure at this pronouncement. Yet I was puzzled about the origins from which this heretofore hidden compassion had sprung.

Jamie moved into Allen Parkway Village with several other squatters. When the police and National Guard and swarms of reporters arrived, I watched anxiously from the freeway, under the August sun, sweating and fretting as helicopters circled overhead. Inside were twelve or fewer families who had refused the relocation. I saw them interviewed every day on local news. There was the Vietnamese couple—elderly, dressed in black shirts and pants, wearing straw hats—tending their garden, which was lush with fruit and vegetables and herbs. There was the eighty-year-old black woman who cried before the cameras, her grandchildren—twelve, nine, and five—grinning and jumping around behind her for the cameras as she said she would rather die than move. And there was my nephew's comrade-in-arms, Nickie, who called himself a professional squatter, who was a white kid with dreadlocks.

Allen Parkway Village was under siege for a week. Parked outside the chain-link fence that had suddenly appeared overnight, I watched as young men dressed in camouflage trotted into the area with large guns, taking their positions along the fence that cordoned off "the projects" from the lovely meandering bike and jogging path along the bayou. Helicopters buzzed the area.

I was proud.

Jamie, nineteen years old, a spokesman for those with no voice.

I read what he had to say in the article over and over again. Recknagel said, "The residents have asked for our help." Recknagel said, "We will stay here as long as they want us to stay." I remember sitting back and looking around the coffee shop, wanting to tell someone, to take the paper and show my nephew's words to the man hunched over his laptop. I'd thought then about the boy who had come to me three years earlier, who had once, in a moment of disclosure, lamented his passivity, who had told me that mainly, that the main thing, that what really shamed him most of all was that he had not left his parents sooner. That he expected so much of himself was a torment to me. It was our fault, I'd thought. My family and I had been the passive ones who should have done more to save Jamie. Now, I thought, in trying to save others, he was escaping the family legacy of passivity. Now he had become an activist. I spread the paper out with my hands as if to touch him.

14

the fog

Jamie called me one afternoon, and said, "I have to tell you something." He always had to lay the groundwork for telling of trouble, thinking, I suppose, or hoping, he could control my reaction. But his strategy always backfired, and only fanned the flames of my hysteria. He was immovable, though; no matter which angle I took to try to wheedle his news out sooner than he was ready to tell, he would not yield. He was teaching me patience, and I got better at waiting, at not having to know everything right away. Everything was what I'd always wanted to know. And right away. He taught me to sit on my hands and wait for him to come to me.

In my life, I'd gained control by knowing, by learning, by accumulating information. I mistook this for wisdom. Through most of Jamie's childhood people had discussed his fate without consulting him, yelled and screamed at each other about what was best for him, spoke of him as if he weren't standing there, talked over his head, or out of his earshot, whispered words he could barely make out. He would now control the flow of information. I learned that if I waited, he would tell me what I needed to know and what he needed to tell.

I took him to dinner at the Black-Eyed Pea, a franchise that boasts home-cooked country meals, which are pictured in garish colors on the large plastic menus that the waitress handed us. I have no nostalgia for pot roast and green beans. Chicken-fried steak and mashed potatoes. Creamed corn. Spaghetti. Yet I wanted Jamie to have something beside pizza, which was his daily fare.

Pale and pasty, Jamie's face was the color of the inside of raw potato. I looked down to study the bright false food on the menu, a contrast to his pallor.

"Marsha," he said, cracking his knuckles. "You have to promise you won't overreact."

I looked down at the picture of the bright orange spaghetti and thought before I spoke. I knew, because we'd had this argument before, that there was no sense explaining—again—the difference between re-action and overreaction. For him, the two were one and the same. So I told him that I would remain calm no matter what he told me, and I tried not to imagine the possibilities.

"See," I said, smiling, "I'm calm, I'm happy." I'd recently started tak-ing an antidepressant that helped me be more patient with him. I didn't percolate and build up steam as often as I'd done before, when I'd spend three days away from him deciding that he was lazy, taking advantage of me, not trying, so that by the time I saw him I was ready to blow. And he'd walk right into my temper tantrum, my vast plans for his self-improvement, with no warning. But recently I thought that I could, with the help of drugs, handle whatever he was going to tell me. Hadn't he, I thought, already told me the worst—that he thought he was incapable of love, that he had no conception of empathy, that the world could blow up tomorrow and he would say good riddance? What else could he tell me that would cause an overreaction?

"Let's get comfort food," I'd said to him as I drove into the restaurant's parking lot, but the pictures and the smell of the food only depressed me. I'd never cooked because the smell of cooking food makes me sad, reminds me of family meals in Shreveport. "Your yuppie food," Jamie called what I like to eat, the food that I'd never even seen growing up—kale and quiches and spinach salads, Thai food and tofu.

"There's this thing that happens to me," Jamie began, wrinkling his brow and brushing his hair from his face. "It's hard to explain."

"Just say it, Jamie," I said.

"Fog fills up the room when I'm talking to people," he said.

"Fog?" I asked.

"Like the fog they have in plays. It rolls in and I can't see whoever I'm talking to."

I pictured the fog, thought of it as an evil presence, seeping under the doors of our lives. I see it even now, remember it from some black-and-white movie as it rushes in and begins to take a human form.

Then he told me about the numbness, which he said began in his fingers and spread to his hands, his arms, until finally all of him was numb. "Dead," he said, pinching his arm. "You could operate on me without anaesthetic."

First I thought: *All this time and he hasn't told me anything about fog and numbness. He had been battling alone to see, hear, feel.* I thought back, filling the past two years with the fog Jamie described, thinking that all the times I shouted, he could barely hear, all the times I had tried to look him in the eyes, he could barely see, all the times I had touched his arm, he could barely feel.

He watched me, not trusting that I wouldn't get up and call for the straitjacket. "And sometimes," he said, "people become very small and it's as if they are receding, getting very tiny."

"Dissociation," I said. "You are dissociating." I went on to explain what I'd learned in psychoanalytic training about how the mind and body splits as a defense against intolerable situations and pain.

"I thought," he said, "that maybe in the mental hospitals they had put in a computer chip. Like I was in an *X-Files* deal."

"It saved you," I told him, wanting him to know that he had activated the process, and that it had saved him from cracking up and that it was not coming from outside him.

"Jamie," I said. "There are things that can be done." In ten minutes much of the last two years made sense.

His brown eyes went wide with wonder, with hope, then with doubt.

This will be the conversation that will change his life. Yet I don't realize, don't even come close to realizing, how resistant part of him will be to coming alive. I should have anticipated that reaction. I'd read about people who were blind for their whole lives and then when their sight was restored they begged to be blind again. The light was too bright. The world too shiny. It hurt their eyes. And when I worked at TRIMS, I'd heard lectures on heroin addicts, about how an addict becomes so deadened that when he comes off heroin even sitting on a chair is too painful to endure. When Jamie finally began to feel the world around him, he hated the hurt; it was such a surprise, to feel.

That day I told him, "It was a good thing." I told him that it was once a good thing. But now it had outgrown its use, now the fog and numbness came as if on their own, against his will, or so it seemed to him. Conditioned response to stress, I told him.

"How often?" I asked him.

"Ninety-five percent of the time," he said.

"Fugue states," Mrs. Samish called them. "Self-induced trances." For nearly six years Jamie had been in a trance. Before he came to me and for the three years since.

What sets it off? we asked him. He'd never thought about it, he said, since the fog just came and went seemingly randomly.

He considered our question, scrunching his brow, thinking about when the fog was the thickest.

He realized that loud voices, perhaps rising in anger, would make it happen. Or if he saw someone across the room that looked like his mother. Or if someone told him what to do in a certain tone of voice. I'd seen the symptoms—he would begin to yawn, taking in giant gulps of oxygen, then his eyelids would flutter, and he would seem to slump into wherever he was sitting. Then he was gone.

From Mrs. Samish's, Jamie and I went immediately to the bookstore and bought the book she recommended, actually bought two of them, one for me, one for him.

He would have to, he said, laughing, do the opposite of what most of his friends wanted. They wanted to be out of it, loaded, zonked, stoned, blitzed. They wanted to learn to be hypnotized, go under to the droning voice of the hypnotist's "You are getting very sleepy." He wanted, he said, to get unhypnotized. To come to.

The next time we went to dinner it was at a place where there was much chatter and clatter of silverware. I saw Jamie's eyelids begin to lower and saw him fight to keep his eyes open.

"Can you hear me?" I said as if speaking to someone who just fell overboard into the night sea.

"Yes," he said. "But muffled."

"Here is the table," I said, putting my palm down on the surface. "Here is the salt shaker," I said, pulling it toward me.

The book had given us ways to bring him back. By focusing his attention on the particulars of the room, reorienting him by adding solid object after object, I could lead him back to the room, to me.

"How often now?" I would ask him over the next year.

"Seventy percent," he'd say.

The best thing, he told me, was that his condition had a name. He was not an alien with an alien malady. He was a child who had saved his life by leaving the room where he was being hurt. "You taught yourself this," I said. "You can stop it."

I will think over time of the fog as a thick shawl or blanket that protected him from pins and needles, from heartbreak, from the pain that comes each day until we get tougher. As I began to help him strip away the bunting, the buffer, the armor, the blanket, I saw him become a raw exposed self, someone whose stubbed toe had never throbbed, whose strep throat had never burned, whose heart had never filled.

"Why," he asked me one day, "would anyone want to live like this?"

The other way, he said, was better.

Sometimes I argued. Sometimes I agreed.

15

weddings
and funerals

In the summer of 1996, one niece got married and the other died.

Jenifer, Jan's daughter, made the perfect bride, and she and my sister hosted the perfect wedding in Shreveport. They had wanted Jamie to attend and began a campaign months ahead of time to include him. My instinct was to say no, but as the date grew nearer I started to urge him to go with me. Perhaps I wanted to show him off, perhaps I just wanted company. He grumbled through a shopping trip to Banana Republic for a coat and white shirt, but he seemed agreeable. We were on the outskirts of Shreveport when he began to grow numb. I should have turned around, but I didn't.

At the reception, I mainly remember movement, the faces flashing around me as if I were riding a carousel: There was Jan's ex-husband, whom I hadn't seen in ten years. That was the second glass of wine. We had once been great friends, before the ugly divorce. The rest of the cast of characters spun by and with each rotation I had another glass in hand as if by magic. There was an old business partner of my father's, and his wife, and now-grown daughter, with her teenage daughter. I couldn't remember if I was supposed to hate this partner or not, but before I could decide the carousel had circled round and there was Gail and Bobby, and Scott and his wife and three-year-old daughter. "Jamie," I heard myself say, high and screechy in response to the question: "Where's Jamie?" "Out on the patio. I think," I said, turning into the next wave of faces breaking over me. Flying past were my father's bankers, now our bankers, and my father's lawyer, now our lawyer, and all the widows of all my father's business friends and old golf buddies. I remember birdseed scattering, hugs and kisses, and Jamie, looking mournful, his shirt half in, half out of his slacks. I remember dancing, turning round and round and seeing Jamie's face, a still point in the spinning room.

Later that night in the hotel, where I thought I'd been so wise to put us away from "the family," I woke dry mouthed and frightened in my room barely remembering how Jamie and I had gotten home. I splashed water on my face and went down the hall to Jamie's room, and knocked, hanging my head when he answered the door. Through sobs I walked into his arms, apologizing for being a fool, for drinking too much, for risking our lives on the way home, for embarrassing him by dirty dancing with the best man. He went over to the TV, turned it off, and plopped on the bed. "You were pretty crazy," he said as I sat before him and hung my head again. "Please," I whispered from beneath my hair, my face averted still, "please forgive me."

"Hey," he said, dropping his hand on the top of my head. "Let's just get home."

We ate cold pizza and talked until sunrise. I explained that I'd never thought about taking care of myself for someone else. Never felt the way I did now, realizing that two lives were in the balance and my behavior could topple two. We talked about family and how I wasn't immune to its power. In fact, I told him, he was further along than I was at resisting the family's pull. Too often, my escape had been self-destructive. I kept my distance from them through connections with men, by drinking, by living too furiously, as if I could outrun their influence, outdo them in outrageousness, be myself by totally losing myself. I saw this more clearly as Jamie and I spoke.

"Detachment," he said. "That's the key."

"Yeah," I'd said, repeating his word. "Detachment." Something he could teach me, and was, actually, teaching me. I realized that to be clear and solid and myself I needed to be far away from them. To guide Jamie to sanity, I had to be sane and I was not sane within, among, around my family. I saw that through his eyes.

But before we left town, went home, there was one more family duty for me to perform.

On the Sunday morning after the Saturday-evening wedding, I went with Mother and Jan to see Stacy in the hospital. Gail's daughter, Stacy, had been dying of cirrhosis for so long that it was hard to believe death was imminent. I'd been called many times over the last ten years to rush to a deathbed scene. She'd always pulled through. One week Mother would tell me that she was hallucinating and plucking at the bedcovers like a dying person, and the next week she'd be propped in the recliner in her apartment, drinking vodka. Yet something told me that I better go and see her, and I was right.

Mother, Jan, and I went to the charity hospital where she'd gone to have the blood vacuumed from her stomach. The sign on her door looked like one of those Danger Radiation signs. Quarantined because she'd been diagnosed with hepatitis C, Stacy was bloated, yellow, and full of southern cynicism and self-mocking. "Doesn't this beat all," she laughed, gurgling from her raspy wraithlike chest. Stacy, the Gerber baby, Stacy who had played the clarinet in junior high, who had won the state poetry contest judged by the Louisiana poet laureate, who'd had chubby cheeks, blue eyes, and who could have, as my mother says again and again, "gone far," lay propped in the bed drowning in her own bodily fluids, each move making her flinch and groan in pain. All the vessels between her stomach, spleen, and liver had begun to leak fluids into her body cavity. She was bleeding to death, dying the slow torturous death of the chronic alcoholic. She was thirty-five years old.

Ever since I can remember, Mother had begged me to talk to Stacy. "She'll listen to you," she said after Stacy quit the band, after she'd started skipping school, after she quit school, after she quit beautician's school. At seventeen she'd married a welder from Michigan who bought her a Corvette that she flipped and totaled while he was at work. He went back to Michigan and the marriage was annulled before I'd ever met him. After an underage stint as a topless dancer, she married a rough-neck, a driller who worked for her stepdad, Bobby. A rig collapsed and two men died and Stacy's husband broke his back, but he got enough insurance money to build her a ranch-style house on several acres and start a wrecker service. But Stacy didn't like sitting home alone at night listening to the police band radio for wrecks so she started drinking even more than she had before, more than when she'd been her mother's drinking buddy. She had four Dobermans, a catfish pond stocked with fish, and a whirlpool in the bedroom. She kept getting swimmer's ear from going under. Then she was diagnosed with cirrhosis. Stacy loved to be loaded. She tried to wean herself from alcohol with cocaine, then went on to crack, then hooked up with the guys who sold it to her. "Talk to her," Mother would plead with me.

As we stood around her bed, Stacy laughed and complained of the hospital food, the beets and carrots. She spoke with her hands gliding through the air like white paper airplanes, the movement beautiful and arcing. I kept my attention on them while we all talked, gossiping as if she weren't dying, as if she hadn't had her best friend, Ronnie, pick her up and carry her outside to his truck and take her on a ride to the liquor store just yesterday. Stacy was a storyteller. She started telling us, graph-ically, about the drainage device put in her stomach to drain the toxins that her liver couldn't. Stacy's stories were always down and dirty. She loved the word "shit" and could say it twenty different ways to express the same amount of emotions. It could be three syllables' worth or a short swift dart.

I'd heard about the minister's visit: he'd stuck his head in her door and asked if there was anything he could do. "Yeah," Stacy had told him and then retold it over and over to whoever would visit, "get me a gun."

Mother had used the anecdote to assure me that Stacy, as Mother put it, "still had her sense of humor."

"Sense?" I'd asked. "Humor?"

When we filed out of her hospital room, we'd each cheerily said "See ya," as if the comings and goings would continue infinitely.

Mother went to find a rest room, and Jan and I stood in the hallway and stared at each other. There were no more words to speak of the ruin that lay behind the closed door. I struggled to find one as I held my hands against the wall and dropped my head: Do you think we should get vaccinated? I asked Jan, who shrugged her shoulders. Mother, dressed in a beautiful suit, her white hair a perfect parfait, her fingers glistening with jewels, walked toward us. We joined her and walked out of the hospital together without speaking, walked past a black family with six children in denim overalls and cornrows, past old ladies strapped in wheelchairs who were fallen over into their laps. We would walk past all of them and get into Mother's Lincoln Towncar, and we would pretend that Stacy was not dying a derelict drunk's death.

Jamie and I went home that afternoon. Hungover, tired, and racked by physical waves of remorse, I thought about what had happened. I'd acted just like a teenager because I was scared of the responsibility of raising one. By drinking too much, I'd embarrassed Jamie in ways with which he was all too familiar. My family was a habit I had to break if I was to be someone Jamie could trust. As we came onto a freeway loop to see the Houston skyline piled before us, I thought about what is passed down, what possesses us, what we choose to own or own up to.

"Jamie," I said, touching his arm gently to wake him.

"What?" he asked, rubbing his eyes as we came upon our exit.

"I'm sorry," I said. "You will forgive me? Right?" I asked.

He put his hand on the crown of my head and patted me twice before reaching over to turn on the radio.

⌒∴∾

Stacy died three weeks after the wedding. For three months before her death, she had been in a nursing home in a bad part of town where Mother had been scared to visit at night. The building was behind a chain-link fence that had razor wire folded in bundles across the top like at prisons. Her hepatitis C diagnosis had kept her from, as my mother said, "the nicer homes." Mother complained that so far all her new nightgowns had been stolen.

My mother had told me that Jimmy and Dayna had visited Stacy often. She told me that Jimmy washed Stacy's hair. I still try to imagine the scene: my brother scooping Stacy's hair into bubbly piles of froth, touching her head tenderly, saying good-bye. Forgiveness, I've discovered, sneaks up on one, was sneaking up on me.

Mother had always nagged Stacy about her hair. She seemed to think a color and cut could solve many problems. In the last five years of Stacy's life, Mother spoke to me more about the state of Stacy's hair than the state of her health. I could picture Jimmy walking down the hall to Stacy's room, knocking and entering, calling out in his booming voice, his tone mocking yet tender: "How's the black sheep doing today?" he might have said. Because Jimmy had become so hefty, his stomach was like a bass drum, giving his voice the sonorous tones that the combination of cigarettes and sadness had amplified.

The call came at six in the morning. I had come back two weeks after Jenifer's wedding to help Mother through cataract surgery. Mother and I picked up the phone at the same time—I was in bed, Mother in the kitchen, and I heard the nurse tell Mother that Stacy had died in the ambulance on the way to the hospital. Someone needed to identify the body that was already at the funeral home.

Jan and I pulled up to the home and checked the address. It looked like the funeral home version of a Las Vegas marriage chapel. We walked in and a man with a built-up heel on his shoe came limping out to greet us. A small sign with white letters stood in the corner with my niece's name misspelled on it. *Stacey.*

"Come on in here," the man said, leading us into a conference room where a family already sat among crumpled balls of tissue. "Oh, excuse me," the man said in his oily sympathetic voice, closing the door and ushering us into an alcove where a Coke machine hummed. "I just need to ask you all a few questions," he said. Jan and I sat humbly before him, ready to perform this task like good students. "What was Stacy's profession?" he asked. "She didn't have one," I said. "Well, what was her last job?" he asked. Jan and I stared at each other. I remembered I'd heard that she had gathered limbs cut by a tree service about five years before. I wasn't sure if that job had a name. "Look," I said, "Could you spell her name right on the little stand?" That may have seemed like a futile effort since Jan and I were the only people who were to view her body before she was cremated. But it was important to me that her name was spelled correctly. Easier to do than figure out what to write down on his forms about what she had done with her life.

"You absolutely can't touch her," the man told us twice. "She has the hepatitis C virus and could be contagious." Jan and I stepped into a dimly lit room where Stacy was draped in a sheet. Her hair fell from her face and the red rash that had covered her neck and forehead was gone—her skin was its original milky tone, her lashes curling beautifully. I felt like a voyeur peering down at her with my hands clasped behind my back.

Sometimes I wish I could show Gail and Mother, who had decided not to see her, exactly who I saw laid out on that table. She looked the best she'd looked in years.

We were waiting for the ashes to arrive, sitting in the den where Mother has each surface covered with family photos. Over the years, I have given her photographs of me—ones that I liked of myself, always the snapshot, my life caught on the fly, not made ready for the moment of the flash. I looked around the room and was stung, as I am every time I come home, that not one of those pictures was displayed. Instead there were the stylized studio photos taken by professionals of Jenifer, of Jan and Jenifer head to head, and the portraits of the other grandchildren, and great-grandchildren. There is always the perfect background in these pictures—no mess, no sign of what looms behind.

There is a large framed photograph of Stacy that has been in a central spot for three years. It is one of those glamorous studio portraits in which the photographer turns you into a model—the hair is big and blown as if by fans. Glam shots, they are called. Stacy had this picture made as a surprise for Mother.

Mother believes in this picture of Stacy.

Gail and Bobby had driven from Tyler to pick up Stacy's ashes, which Gail said she planned to scatter in the lake in front of her house. My brother, who could not be in the room because he and Gail and Bobby despised each other, hated each other over Jamie, had already groused to Mother that Stacy hated that lake.

Jan and I had thrown together some sort of spur-of-the-moment memorial service to take place in Mother's den. Gail had made it clear she did not want a funeral. So Jan asked a friend from her church, a young black woman who sings spirituals to hospice patients, to come sing for us. A born-again Christian, like Jan, Liz prefaced her singing with a prayer, and Gail shuffled uncomfortably in her chair, turning her hip to the side and crossing her legs—a clear indication that she was annoyed. Gail was making it clear that it was not lost on her that she had been railroaded into what she saw as a sham, a ceremony not applicable to Stacy and her death. Also, I suspected, Gail bridled that Jan had gotten control of what was hers.

Gail's heartbreak was beyond the room. For Gail, the family holds no consolation. Her heartbreak seemed to me to be the only real thing in the room, where we were surrounded by dozens and dozens of frozen smiles caught in the flash of a stranger's camera lens.

———

I have stopped trying to mesh and mold and meld into the picture that my mother carries of us in her head. When younger, I found it excruciating to perform the necessary split required to survive or thrive in my family. Yet I did live the two lives—painfully. Two lives are too many to keep track of in oneself. I've come to like the one that Jamie likes. I like who he sees and I want him to see the best of me.

There were two parallel universes in the den during the service in which Liz sang along to a tape that she played on a small plastic cassette player. There were the clutter of photographed faces on the tables that smiled—gruesomely, I thought—at the real people whose grief took various forms. In my memory, my family's faces are always laughing or crying—rarely much in between. And in motion. We did not, I thought that afternoon, even know what exactly we were consoling each other about. The loss of Stacy, I imagined, meant something very different to each of us—something private, representative, and for me, symbolic.

Burned down to bone, she was before us in a box.

What remains.

My brother said that near the end of her life Stacy had spoken compulsively of the money—how she should have gotten as much of Daddy's money as "the real kids" had. Finally, I thought, it is over, the whirlwind of envy and sadness that had been with her for so long.

I've always thought I could have lived Stacy's life.

That's why I stayed away from her. Not because I might catch her sickness and sadness, but because I already had it and feared the contact might activate my own.

In the den we all sat in our isolation. Gail, antsy to get away, "to get on the road," as Bobby explained as they gathered the bouquets. Mother couldn't believe they wouldn't stay and eat, though they never do, and she repeated that it was just such a shame. After Gail and Bobby left,

Mother sat on the couch to go through old photographs, looking puzzled. "Stacy," she said, "could have done anything she wanted." She repeated, "She was so smart."

"No she wasn't," I said, surprising myself.

Mother's head jerked up. "What do you mean?" she asked. And without waiting for an answer began her recitation. I thought I could not bear to listen to it one more time.

"She won the state poetry contest in junior high. She played the clarinet."

"She was stupid!" I screamed. My mother, who loves the halt and lame, looked sadder than she did when she'd learned of Stacy's death. Looking at her sweet face, I hated myself for wounding her—an old lady, I thought, I'm abusing an old, old lady. She *only* loves the damaged ones, I realized. Let her be.

Most of my life I'd had to fight the urge to trip and fall, to stumble and stray, to falter and fail. For she would be there, happy to pick up the pieces.

Late that night in the den, after Mother had gone to bed, I wandered around and studied the photographs. Just as earlier in the afternoon, there were missing faces: no pictures of Jimmy and Dayna. Their picture was in her bedroom, where it wouldn't offend Bobby and Gail. Mother had often said in these last ten years: "All I want before I die is for the whole family to be able to be in the same room together." It is, I think, too much to ask.

It is a request that is beyond her right to ask.

That I have rights is a new thought for me. Jamie taught me this by example. He thinks I have guided him, but he has been my guide, showing me how one can choose which life one wants. At sixteen, he didn't drift. He decided.

All of the photographs of Jamie are of him with Bobby and Gail, when he was six and under.

I surveyed the room—there was little evidence of my father. No pictures. No favorite chair.

"This your daughter?" a sales clerk asked Mother the day before when we'd stood in line at the grocery. "You look alike," she said, smiling at my mother.

"No, no," my mother said. "She looks just like her daddy."

Always she handed me back to him.

Perhaps it had not been my decision, or his, that I be Daddy's girl.

My analyst had thought it was a family decision. I'd been given over to my father so they could all go about their business.

"Was it really such a blessing?" he'd asked one day.

To be, he meant, the one to measure up.

My father's expectations had separated me from everyone else.

My brother had once said, "Daddy didn't expect a thing from me." Always with my brother we turned the memories of my father this way and that, looking for the angle at which all might become precise and clear.

As I sat in that den, after four years (had it been five?) of being with Jamie, I thought about how different I had become over time. Time had become a blur, not a linear unfolding of a calendar but leaps and bounds and backslides that had to do with Jamie's life, my life, and the life we were building together, brick by brick, until there was a solid place for us to stand together and apart.

As for this family which was grinning back at me, I thought I loved them and hated them. My life now had a different center that was far from Mother's den. My internal compass had shifted and reoriented. Turning away from the family that had held me too tight, too long, I saw Jamie's and my life open up before my eyes as if someone had walked across the stage with brand-new scenery.

I knew that Jamie's escape had been my release.

16

the fog lifts

After Gail and Bobby drove back to Tyler with Stacy's ashes and her little dog, Tinker, my brother came to Mother's house. Mother and the woman who's worked for her for twenty years, Pearlie, stepped back and made my brother and me center stage in Mother's kitchen. My brother held out his arms and I walked into them. Where there should have been drama, there was none, or not outwardly so. If you could x-ray my insides, there was fluctuation, movement of the blood, synaptical pops and snaps, the inside of me overcome. But on the outside, I reacted to a mold laid down forty years before. He was my brother. I was his sister. Some things don't change.

First we sat in the kitchen and began to argue about money, the taxes we all owed for a recent gift of money from Mother, and Mother started to interpret, to act as if she were a U.N. translator, repeating back to us what we'd just said. Mother was still in her robe, her small feet in little terry cloth slippers, and she kept shuffling a deck of cards. I could tell that Jimmy needed to smoke—he was worrying a place on his hand. What is that? I asked, looking at a knotty growth on his finger.

"Spider bite," he said.

"Spider bite!" I yelled.

He told me that the house he'd recently bought, two blocks from the old house, was infested with spiders. "Brown recluse," he said, seeming to enjoy my reaction.

"Does she know about the bones?" he asked Mother, his eyes filling with delight, opening wider as he was about to be able to further shock me.

The first week he was in the house a sewer line broke, and the plumber found a wooden box full of bones buried in the backyard. He'd called the coroner, so sure that the bones were human.

"And?" I asked.

Enjoying the moment, my brother stretched it out.

"You remember that ghost? The one in the old house?" he asked.

"The bones," I shouted. "What were the bones?"

"Dead dog bones," he said, rising up from the kitchen chair and grinning, coming to life before my eyes, changing from the zombielike man who'd walked into the door to the teasing boy with whom I'd grown up.

I followed him out to the patio so he could smoke and to get out of earshot of Mother, who wants too much for us to love each other.

We went out the sliding glass door and sat around the round wrought-iron table, facing each other across years of acrimony.

"Well, Stacy's gone," he said. "And when Mother goes, I'll go," he said, fingering the pack of cigarettes.

"Where is she going?" I asked, confused for a moment.

He lifted his eyebrows as if prodding me toward understanding.

"Goes," he said again in his husky baritone voice.

"You mean dies?" I asked.

He nodded his head solemnly.

"And when the trust goes, I'll go," he said.

I stared at him as what he was saying seemed to be poured over me like a sickening sticky substance. My brother had tied his lifeline to the longevity of the trust in the bank. My father, I realized, still lived for Jimmy through the monthly disbursements. Jimmy was supported emotionally as well as financially by the money my father had tried to keep safe for him. Jimmy must know, I thought, on one level, that Daddy put all of our money in trust so as not to be impartial. He knew Jimmy was going to need help managing his life. Mainly he'd needed help managing his wife, who sometimes had as many as four seizures a day, who needed around-the-clock care, who had overdosed twice in the last year, one time going into a coma and put on a respirator and not expected to make it through the night.

The year before, Jimmy had had a heart attack and had told mother he'd never forgive Jamie for not coming to see him. On my mother's patio, Jimmy told me how the pain had shot through his chest and down his arm as he drove for his checkup that had been scheduled a month before. In agonizing pain—like electric shocks, he said, a cattle prod to the chest—he'd parked and entered the waiting room where he'd gone up to the receptionist, and said, "I need a doctor." All six feet six and two hundred plus pounds of him then fell forward onto her desk—out cold. He always chuckles when he tells the punch line: it was the receptionist's first day on the job.

"I don't want to live," Jimmy said as we sat silently across from each other, stunned by the heat.

"I've made a mess of things," he said.

"No, you haven't," I said, lying, wishing there was some way things could have been different for him. If only he hadn't met Dayna in the hospital, if only Daddy would have been more patient when Jimmy was a child.

We sat for a few minutes in silence. I stared out at the yard and Jimmy stared at me, studying my face, perhaps deciding if it was the time for broaching the subject we'd avoided for thirty minutes.

"How is Jamie?" he asked, the question hanging in the summer heat like a mirage. Maybe, I thought, because it was 110 degrees, because Jimmy had smoked five cigarettes in so many minutes, because I could so easily sit across from my baby brother and worry that he'd already had one heart attack and was sure to have another, I began to think that maybe it was all a dream, a story I'd dramatized over the years, added to until it was out of proportion, the sweep and scale and scope not what I thought. To say Jamie was great would be to gloat, I thought. Perhaps to speak of Jamie at all would be a betrayal of Jamie.

I couldn't speak.

As the sun began to set over the gazebo and glisten through the pines, he said, "Jamie should call his mother."

When I sat silent, surprised that nothing inside of me had lurched, he said, "You know she *is* his mother."

I stared at my brother and kept comparing his eyes to Jamie's eyes.

My brother's eyes had grown sick, bulbous, as if something were pushing on them from inside. All of the pressure, I thought, pressing against his face, against my heart, which I was holding together by touching my chest with two fingers. Sometimes I'd move my fingers to my forehead and press. It was as if I were clay that I kept shoving back into shape.

My brother, over the years, had ballooned, his stomach seeming to have a life of its own. There had always been a hunger in him for sweets and sodas. His face seemed bigger, twice the size it had been when he was thirty, yet handsomer, actually a strong yet sleepy and faintly surprised face. There was no longer any confusion in my mind between Jamie and my brother.

"She thinks of him every day. She will always be his mother, you know," he said, his huge eyes filling.

"That's true, Jimmy," I said, looking across the yard and wondering how I could get up and out and away.

"That is true," I repeated, nodding my head. I felt no need to fight anymore with my brother or with his wife or with my mother. I knew

Jamie. That was my secret, what life had blessed me with, the sacred secret that was Jamie and all his secrets.

It was true, I said. I was not Jamie's mother. I was something else.

"You made it out, Marsha," Jimmy said, reaching for another cigarette, looking at me with his huge basset brown eyes, his mouth full of gold, his white hair standing like straw on his head, his gray beard beautiful, just like his laugh.

"You should write about all this," he said.

"I probably will," I said.

⋄⋄

After Jamie moved to Houston, Gail and Bobby moved next to a lake in the country outside a small east Texas town. Mother had always clucked and said "I just don't understand," when she spoke of her girls' love of lakes, oceans, rivers, the country—nature. "I just don't know why anyone would want to live in the middle of nowhere," she'd said about Gail's move, as if Shreveport were the middle of everywhere.

Gail and Bobby had lived in the country, outside the small town of Many, Louisiana, when they were first married and Bobby worked the oil wells. Their move ten years later to Shreveport had been disastrous— Scott and Stacy had been eleven and twelve and Daddy had wanted Bobby to move up to management. Gail always spoke of going to Shreveport and the renting of a house a few blocks from our parents, as a move from paradise to hell. It was during this time that Stacy began to skip school, Gail drank even more—"taking to the bed" we all said. Bobby's management position was to be, it turned out, mainly a matter of managing my brother. Daddy had bought the downtown garage with hopes of putting my brother to work. Bobby was to supervise the garage—and Jimmy. (My brother had had a string of disastrous jobs, from managing a small gas station where the condom machine was constantly raided in the men's restroom, the cost of which the owner subtracted from Jimmy's paycheck. At the end of three months, Jimmy was in the hole.) Soon

Bobby left the job at the parking garage—"ungrateful," my mother declared—and went to work back in the field and moved his family to the outskirts of Shreveport, a good thirty-minute drive from our house to theirs.

This small house on the edge of cotton fields was where Jamie spent his first six years. They kept that house for the ten years Jamie was gone. I think they stayed put so that if Jamie ever left his parents he'd know where to find them. Once he was safe—away from his parents—they felt they could move on.

Two years before Stacy died, they'd unfolded the plans in Mother's kitchen on Christmas day. Bobby pointed out the way the windows would be floor to ceiling facing the lake. "An A-frame," Gail said, pride blooming, new beginnings giving her voice an edge of excitement, like a teenager planning for a prom, a sound heartbreaking in its unfamiliarity. It was to be right on the water where you could step out and feed the ducks or go fishing or watch the hummingbirds swarm the feeders that would eventually surround the wraparound deck. After they'd moved, their gossip was of new goslings, the threat to the family of ducks by coyotes, the problem of nutria that were digging away the lake's fragile coast. Later there would be stray dogs and a cat who arrived pregnant who wanted to give birth in Gail's lap.

I was spending a month in New York, my first extended length of time away from Jamie since Montauk, when Mother called to tell me Gail had pneumonia. She liked her doctor and with his encouragement, I imagine, she decided to stop drinking. When she came out of the hospital, her body was free of alcohol and she hasn't had a drink since. She doesn't talk much about the not-drinking any more than she'd talked about the drinking. Sometimes she smiles and says in wonder that she doesn't miss it at all. So I'm left with wonder also: I wonder why she drank so hard for so long and I wonder why she quit. Why don't I ask? Over the years I've become conditioned, I suppose, to honor her privacy over everything. She's been through so much, my mother would say, and that used to be an explanation that sufficed. Lately, however, the heretical thought has surfaced in my mind: What about what she has put us through?

Jamie and I were building a life of layers in which each week brought something new to light, not to shadows and subterfuge. We peeled back to a place nearer to the heart of the matter. Sometimes we saw each other daily, sometimes weekly. "Touchstone," Mrs. Samish told me. "You are his touchstone." And so I waited for him or sensed when a call needed to be made.

I remember the day Jamie said, "Okay, I need some medicine." The therapist had said that it had to be his decision. Too many people have imposed their wills on him, she said.

We went to a neuropsychiatrist.

We sat in an office and as I sat down I thought of how we had sat in so many offices. This one had good magazines, but I'd just turned to my horoscope in *Vogue* when Jamie handed me the form he was to fill out.

"I need to smoke," he said. "Will you do this?"

When the doctor called us in, the first thing he said was, "What was that all about?"

"What?" Jamie and I asked back in unison.

The doctor tried to trap Jamie's eyes. "That she filled out the form?"

"She always does," Jamie said. "She's faster."

After a cursory check of the form, he began to pepper Jamie with questions. Very quickly my palms went sweaty and my shoulder muscles tensed as if for danger. Jamie seemed nonplussed.

"Do you ever want to kill someone?" the doctor said, sitting unnaturally upright and stiff in his chair.

"Kill someone?" Jamie asked with a lazy double-take, blinking wide-eyed.

"Yeah, buddy," the doctor said. "Just take someone's head off. Ever get that mad? Huh? Do you? Do you?"

"No," Jamie said, simply.

By this time I was about to take the doctor's head off.

"Never get so mad you just want to punch someone?" he asked, his eyes squinting and holding Jamie's in a menacing challenge.

Jamie smiled. "No, not really," he said.

The doctor was surprised that there was not tremendous rage lurking beneath the surface of Jamie's psyche. He tried to provoke it on several visits, but Jamie would just stare back at him—confused, wary, hurt. And after a few of these taunts, apparently to see if he could prove Jamie wrong, Jamie would get sleepy and begin yawning wide-mouthed, full-body yawns.

The doctor ordered an MRI of the brain and an EEG. Some unusual activity, he said in our next visit. He talked eloquently of the limbic area of the brain.

He explained that the primitive part of Jamie's brain had gone on overdrive, the cortical area that reacts to danger. Although Jamie might seem very still and sleepy, he is not unaware of his surroundings, which he is always monitoring for surprise attacks.

That's why he must sit with his back to the wall. That's why he jumps when touched. He is on hyperalert, the doctor explained. Posttraumatic stress disorder, he said. He would, he said, be good at triage, wartime service, emergency-room work, paramedical stuff. Anything to give him the grist for his mental mill. Or medication could calm his system down, wean him from what had become a biological need to protect himself from assaults. His system, the doctor said, thinks he's still under siege. It thinks he is still with his parents.

Sense was made of what had been a riddle to Jamie. Why he was still exhausted after twelve hours of sleep. The doctor explained that his body kept watch through the night for danger. Sense was made of the paranoia that undermined his relationships. There was a creature—a wary damaged child lurking at the back of his brain—who told him, "Don't let down your guard."

Jamie began to take an antidepressant. I imagined his system being flooded with a magic potion. I imagined the blackened nubs of his receptors coming to life, beginning to wave small tentacles as if they were sea plants reaching for this particle of peace, this molecule of joy.

"Look," I said to Jamie one afternoon, "look at the way that tree's branches have leafed overnight!" And he smiled at me. He told me he felt the slow churning of change, a tingle in his fingertips, a smile that tries to make its way to his lips. Now, he said, he sees a little of what I see.

Jamie entered college in the fall of 1997. He'd try part-time, he said nervously, not sure if he could do it but declaring his interest in anthropology. I waited in line with him during registration until I tired of standing and went to sit on the bleachers of the gymnasium where I could watch him from afar. I saw a pretty African-American girl in a miniskirt and high, high wedge heels get in line behind Jamie time after time. Finally, I saw her ask him a question, flip her hair with a hand, laugh and smile. I smiled.

Three months before he'd asked to join a health club, and I couldn't write the check fast enough. He'd completed a six-week boot camp, working out with a trainer every day, and the transformation was stunning. For the first time in his six years in Houston, he'd begun wearing shorts and short-sleeved shirts. Peeling back the layers, I'd thought, coming out from hiding. He now stands tall and handsome, his beautiful jet black dyed hair pulled back in a ponytail that reaches the middle of his back. He looked around to catch my eye right before his turn to step forward to register.

Afterward, he walked across the room toward me, smiling.

"Let's get out of here," he said, changing his heavy book bag from one shoulder to the next.

The last five years rose into my mouth until I tasted them, then I tasted victory, ours.

"What is it?" he asked, frightened.

"Oh, you know," I said. "Emotions."

He rolled his eyes, then smiled. "Let's go," he said, pulling me up from the bench dramatically as I dabbed at my eyes.

As we walked out, he said in disbelief, "I think that girl was flirting with me."

"I *know* that girl was flirting with you," I said, taking his arm possessively, protectively, proudly.

In five years, Jamie has changed his name three times. He arrived in Houston as Jamie. Then, within a year, he asked me to call him Jimmy, which I found strange since it was his father's name. "Anything but Jamie," he said, grimacing.

When soon after he changed his name to James, he told me he'd understand if I couldn't make the transition.

Two years ago, he became Dante. "Why Dante?" I asked with a whine, feeling I could never call him that.

"Because of the Inferno," he said.

To his girlfriend and his professors, he is Dante. Often I call him "Jimmy, Jamie, Dante, whatever," all in one string just as my mother used to call me Gail, Jan, Marsha when trying to get it right, work through the ones who'd come before and lodged in her memory ready for retrieval when a name was to be called. I was third on the list. Finally, I understand her three-step litany. The name changes represent his accelerated development, the way Jamie's transformed himself, made himself up over the last five years.

"Dante suits him," a friend of mine says.

"It does?" I say, having lagged behind myself, stuck in the Jimmy phase of his life, the one that he has gone through and moved on from. Why would I stall right there, at Jimmy, the name of my brother? Has Jamie, James, Jimmy, Dante finally become the correction, the replacement, the substitute for the other Jimmy, the boy, the man who wants to die, who measures out his life in the dwindling assets of a trust? Maybe to call Jamie by the name of Jimmy I can keep the memory of my brother near me. I know I should call Jamie by the name he has chosen. "Dante," he told me. "He went to hell and made it back. Just like me."

Midway through his first semester, I'd not heard from him in a week, when he called frantic from the phone booth right outside the liberal arts building and told me that he was sure he would flunk his upcoming English midterm. He had walked directly from his classroom to the phone. I said I was sure he would not flunk the test, and to come over, I'd make coffee and we'd read the stories. I had the same book his teacher was using and when Jamie came over, we sat in my bedroom, and we both read Flannery O'Connor's "A Good Man Is Hard to Find." "I don't understand one thing about this story," he said, putting the book down with a huge sigh and reaching for his cigarettes.

"Jamie, listen. This is a story about a family on a car trip with a selfish grandmother who wants everything her way and who wouldn't leave the cat at home and one thing led to another until the whole family ends up in jeopardy."

"Sounds like June," he said, meaning his mother's mother. "But where do you see in here that she is selfish?" he asked, staring at the pages.

"Look," I said, and read several passages in which the grandmother reveals herself to be shallow, vain, and selfish.

"That's just like everybody," he said, his eyes a swarm of confusion.

"No," I said, my voice rising in frustration.

"You don't have to yell, Marsha," he said, looking as if he were about to cry. Reading the world had not come easily for him and now he must read an echo of the world in worlds of words.

The story is about all the crosscurrents in a family, I explained—the mother, father, two children, and grandmother have a long history that has been compressed into a day on a car trip. "It's considered a funny story," I said. "Historically."

"Funny?" he asked in complete bafflement.

"Jesus," I said, suddenly realizing we hadn't even come close to reading the same story—the story of an extended family. "You don't get the jokes, do you?"

"Jokes?" he asked. "There are just so many people I zoned out."

"I don't understand," I said.

"The story is crowded. There are too many people in there. And they're all talking at once," he said, rubbing the heels of his hands into his eyes as if trying to clear his vision of O'Connor's chaos. So many people in a story confused him as much as too many people in a room.

"You know," he said, "I think I don't understand stories where there's more than one person in it." I would learn that just like in a room, if a story is too crowded he can't read between the lines, can't detect sarcasm or irony.

Allegories, he said, are his specialty. Black or white, he said, smiling at the thought of no gray areas in which to get lost.

We drove to our favorite café, owned and mainly frequented by lesbians, most of whom Jamie thinks are darling. "Too bad," he mumbled just like every time we arrive, shaking his head as we sat down in a booth to eat and talk about Shirley Jackson's "The Lottery."

"Let's," he suggested, "take each of our family members and think of them as having one characteristic, like in an allegory."

That Jamie wanted to do such a thing amazed me. We'd had a moratorium on family talk from the beginning of our alliance. He hadn't known over the last six years the ups and downs, the hospitalizations, the crises and resolutions that was the drama of my family. Which was not, he had made clear in the early days, *his* family.

I said for him to go ahead and start. He made some broad-brush characterizations that made me laugh hard and guiltily. Mainly he poked fun at his mother's mother, who is remarkably like the clueless character on *The Golden Girls*. And he spoke of my mother's fondness for speaking over the phone to him almost exclusively about the weather. We did not speak of his mother and father, but their presences floated between us, their lives the stuff of stories. I put my hands around my cappuccino cup and stared into the foam, thinking that I didn't want to make fun of my brother, hoping that Jamie would not, when suddenly he said, "You know, sometimes I feel sad for my father."

"Me too, Jimmy," I said, using the name I call him by although I know I have to begin calling him Dante, soon. The sadness swelled between us like a balloon about to burst, stretching our mixed emotions to the breaking point.

"Let's go outside," he said, jumping up the way he does when the emotions propel him up and away from them.

We repositioned ourselves at a table outside, Jamie being careful, as he always is, to be downwind so his smoke won't bother me. He lit a cigarette and blew out the smoke before he spoke. "You know, I felt bad even as a little kid to be embarrassed of my father," he said. "What did you think of me? At first? When I first got here?"

I looked across the table that had chips of ceramic swirling into a picture of some feminist spiritual earth mother, and traced the grout around the edges of the broken tiles that had been placed piece by piece together to create the picture.

"Sometimes," I said, "I was embarrassed." I felt the skin at the edge of my forehead go hot and prickly with the heat of the truth—the shame of my shallow shame.

"About what in particular?" he asked.

To Jamie we were talking about a long, long time ago, though to me the boy on my doorstep, the boy who ate that first meal we had together like a ravished wild child, was still close by, only, in my mind, a year or two away, not, as in Jamie's, a page turned, the distant past as in Once upon a time a long, long time ago.

I thought about his question, about the nature of shame, and the pact I'd made to myself five years ago to never lie to Jamie—ever.

"The smell," I said.

Jamie lifted his arm up and smelled, then grinned at me.

"It reminded me of your father," I said. "And I worried about what my friends would think."

"I didn't even know about friends," he said. "My parents didn't have any friends," I don't think Jamie had a friend over at his parents' house once in ten years.

I could not look at the picture he had handed me of the solitary childhood; instead I thought of who sat before me, chatting about allegories, Flannery O'Connor short stories, the merits of what he calls "heavy-handed" prose, like the circuitous sentences of D. H. Lawrence compared to the dialogue of Raymond Carver. Never had I dreamed I would talk literature with a member of my family. And never had Jamie let me indulge in pawing through the past with him. I felt the pleasure of two travelers going over a trip they'd shared.

"Remember," I said, "when you first came, how you wouldn't trust my motives? Always thought I had some big hidden agenda?"

"Yeah," he said, smiling. "But that's over and done with now." He spoke like a very old man who had come into newfound strength and wisdom, which he had.

"Why," I asked, "do you think I did it?" I knew he would understand I meant letting him come into my life, deciding to love and care and worry over him.

"Identification," he said quickly, his knowledge of me deep and wide and breathtaking in the relief of being known.

"Yeah," I agreed. "At first. But then it was just love for you, not anyone but you, who you were, that guy, that big mess of a guy, that particular guy. You."

I looked over at the next table and saw a pair of sunglasses that someone had left. "Would I be a terrible person if I took those?" I asked Jamie, pointing at the glasses. Now I was the one who changed the subject, who couldn't stay there anymore, who would not press what I had found.

"Marsha," he said, surprised. "You can't do that."

"Oh, well," I said, admonished by his morality. "You're right." We got up and crossed the lot to get in the car.

"I'm just a thief at heart," I said, half to him, half to myself, mulling over my flawed nature.

"A thief of hearts is more like it," he said, slyly, proud of his word-play. He grabbed me around the neck, then left his arm linked over my shoulder.

↔

A year later, after two semesters of college, on a late afternoon, Jamie and I sat in my car in the parking lot of the community college. We were talking about his girlfriend who complained of his "numbed" state, the lack of emotion he presented to the world, the way he could become so unfeeling that it was frightening, it frightened her. He'd just read a book, he said, that his girlfriend gave him. He told me that the author of the book wrote that all relationships take as a model the love one had with one's mother.

"I didn't have a mother," he said, worried that he was missing the blueprint that would let him love.

"But you had mother love," I told him, explaining that if he hadn't had love early on that he wouldn't be able to love me, or his girlfriend the way he clearly did. He thought about that and shook his head. "I don't feel things like you do," he said mournfully.

"You were once different," I told him, seeing in my mind's eye the boy I'd known, the boyhood he couldn't remember. This was one of those rare times when he'd wanted to talk about the past, had asked me questions, had tried to look back, and I was nervous that I'd say too much or the wrong thing, let loose the memories that could send him retreating far, far away.

"Lately," he said, "I've been remembering." He'd told me several times over the last six years that he had no memory of his childhood before being with his parents, that he didn't remember the trips I'd told him about that he'd taken with Gail and Bobby to the seashore, didn't remember the backyard with the swimming pool and slide and the miniature oil derrick Bobby had built.

"I remember you now, a little bit," he said, looking straight ahead at the windshield, speaking to the speck of me, barely visible in his past. "You were always dressed in black," he said, squinting. "You were sitting in Nana's backyard by the pool." He spoke as if he were a fortune-teller who could make out the shadows of the past life.

I looked across the parking lot, thinking back on those summer days in Shreveport, the weekends of watching Jamie fly down the slide, cannonball into the water, beg me to come in and swim. He had been Gail and Bobby's boy, who had moved into the world they laid before him, one full of love and neighbors and toys and pets and faux oil derricks and rose beds and chili steaming on the stove and meat sizzling on the outdoor grill, and Letha from down the road bringing vegetables from her vegetable stand and homemade fudge. There had been Fat Cat, a stray that had appeared at Jamie's window screen, and Charlie Brown, the chocolate poodle that lived to be eighteen. And there had been the Pomeranians—501, FizGig (that Jamie'd named after a little furry creature from the movie *The Dark Crystal*) and Lajitas. There had been a home.

Like the fortune-teller's supplicant, I encouraged him to keep looking at his past. "Yes, yes," I said, excited. "Yes, I always wore black. Mother said it suited me, set off my brown eyes and white skin, and I thought black made me look urbane and intellectual."

We laughed together because of my poking and prodding at him to branch out from his black wardrobe.

We sat quietly looking before us as if watching a drive-in movie.

Suddenly he said, "And Nana always had on those sundresses with big flowers on them. And floppy hats."

"Yes, yes!" I said, laughing at the memory of my bohemian outfits, and Gail's sun hats and her smile, that lovesick grin she had on her face throughout her years of raising Jamie.

"You were once the center of her universe," I told him as if now I were the fortune-teller.

I looked out at the wide expanse of concrete, at the students going to and fro, and felt my heart come together as if flexing a muscle.

"You were beloved," I said to the windshield. I said to Jamie.

Gail and Bobby had made this conversation possible, I thought. The possessiveness was like a wince inside of me, the thought that he was always, already theirs.

Jamie's relationship with Gail and Bobby had gone from strained to nonexistent as he struggled to define himself as not-them, not good ol' boy. I'd had to be careful not to pressure him to reconnect with them, call them, write them, visit them. But I often thought of Gail's sadness, how hard it must be to let him go. She had been valiant, only thinking of him as she sat offstage and waited for him to come to her. I believed someday they'd work it out.

Jamie was taking his first steps toward being a loving man, thinking about the place from where love springs, and frightened that his well was dry.

I wanted to give him back that beloved boy, crack open the carapace that had served him well while he was with his parents, and let the boy he'd once been venture out.

"You were once different," I said. "Inside you is still the boy. Sometimes I see him behind your eyes, your smile."

"I loved you, Jamie," I said. "Not a day went by in those ten years that I didn't think of you."

"I never knew," he whispered, tapping the end of his boot with his hand. "I never knew."

We stayed quietly together in the car, the past like petals falling around us.

17

nearing the end

I was in the kitchen about to pour a cup of coffee when the phone rang.

"Marsha?" Jamie said.

"What is it?" I said, my heart beginning to pump in reaction to the timbre of his voice, my radar for his sadness fine-tuned over the last six years.

"You know you always told me to call you if I thought I might do something to myself. Well, I'm calling you."

"I'll be right there," I said. I poured the rest of the coffee in the sink and went out to the car still dressed in my LSU jersey and sweatpants, the clothes I'd slept in. I drove the four blocks to Jamie's new apartment—1820 Hawthorne—the same complex I'd lived in when I was his age.

Jamie was waiting by the curb. As he got in, I saw Willy, my old friend, the maintenance man, rest his elbow on the rake and raise his hand in a salute: Repetition compulsion, the psychologists call it, the desire to return again and again to the same scene. I liked that Jamie lived where I once lived, felt a deep sense of satisfaction that there was some lineage for us, a common place we have both called home.

Jamie sat in a welter of worry as I drove off, watching Willy in the rearview mirror growing smaller but no less distinct. Echolocation, I thought, playing with words like worry beads. The invisible sonar that helps dolphins locate each other by measuring the time for a sound to return. A sonar net, like memory, catching echoes, sending them back. Jamie and I spoke within our high-frequency silence until he broke it, finally, with his story.

Jamie had just learned that his girlfriend had slept with his friend, her upstairs neighbor.

The heart Jamie had sworn those years ago that he didn't have, or couldn't feel, was now alive but not well. I heard his unspoken accusations break the surface of his story: I had talked him into this heart thing. This was my fault. See, I heard him say across the space between us, numb is better. To be alive is death.

For five hours I told him why he should want to live. I calculated, making a rational list for what was clearly beyond reason. One—because he had spent so much hard work and effort to want to live, he couldn't give up now, I reasoned. Couldn't, shouldn't. "You will not," I said to him, "give up." Then I smiled at him: "Over my dead body," I said. "Over a girl." My forty-six-year-old's perspective made no sense, I knew, to a young man with a freshly broken ripe heart.

I took us to the coffee shop where we sat in a booth, and I continued my appeal, reaching for reasons I didn't know I had until they spilled out of my mouth and onto the table like marbles, the sound harsh and popping, one explosion after another, unexpected, like us, like life.

"Most people," I told him as I looked down at my cappuccino, "go through stages of loving." I explained that by the time most people are his age they have grown thicker skins. He had gone, I said, from having a suit of armor to being all exposed tender self. I looked across at him and imagined a burn victim, seared of the flesh, my touch, my words, like fire.

"I don't see the point," he said, looking away, his eyes filling full of tears.

Salt water, I thought. *Don't cry,* I wanted to cry. *They will burn. Those tears will burn you.*

I took him to the park where we'd gone so often the first two years he'd been in Houston.

I lay on my back looking up into the lacy web of limbs of an exotic fir tree and came up with a variety of reasons why he should not kill himself, while he sat with his back against the tree trunk and smoked one cigarette after another. The hair that he'd hidden behind for years now opened like a curtain for the announcement of his face, his eyebrows wavy with worry and intensity, his gaze that of a young Indian warrior, convinced that he will die in battle.

I'd once slept under this fir tree, having left my house with an ungodly hangover and gone to lay my shame under the shade of the fir. I didn't tell Jamie that under this tree I, too, had wanted to die.

Instead, I told him to pretend I had a crystal ball and in it I could see a lovely woman in his future who would see who I saw, who would love who I loved—Jamie.

Rising up on an elbow, I looked at him, tried to be the mirror he needed to see himself more clearly.

I told him that if he died I wouldn't want to live.

I stretched out again and looked up at the tree, trying to imagine life without him.

I'd grown used to my worry for him. I think I'd always wanted someone to worry about as much as I worried about him. To make a gift to him of what I'd learned during my years of befuddlement through the same terrain, to share with him my past and the times my heart had been broken, was a gift to me, also.

He put on his robot voice of reason and said that if I truly wanted to die—if that was what I really, really wanted, then *he* would let me die. If the positions were reversed, he would let me have my way.

"Thanks, Jamie," I said. "Alias Kervorkian." I got up and brushed the pine needles off my sweatpants before starting to the car.

"Some conversations," I yelled back at him, "are for their own sake."

"Like masturbation," I said as I walked away. I didn't, I said, want to argue the fine points of suicide.

"You wouldn't ever kill yourself," he called to me. "You have too much self-worth."

"Oh, Jesus," I said, mostly to myself, not bothering to turn around. I knew where he was headed—could tell by the tone that the hardheaded burrowing had begun. He was digging himself into his position.

"Don't make assumptions," I turned and yelled at him, shaking my head at my own descent into an argument *about* our argument.

It was an accusation we'd flung at each many times over the years. He'd make a casual remark in a restaurant about men in suits, and I'd rail at him about his quickness to stereotype. Then when one day I made a pointed remark about the padlock one of his friends sported around his neck—"A political statement?" I'd asked. "He wants to be led around by a leash?"—and Jamie had quickly shot back, "Don't make assumptions."

Jamie followed me to the car and got in. He slit his eyes toward me, then smiled, then laughed, and I knew that he would live until the next day, which would mean he would then live for the next and the next.

I had hauled him back beside me. Part of me had known that he meant he wanted to die because he was still, and always, the child whose mother made him hold his arms up in the air for hours—to try to touch God, she'd told him—and the child whose mother made him kneel in a corner with bare knees under which she'd placed uncooked rice. That child will always be there, questioning the punishment, bewildered about the crime. But now, six years into knowing Jamie, loving Jamie, I knew that he was also a teenager—although twenty-one—who had a broken "Oh—God!—I—can't—go—on!" heart, as is the case with all teenagers who can't and do and will.

At five that afternoon I went home and crawled into bed, reminding myself that Jamie and I'd had worse days than this and gone on.

◆:◆

I saw my former analyst, Dr. C., at a cocktail party, and we found a corner of the room in which to catch up.

"I did it. I almost finished the book," I said, grinning, clearly much more surprised about my announcement than he was. I'd quit analysis before Jamie's arrival, wanting to step out of myself and into another world, another's world, never suspecting the way my wish would be fulfilled, with Jamie. Or that I would one day write it all down.

That evening I told Dr. C. that a friend had told me that she thought our story, Jamie's and mine, was about redemption.

I told Dr. C. that I'd circled the dictionary for two days before opening it to the *R*'s.

I wanted to know the dictionary's definition.

"I didn't know what it meant," I said. "Redemption."

"You know what it means," Dr. C. said, looking up over his glasses with a smile.

"What?" I asked. "You tell me what it means."

"Ask Jamie," he said.

◆:◆

Sitting on my porch on a morning in April, I figured and refigured the time from when Jamie first came to Houston until now. I thought about the way the years expand or shrink like Alice on her potion, depending on which scene I was working on in my writing about Jamie and what actually was happening in our day-to-day lives. I might spend an evening, like last night, rewriting the scene in which he helped with the renovation of the house. He'd spent two whole days jack-hammering part of the driveway that eventually was turned into a garden. He'd been the one, I recalled, to suggest using the chunks of cement to delineate the path. I looked over at the rocks with which he lined the sandy path on the side of the house six years ago—continual reminders of the time between then and now.

Lately it had become a comforting ritual, the counting on my fingers: 1993, '94, '95, and so on as I added up the years, trying to come to terms with time past, time present, as I come to the end of writing this story.

I could cut the cord of this here, now, today, I thought as I padded barefoot to the center of the yard to pick up the paper.

A miracle, my friends say. Night and day, another friend says of Jamie's transformation. Who would have imagined? One would have to *imagine.* Thinking had sometimes gotten in the way, I'd said.

I went back to the porch with the paper, picked a leaf out of my coffee cup, and then drew a circle in the pollen that dusted the walkway, the paper unread and beginning to ruffle and blow—perhaps, away—with the next gust. Birds were at full morning throttle and a mist of pollen fell like rain around me as I watched my cats—one fat and stern, the other an adolescent—tackle one another. My dog's hairs floated by after I scratched his head upwind. I did a yoga stretch, then walked farther out into the yard and sprawled out under the ash tree.

And what am I to do, I wondered, suddenly with more time on my hands than I've had in years?

Spring seemed to be fast-forwarding as I watched, Easter approaching quickly. I thought of St. Charles Street in New Orleans, the dogwood in bloom. And azaleas. Camellias. Wisteria.

I jumped up and called Jamie, who, with me, was on spring break from college. I asked if he'd like to go to New Orleans.

"Cool," he said.

In a moment of spring-induced magnanimity I told him to ask his new girlfriend to come along too. I didn't realize until after I'd spent all morning calling a friend who lives in New Orleans, making plane reservations, finding us lodgings in the Quarter, what I was really doing. I was going back, returning to the place where much of it began.

࿓

On the plane, Leah sat between me and Jamie and napped as Jamie talked to me across her. He tickled her nose to make her wrinkle it and then grinned at me.

"Don't," I told him. "Leave her alone."

"She won't wake up," he said. "Watch." He then proceeded to brush her nose again, and when she made a funny twitch he smiled. "She sleeps like a rock."

In this small display of intimate knowledge, Jamie was showing me that he knew Leah, knew her secrets, shared her bed. Leah, who at eighteen is four years younger than Jamie, is five foot two and voluptuous. "A little Lolita," I've told my friends. She has dark olive skin, a heart-shaped face, and a bubbly nature undercut by sadness: an alcoholic father, a diagnosis of attention deficit disorder.

My nostalgia for the early stages of tenderness surprised me. The way his hand rested nonchalantly on the top of her head, the way he got her a Coke and handed it to her as if it were second nature for him to give her what he knew she needed right then made me turn my eyes away as if it were something I shouldn't see.

After landing, Leah and I headed for the rest room while Jamie walked at his usual deliberate pace several yards behind us. I was first out of the stall and was standing surveying my face—not happily—when Leah joined me at the next sink. I'd raced through the morning—I'd had to write a student a recommendation, had to find a last-minute replacement for my usual house sitter, and had spent fifteen precious minutes at the pharmacy drive-in lane begging for six Wellbutrin because Jamie had run out of pills. "Marsha, I really don't need them," he'd said as I tapped the steering wheel nervously, thinking we just might not make the flight. Leah and I had exchanged looks in the rearview mirror agreeing silently that the pills were crucial. The whole morning showed in my reflection in the mirror: in the dark circles under my eyes, the puppet line from nose to mouth, the groove that had recently appeared between my eyebrows as if gouged there.

Leah took out her little makeup case and began to apply mascara. I knew Jamie would become frantic if we were gone too long, and I considered hurrying her along, but then stopped myself. Our therapist had said he should push himself through some of his anxieties, try to stay in a crowded room one minute longer than he could stand it, try to not call his girlfriend the minute paranoia began to crawl like bugs across his skin, try to sit through the math class when the teacher got sarcastic. She said it was actually possible to grow new neural pathways, that his mind would let him venture further into, and then maybe away from, his worst fears. One of his fears is that those he loves will disappear the minute his back is turned. He'd told me about the time he came home from the third grade to an empty apartment—all of his parents' furniture gone, as well as his parents. What did you do? I'd asked him, not being able to imagine what I would have done. "Sat down on the steps and waited," he said. Leah, free of the burden of these stories, just giggled and hugged him when we came out of the restroom to find him pacing and frantic. "Where have you all been?" he said, as if we might have crawled out of the window of the rest room and gone on some secret adventure, leaving him behind. "A girl's thing," Leah'd said, and rested her head against his chest and pulled him along and onto the other side of his worry.

I walked ahead of them and out into the thick New Orleans air, full of heat and diesel fumes, to get into the taxicab line. I glanced behind me to see where they were and saw Jamie lifting Leah's shoulder bag off her arm to take it on his own. As the line inched forward, I craned my neck to find them, hoping they'd show up before I got to the front. I saw Jamie light her cigarette, the two of them huddled close as if in front of their own campfire.

In the cab, Leah was again in the middle, squashed in the backseat between Jamie and me. I felt shoved onto the outskirts of Jamie's affection, and flickers of such fifth-wheel feelings came and went as we drove past familiar landmarks. The cab driver, an older black man with grizzled gray hair and thick arthritic knuckles that wrapped casually around the steering wheel, started to chat with me as if he sensed that a life preserver should be thrown—to me.

He hadn't made it to Mardi Gras this year, he said, catching my eye in his rearview mirror. He grabbed the bundle of beads that hung from the mirror, touched them fondly, and said, "My grandkids got these for me."

I looked at myself in his mirror, and again his eyes studied mine. I wanted to tell him how Jamie and I had come to New Orleans six years ago in a wild escapade that had changed my life—our lives. I thought back to the strange hotel with the Abbysinian cats. We had been a similar couple of strange creatures then, warily walking around each other, both, I know only in retrospect, having deeply held notions of independence.

I'd become accustomed to our dependence on each other, loved when our mental telepathy shows up in knowing looks, phone calls in sync. I thought of the invisible wires between Jamie and me: sometimes they were taut and singing—tight wires we made our way across with cautious steps—and sometimes loose and lank, giving us both free rein while still safely tethered. Looking across at him, I wanted to tug the line.

Jamie bent his head down to Leah, pushing her hair over the rim of her ear, and whispered, then looked up at me. "Jambalaya," he said. "I want her to try it."

Our therapist had explained that once there was a safe environment that Jamie's development would unfold quickly. She had been right. Like in time-lapse photography, he'd jumped ahead, sometimes growing up a year's worth in a crucial week. I'd come to realize that his time with the street kids had been his rebellious teenage years. Lately I couldn't keep up with where we were, where he was, which left me displaced. "You're patronizing me," he'd said recently. "I'm not that person anymore." In the last year he'd gone from being a big awkward boy to a dignified young

man. Gone from Jamie to Dante. Gone from needing me completely to
needing me as a home base, an absent presence, an idea.

My flesh-and-bones mother-self had emerged stiffly and with false
starts over the last six years. But once the maternal motor had kicked
in, it had a tendency to get stuck on overdrive. The first time Jamie had
gotten sick, the first year he was in Houston, I'd gone to the store and
bought three huge packages of throat lozenges, enough to last a couple
of years. In the last two months, I'd gone to IKEA several times and
lugged out cartloads of gifts that I left at the door of his apartment: rugs,
wineglasses, picture frames, pillows, a bath mat, a rice cooker. Then I
went to PETCO and inundated him with presents for his cat—catnip, a
fancy catbox, a giant sack of cat litter, a dozen toys. And then I came
bearing new girlfriend gifts, leaving a card along with toilet paper—(girls
need more of this, I'd told him) special soaps, Comet, sponges (girls like
a clean bathroom, I'd told him).

Over the years, the time I had used to mull over my own future had
been filled with planning Jamie's. But lately, when I stepped into the
bath, stretched out into the water and let my mind wander, it didn't
know where to go.

As I stared out at the throngs of tourists—a woman in Bermuda
shorts zipped across the streetcar lines to join her husband on the other
side, the conductor rang the bell—I thought about Jamie and what was
coming to pass: his needs would be fulfilled by others, his dependence
on me would shrink. The thought made me feel small, as if I had only
been inflated by his need for me. I straightened my shoulders, put on
more lipstick, and asked the cabbie what convention was in town.

Dermatologists, he said. Eighty thousand of them.

I often said to Jamie in his first years in Houston—particularly when
he was bereft, feeling hopeless about making it to college, or finding a
girl—that someday he would have lived longer away from his parents
than he'd spent with them. When that watershed moment came, I'd tell

him, then the good memories would outweigh the bad. In my mind, each day away from them diluted the days he'd been with them. There was a scale in my imagination I'd been waiting to tip in our favor.

As Jamie moved further from his past, I was going over it in my mind. For me to move forward, I'd always had to move backward. Pawing through the past. At first I'd tried to make Jamie follow suit. Our therapist's words came back to me: Your way will not be Jamie's way. That had been in response to an argument Jamie and I had had about books. "She thinks if I just follow in her footsteps, do what she did, read what she read, I'll be a success," he'd complained to the therapist. Why not? I'd thought. It had worked for me—the trail of books I'd followed had led me away from my family and into a clearing. I remember the session in which the therapist said I had to loosen my grip, let him flounder. Again, I had to learn to let him be.

I looked over at Jamie who was pointing out something to Leah. The riverwalk, he said, turning around in the seat, is back that way. The Café du Monde, over there. Now he was the guide.

As the cabbie turned onto Canal Street and got stuck in five o'clock traffic, he put his arm across the front seat and turned around to me, and said, "Where did you say you were from?"

"Originally," I said, "from Louisiana."

"Your grandfather," I said, turning to Jamie, "My daddy—your grandfather—loved barbecued crayfish."

"Really?" Jamie said, lifting his head up from nuzzling Leah's neck. Jamie loves crayfish.

Mud bugs, my daddy had called them.

I don't think of New Orleans as my father's hometown. Maybe because I'd never been able to imagine my father as a child. I think of him as having emerged fully formed as an adult from somewhere in the Texas Panhandle. He didn't have childhood photographs. I'd never seen a picture of his mother.

———

After his death I wanted a sign of sentiment. There had been nothing in the will—no personal bequests, no passing on from one generation to another of any object that resonated with the sense of him. It was two weeks after the funeral, and I was about to return to Houston when the banker called and said he'd discovered that my father had a safety deposit box. My mother and I went down to the bank. The metal box was set down in the middle of the table, the scene with the substantial clanking of the box, familiar from old movies.

My mother and I had different desires. My mother wanted some evidence of why he had been stressed to the point of imploding, then dying. Were there financial matters she could trace back through in order to understand why? Why he was gone at only sixty-five? Why she was on her own? Were there secrets that once known would make sense of things?

I wanted letters.

I realized that my fantasy was for the banker to unlock the box and pull back the top to reveal old love letters from my mother that my father had kept. Or letters he wanted read at the time of his death. I needed some of his words. I needed pen on paper, the personality of a signature. I wanted dusty, yellow, crinkled letters professing and expressing.

There were no letters in the box.

There were some old municipal bonds and the deed to the house on Centenary, sold ten years before.

Two weeks before his death, my father had surprised me as we stood in an airline terminal where he was seeing me off. I was going back to Houston. "I think," he said, "that you should buy a house."

"A house?" I'd asked.

"A *home,*" he said. "You should have a home."

Then he'd offered to put one hundred thousand dollars in the bank in my name and have me buy the *home* with the interest. I was too shy and startled to look at him so we'd stood looking out the window at the planes in the distance.

Later, sitting on the plane, I'd thought about his offer, surprised about his newfound empathy, wondering about how he envisioned my life: *He must think I'll never marry. He knows I'll never marry. Oh, dear, I suppose I'll never marry.*

There couldn't be, I decided, another reason he would bend the age-old rules of equality. Always what one family member received, the others got in kind. Circumstances didn't matter. Had there been, I wondered, other deals made under the table? Something, I sensed, was different. He was imagining other rooms, other homes, and perhaps, I thought, he was considering another life himself. There was about to be a change. Yes, something was definitely different.

I never got to find out what.

From the bank, Mother and I'd walked across the street to Daddy's office, one that he'd only been in for a year. Inside was a large new desk of polished wood—not a real antique but a replica—and fake ferns flowed from a gold urn in a bookshelf that held a set of leather-bound books with gold-inscribed spines, clearly bought from the furniture store. Inside a cabinet we found a large stack of yellow legal pads.

We'd struck gold, I thought, sitting down Indian-style to thumb through the pages that I hoped would read like journals, revealing my father's day-to-day life. My mother and I didn't speak of it, but I knew we were looking for evidence of an affair. He had been so different lately—staring at sunsets, buying new clothes, a preoccupied air about him. It was as if he had a new inner life, a place that sustained him when he was with the family. I turned page after yellow page, my mother looking over my shoulder. Each and every page was filled with numbers—columns and columns being added and subtracted. His secretary, who also worked for the two other oilmen in the office, opened the door to offer us coffee. "One a week," she said, nodding at the pile of legal pads. She said she put a fresh one on his desk each Monday. While he talked on the phone to investors—thirty years of friends in the oil business—he had calculated: what percent of what well for how long to pay out how much?

Sitting with my father's days stacked in my lap, I looked up at my mother, who was picking up mementos from his desk and bookcase, touching the presents that had been given for birthdays, and Christmases. There was an oil derrick pen-and-ink stand, a small sculpture of a man playing golf made out of scrap metal, and numerous paper weights. On his desk sat the heavy brass apple I'd given him. I took the apple home with me. It fit in my palm and felt solid.

I opened his desk drawer and at first saw only paper clips and rubber bands. I pulled it all the way out. In the far back corner, I saw a piece of paper that looked like a high school love note, a teenage missive folded into a tight square. When I unfolded it, I stared at the writing, seeing the actual handwriting before the meaning surfaced. The fat loopy letters seemed mismatched to my expectations of a love letter from a mystery woman. The handwriting seemed familiar, yet not. "Dear Daddy," I read. "I want to thank you for . . ." Though written in script, the letter looked as if it had been written by a child, the letters fat to bursting. Many of the girls who I taught wrote in this way—feminine flaky, I'd called their self-conscious bubbled scroll. With a jolt of recognition, I realized the letter was from me to my father and had been written ten years before.

I wrote, "I can not thank you enough." The misspelling of "cannot" was a common error I pounced on when I found it in student essays. I put my hand to my forehead as I thought of this letter sitting in his desk, kept for ten years, maybe even cherished. I was thanking him in my bumbling fashion for my education. I held the letter in my hand, reread the handwriting of a stranger who had thanked my father for sending me to college. I told him I knew how hard he'd worked. I said I thought I should tell him because he might not know. If only, I thought, as I stood holding the paper torn out carelessly from a notebook, I'd known. If I'd known my words would have been read and reread over the years, I would have written him many more.

———

The lobby of the Bienville House had trompe l'oeil paintings on the old concrete walls, and two newly upholstered love seats facing each other across from a bronze table topped by a giant vase of flowers. Two gay men stood at the checkin desk, raising their eyebrows at each other in amusement as a man ranted in Greek at the desk clerk, who clearly didn't understand a word, but who was explaining that there were no reservations for this man in the computer. The man's wife, who sat on one of the overstuffed brocade love seats was beautiful, even with the dark circles under her eyes. Her sweater was knotted in perfect, casual European style around her shoulders, and she wore her impatience with the same elegant flair. Jamie and Leah sat on the matching love seat across from her and leaned into each other, the top of their heads touching.

"Come on, you guys," I said, handing Jamie and Leah their keys as we boarded the small elevator to the second floor. After we found the rooms, I stood in front of my door, they in front of theirs, and before we inserted our keys, Jamie and I looked at each other. In the four feet between us was six years, the time that began in New Orleans, in another room, where we had been strangers. Now we stood and stopped and grinned at each other before walking into our separate rooms.

The bellhop came in to open the French doors to the balcony and explain about the continental breakfast in the lobby in the morning. He had almost walked out when he reconsidered and turned to me to ask if I wanted him to unlock the door to the adjoining room, Jamie and Leah's.

"No!" I said so fast that he laughed. It wasn't what he assumed—that I wanted my privacy. I wanted them to have theirs.

After he left I sat on the bed and looked around the room. I opened the closet. Then I took out some clothes and hung them up before I sat again on the bed and bounced. There were two double beds in my room. The luxury of it made me smile, especially when I thought that in the next room Jamie and Leah were exploring the same room: checking the refrigerator for snacks, rustling through the basket of soaps in the bathroom.

I stepped onto the balcony and looked down at the dark courtyard that was filled with a rectangular pool. The turquoise water was lit by underwater beams of light that threw oscillating water patterns onto the brick walls. The courtyard was empty, but the sounds of the Quarter filled the space with echoes of what was happening in the streets outside the hotel. I could hear the clop of horse hooves and yelps and whoops of laughter, voices rising and crashing like waves against the wall. Jamie walked out onto his balcony, and we stood and listened.

"Do you mind if I smoke?" he asked.

"No, no," I said, bending down toward the courtyard to take one last breath of bougainvillea before he lit the cigarette.

"You going out?" he asked, smiling through the smoke. The tone of teasing made me examine his profile, look for the next question.

"What?" I asked, hitting my palm on the rail.

"I don't want to make you mad," he said, staring down at the patio.

I let the silence bob in the air, drift off with Jamie's next exhalation of smoke.

"Or be sexist," he said.

"What?" I asked, curious but bracing myself for Jamie in truth-telling mode.

"You've been pretty uptight lately," he said, taking hold of the balcony railing where he stood and stared straight ahead the way a man does when he's serious and talking.

"Yeah," I agreed. "I guess I have been."

"I've been thinking," he said, "that maybe you need to get laid or something."

"Oh, for God's sake, Jamie," I said, laughing and putting my hands over my eyes, shaking my head in my what-next gesture, relieved that he hadn't told me he hated my new haircut.

I realized that he'd felt my isolation in the airport, in the cab, in the lobby. He wished for me a partner. In the darkness, I felt his grin and his goodness. I closed my eyes and heard the music coming up the street.

༝ༀ༝

Like the smudgy woman in a Chagall painting who hovers over French villages, I let go of where I am and float into the night, out the front door of the hotel where the black man stands under the green awning and toward Bourbon Street. I hover, my arms outstretched as if about to catch a trapeze, then float through the throngs to a destination, where I fly right into Felix's, the oyster bar my daddy brought me to when I was ten. Look, Marsha, the way they open up the shells, the salty wound, like a present, a surprise, sometimes there's a pearl. Tonight, dipped in batter and fried, served as I watch me from above as I sit at the bar where a waitress who looks seventy bends over with a smoker's hack, the oysters melt in my mouth. Small-fry, my father had teased me, grabbing me around the waist and tickling me into tears. Wiping my mouth with the white cloth napkin, drinking the bottom of the beer, and then going to the place where I'd always gone, to hear the musician on the corner of Bourbon and St. Ann's. Sometimes over the years I've listened to him from outside, lolling at the window with the others, the tourists and ten- and eleven-year-old black boys who will tap-dance for a quarter, pull a trick on you for a dollar, but never, ever shine your shoes anymore, anymore. Tonight I will go there and the singer will take my hands in his and turn my palms up, cradling my hands. Just like the other one, I think, the fortune-teller long ago who looked down into the crisscrossed map in the middle of my hand and told me, I see a boy. And then six years ago when I was escaping from the sixteen-year-old with whom I was sharing a hotel room then—and was about to, yes, about to share a life with, though I couldn't see that far ahead, wouldn't have believed it if Coro Milling hadn't told me years earlier. I remember his name clearly now, like his face, the lines like a puppet. He said to me as he looked into my palm—A boy. Not biological. That was his name, Coro, the palm reader I'd gone to and then returned to, the one that saw Jamie but hadn't named him, but had said, There is a child in your future, he will change your life, your life will change, and I had thought that some man would bring along his child, perhaps on weekends, for summers. I had been looking one way while my whole world was swelling up behind me. The musician will fold my hands into fists and hold them with his own, then brown eyes to brown eyes, will say, "Come." And together we flew up and over New Orleans, looking down into the secret courtyards full of yellow trumpets and scarlet bougainvillea and the wine of wisteria. "Make me an Angel," he sings, a song that almost always makes me cry. Why does that song, looping down like line, the fish hook catching me, make me cry? I've often thought it was a matter of grammar. And who you are or can be or hope to be or pray to be or hope for or pray for. I play with it in my mind back and forth back and forth. Make an angel of me or one for me. It's like when I was little and would ask my mother to make me an egg. "Poof, you're an egg," she'd say, jolting my view of the world for a minute. Just a minute. Just a minnow. My little live bait, my Daddy used to say to me. I am fluid, still posing for you, Father, knowing that I hold the shape of you like a fossil within me, you, the impression of you, imprinted, moving me, being moved, shuffled, retold by me, over time.

I float through the spring night. And then I remember. Remember his words I'd forgotten. The fortune-teller. He'd said, I don't know if he is yours. What, in this life, is yours? I'd thought then, and again, and again. Will there, I'd returned to ask the fortune-teller, be a man in my life? I see love in your life, he'd said. That's all I can tell you. Many loves in your life.